THE BEST OF KEYSTONE TOMBSTONES

JOE FARRELL AND JOE FARLEY

Mechanicsburg, Pennsylvania   USA

Published by Sunbury Press, Inc.
50 West Main Street
Mechanicsburg, Pennsylvania 17055

www.sunburypress.com

Copyright © 2015 by Joe Farrell & Joe Farley.
Cover copyright © 2015 by Sunbury Press, Inc.

Sunbury Press supports copyright. Copyright fuels creativity, encourages diverse voices, promotes free speech, and creates a vibrant culture. Thank you for buying an authorized edition of this book and for complying with copyright laws by not reproducing, scanning, or distributing any part of it in any form without permission. You are supporting writers and allowing Sunbury Press to continue to publish books for every reader. For information contact Sunbury Press, Inc., Subsidiary Rights Dept., 50 W. Main St., Mechanicsburg, PA 17011 USA or legal@sunburypress.com.

For information about special discounts for bulk purchases, please contact Sunbury Press Orders Dept. at (855) 338-8359 or orders@sunburypress.com.

To request one of our authors for speaking engagements or book signings, please contact Sunbury Press Publicity Dept. at publicity@sunburypress.com.

ISBN: 978-1-62006-584-6 (Hardcover)

Library of Congress Control Number: 2015936617

FIRST SUNBURY PRESS EDITION: April 2015

Product of the United States of America
0 1 1 2 3 5 8 13 21 34 55

Set in Bookman Old Style
Designed by Crystal Devine
Cover by Lawrence Knorr
Edited by Allyson Gard & Marc Farrell

Continue the Enlightenment!

CONTENTS

Acknowledgments..iv
Introduction... v
1. **Richie Ashburn** and **Harry Kalas** "The Voices of Philadelphia".....................1
2. **"Babes in the Woods"**...11
3. **Smedley Butler** "The Fighting Quaker"..19
4. **Dick Winters** and **Joe Toye** "Band of Brothers"......................................23
5. **Simon Cameron** "Pennsylvania's Political Kingmaker"................................30
6. **Michael Cheslock** "The Lattimer Massacre"..35
7. **Billy Conn** "The Pittsburgh Kid"..45
8. **Benjamin Franklin** "The First American"...51
9. **Joe William Frazier** "Smokin Joe"...58
10. **John White Geary** "An American Success Story Few Have Heard"..............65
11. **Josh Gibson** "The Black Babe Ruth"..72
12. **Frank Gorshin** "What Does It All Mean?"...77
13. **Winfield Scott Hancock** "Hancock the Superb".......................................81
14. **Milton Hershey** "The Chocolate King"...89
15. **Johnstown Flood Victims** "An Act of God"...94
16. **Mary Jo Kopechne** "What If?"...100
17. **Jayne Mansfield** "The Blonde Bombshell"..105
18. **Mary Pinchot Meyer** "The Mysterious Case of Mary Pinchot Meyer".........110
19. "The Molly Maguires, **Black Jack Kehoe** and **Franklin Gowen**"................119
20. **Herman Webster Mudgett** aka Dr. Henry H. Holmes...............................133
    "America's Answer to the Ripper"
21. **Joe Paterno** "JoePa"...141
22. **Bob Prince** and **Myron Cope** "The Voices of Pittsburgh".........................151
23. **Frank Rizzo** "The Cop That Would Be King"..157
24. **Fred Rogers** "America's Favorite Neighbor"..163
25. **Art Rooney** "The Chief"...169
26. **Bessie Smith** "The Empress of the Blues"..175
27. **Thaddeus Stevens** "The Dictator of Congress"......................................179
28. **Jim Thorpe** "The Greatest Athlete of the 20th Century"...........................185
29. **"Titanic Victims and Survivors"**...193
30. **Andy Warhol** "The Pope of Pop"..210

Acknowledgments

The success of *Keystone Tombstones Volumes One, Two & Three* and the special editions of *Keystone Tombstones Civil War* and *Keystone Tombstones Sports* has led to this volume. We would like to thank all of those who purchased any of our books and encouraged us to continue this series.

Our work has been well-received and supported by many in the media, especially by Pennsylvania Cable Network (PCN). We'd like to thank Brian Lockman, Francine Schertzer, Corinna Wilson and Alanna Koll as well as the whole crew at PCN for their tremendous support and interest.

We are also grateful to Mike Rozansky and Tirdad Derakhshani of the *Philadelphia Inquirer* and Brian O'Neill of the *Pittsburgh Post-Gazette* for bringing our books to the attention of readers at both ends of the state.

We extend special thanks to Stacy Smith, Jill Neely, Kristine Sorenson and John Burnett for having us on "Pittsburgh Today Live" three times. We deeply appreciate it.

We also appreciate the interest, support and contributions of Paul Perrello of LaSalle TV in Philadelphia.

In Central Pennsylvania, we'd like to extend our thanks to Scott Lamar at WITF, and Chuck Rhodes and Amy Kehm at WHTM-TV for their interest and support of our projects. We are also grateful to Debbie Beamer at the Mechanicsburg Mystery Bookshop and Dani Weller at the Harrisburg Midtown Scholar for their continued support.

Many others have been kind and supportive as we traveled around the state, often lost, often thirsty. Frank Rausch at Laurel Hill Cemetery and John Hopkins at Christ Church Preservation Trust, Jim Dino at the *Hazleton Standard-Speaker* and Terry Parris from PennLive were all particularly helpful.

Lastly we thank our wives, Sharon Farley and Mary Farrell, for their tolerance of our folly. It's not easy being them.

Introduction

It was back in May of 2010 that Joe Farrell and I met at Nick's bar and restaurant in New Cumberland, Pennsylvania. Over a few drinks, we began discussing writing a book together. Farrell had recently published a book on his own (*Jesus Runs Away*) and I had just retired, so he had the experience and I had the time. Our first thought to travel the Lincoln Highway, from one end of the Commonwealth to the other, had been vetoed by my wife, so we had to come up with another idea. I suggested a book about famous and infamous people who had been laid to rest in Pennsylvania. Farrell liked the premise and suggested that we visit and photograph the grave sites. I think it's safe to say that our fellow patrons, who were listening to our discussion, thought we had had one too many. Today most of them own at least one of the five volumes.

Work on what would become *Volume 1* began by Farrell putting together a list of approximately 80 people as potential candidates to include in the book. We began visiting cemeteries and taking photos of the graves. Naturally, on some of these trips, we found ourselves in need of refreshments. It was in seeking out spots to refresh ourselves that we came up with the idea to include an "If You Go" section at the end of each chapter. In this section we point out other graves in the area worth visiting and tell of bars and restaurants that we enjoyed. Prior to starting to write the book, we sat down with Lawrence Knorr, the owner of Sunbury Press, to present our idea. He was very enthusiastic, which went a long way toward convincing us to give it a go.

While our original idea was to do one volume, it quickly became apparent that we had far too many people to cover. That is what led to multiple volumes. As of now, there are five books in the series, *Keystone Tombstones Volumes 1, 2, 3* and special editions on the Civil War and on sports figures. The chapters that appear here in *The Best of Keystone Tombstones* were selected from those works. The two of us each made a list of chapters we felt were worthy of being included in *The Best of*. Then, we met (yes, back at Nick's) to compare our choices. We found that we agreed far more than not, so the selection process went very smoothly. As a result, this volume contains stories on founding fathers, sports figures, politicians, entertainers, civil war heroes, and a serial killer, among others.

We used the same process in putting together all of the books. Once we agreed on about 30 people to cover, we divided the writing chores up equally. Once a chapter was finished, it was shared with the other author to review and edit. During the writing process, we scheduled trips to the grave sites to take the photographs. In addition, when possible, we photographed monuments erected to honor our subjects, as well as locations that might be part of their story.

So, there you have it. It's been over four years and five volumes since we started this series. The two of us agree that it has been a real learning experience.

The Pittsburgh Post Gazette said of *Volume 1,* "With more than 30 deceased subjects, the book is hard to summarize, but it's pleasures come with the 'I can't believe I never knew that' moments which are everywhere." It is our hope that, as you, the reader, go through this volume, you will get to share in those moments.

1

"Voices of Philadelphia"

DON RICHARD "RICHIE" ASHBURN and HARRY NORBERT KALAS

Counties: Montgomery, Philadelphia
Towns: Gladwyne, Philadelphia
Cemeteries: Gladwyne United Methodist Church, Laurel Hill
Addresses: 316 Righters Mill Road, 3822 Ridge Avenue

The 1950's has long been considered part of the "Golden Age of Baseball." There is little doubt that the glamour position during that decade was centerfield. Three centerfielders, all of whom played for teams who made their home in New York City, dominated the attention of baseball fans around the country. Mickey Mantle, Willie Mays and Duke Snider were all prolific sluggers and of course baseball fans love the long ball. Songs have been written about the trio, and to this day their fans still argue over who was better. While all this was going on, another centerfielder was plying his trade in a city just down the road. By the end of the 50's, no major leaguer had banged out more base hits during that decade than this Philadelphia Phillie. His name was Richie Ashburn.

The future Hall of Famer was born on a farm in Tilden, Nebraska on March 19, 1927. His father operated the largest general store in the area. Among his childhood friends was a young man by the name of Johnny Carson who would go on to make quite a name for himself as an entertainer. Ashburn was drawn to the national pastime and played for the American Legion as well as Tilden High School. In 1944 he was selected to represent Nebraska in the prestigious Esquire all-star game held in New York City. It was there his talents began to draw the attention of major league scouts.

The Philadelphia Phillies signed Ashburn in 1945. He made that team's major league roster in 1948 when he was 21. In his rookie year he showcased the abilities that would mark his career hitting .333 with an on base percentage of .410 and stealing 32 bases in 117 games. There were many who felt that Ashburn deserved rookie of the year honors, but the award went to Alvin Dark.

The 1950 Phillies team was nicknamed the "Whiz Kids" based on the fact that the average age of the team was 26.4 years. This young team played consistent baseball throughout the season, and by September 20th they found themselves in first place with a 7 1/2 game lead over Boston and a 9 game lead over Brooklyn. It was at this point in the season that injuries began to take their toll, and the losses mounted. On the last day of the season the Phils held a 1 game lead over the team they would play to finish the year, the Brooklyn Dodgers.

Richard Ashburn

The Phillies started their pitching ace, Robin Roberts, in the season finale, and the Dodgers sent Don Newcombe to the mound. Both men pitched extremely well, and after 8 innings the score was tied at 1-1. In the last of the 9th Roberts walked Cal Abrams, and he moved to second on a single by Pee Wee Reese. Duke Snider hit a hard single to center that was fielded by Ashburn. Abrams attempted to score, but a perfect throw from Ashburn nailed him at the plate. Roberts then retired the side, and the game went into extra innings. The Phillies opened the top of the 10th with consecutive singles, putting men on first and second with Ashburn coming to the plate. He laid down a sacrifice bunt that advanced the runners to second and third. Dick Sisler followed with a three run homer that provided the margin of victory as the Phillies won their first pennant since 1915.

The "Whiz Kids" faced the heavily favored New York Yankees in the World Series. Three of the four games were decided by 1 run, but the Phillies lost all three contests. The Yankees completed the sweep by winning game 4 by a score of 5-2. Philadelphia only managed three earned runs in the series, one of which was driven in by Ashburn. While many thought this would be the first of many post game appearances for the Phillies, it would be the first and last World Series for Ashburn. The Phillie centerfielder was quite candid in his opinion as to why this young team failed to repeat: "We were the last to get any black players. We were still pretty good, but they were just getting better." In light of Ashburn's opinion, it is worth remembering that the 1950 World Series was the last in baseball history to match two all-white teams.

While post season honors may have eluded Ashburn he continued to perform during the regular season. He had a fifteen year major league career that included twelve years playing for the Phillies. He was among the most consistent leadoff hitters in major league history and was a terrific centerfielder. Ashburn won the National League batting title twice first in 1955 and again in 1958. In three other years his batting average was good enough for a second place finish. He consistently hit for average, batting over .300 nine times and retiring with a lifetime average of .308. Ashburn was also a great fielder as demonstrated by the fact that he routinely led the league in fielding percentage. In addition he had a good eye at the plate leading the league in walks four times, and he was an excellent base runner.

Ashburn was named to the National League All Star Team five times (1948, 1951, 1953, 1958 and 1962). He finished his career with more than 2,500 hits. He had a reputation for being a spray hitter meaning he could hit the ball to all parts of the diamond. This ability made it extremely difficult for opposing teams to effectively defend him when he had the bat in his hands.

Ashburn was nicknamed "Putt-Putt" by Ted Williams because he ran the bases so fast that you would think he had twin motors in his pants. Later he became known as "Whitey" due to his light blond hair. After he retired Harry Kalas, his broadcasting partner, referred to Ashburn as "His Whiteness."

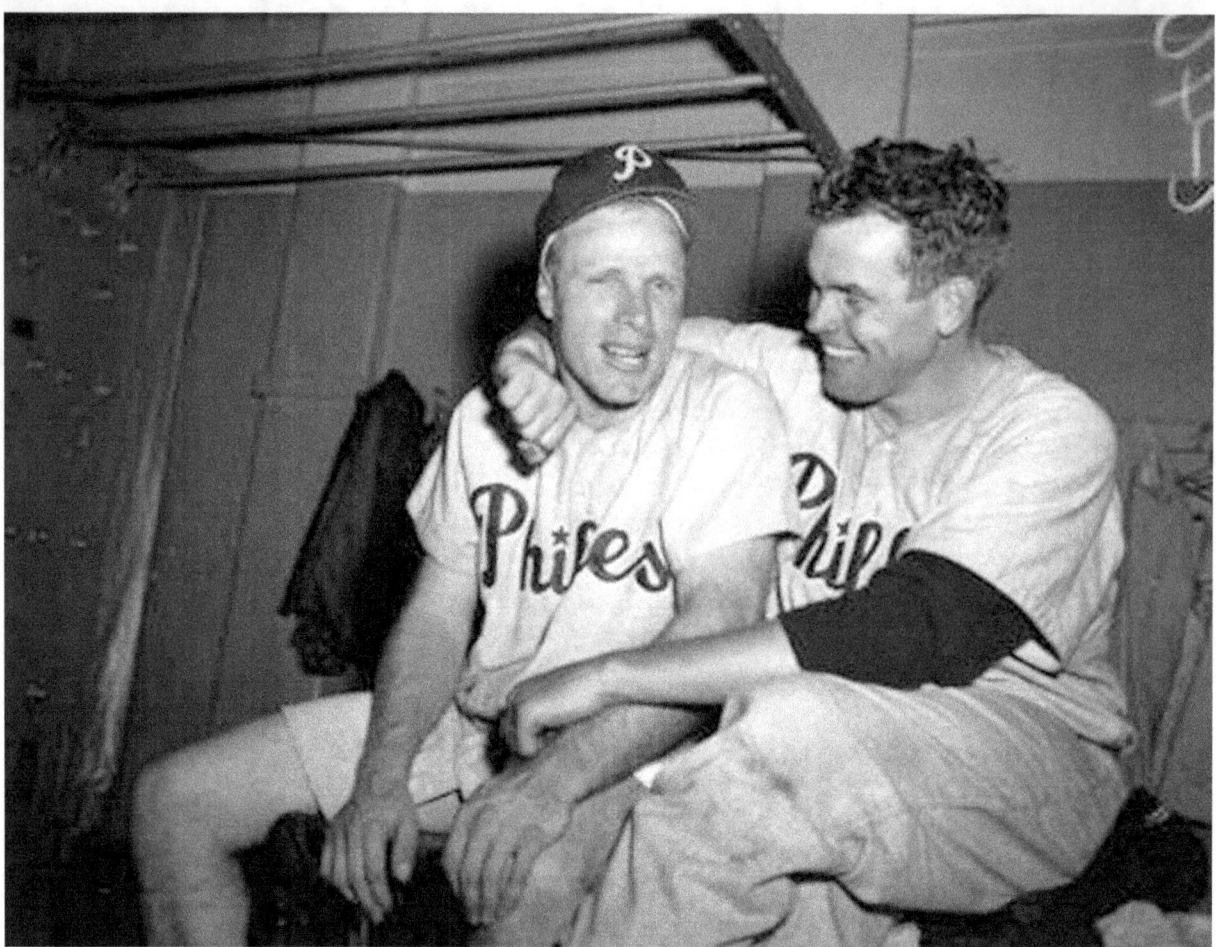
Phillies pitcher Robin Roberts (right) embraces teammate Richie Ashburn in 1956.

One of the great Richie Ashburn stories took place during a game played in 1957. Ashburn was at the plate when he fouled off a pitch into the stands. The ball hit Alice Roth, the wife of the Philadelphia Bulletin sports editor, square in the face. The impact not only stunned Mrs. Roth, it broke her nose. Play on the field was halted while medical personnel rushed to Mrs. Roth to provide assistance. After a quick examination, it was decided that she should be removed from the stadium using a stretcher. As Mrs. Roth was being carried out, play resumed, and Ashburn fouled off another pitch that struck the poor woman yet again. After the incident, Ashburn and Roth became friends and remained so for many years.

After the 1959 season, the Phillies traded Ashburn to the Chicago Cubs. He remained a Cub for two years before being selected by the New York Mets in the expansion draft of 1962. The original Mets who were described by their manager Casey Stengel as "amazing" may have been the worst team in the history of the major leagues. They finished the season with a record of 40-120, a dubious mark that no other team has been able to equal. While Ashburn had a good season and was named Most Valuable Met after hitting

Stan Musial (left) of the St. Louis Cardinals has a big smile for 1958 batting champion Richie Ashburn of the Philadelphia Phillies in St. Petersburg,, Florida, in this March 1959 photo. Musial finished third in the batting race with a .337 average against Ashburn's .350 average. Ashburn also won the title in 1955.

.305, the mountain of losses was too much for him to take. He retired at the end of the season and later remarked, "I just didn't think I could go through another year like that."

Upon his retirement Ashburn soon became a radio and television commentator for the Phillies. He also wrote sports columns for the Philadelphia Bulletin and later for the Daily News. Eventually he was paired up with Harry Kalas to form the Phillies broadcasting team. The two became best friends as well as Philadelphia sports icons. Ashburn and Kalas called Phillies games for 27 years. Ashburn was known for his sense of humor as a broadcaster. He once told a story about a habit he had of keeping a bat that he was hitting well with in bed with him so he was sure to have it for the next game. He ended the story by saying, "I slept with a lot of old bats in my day." He also liked to talk about how he felt about pitchers. "After fifteen years of facing them, you don't really get over them. They're devious. They're the only players in the game allowed to cheat. They throw illegal pitches and they sneak foreign substances on the ball. They can inflict pain whenever they wish and, they're the only ones on the diamond who have high ground."

Years after he retired, Ashburn openly complained about being snubbed by the Baseball Writers Association in their voting to elect new members to the Baseball Hall of Fame. The three famous New York centerfielders, Willie, Mickey and the Duke, were all quickly enshrined in the hall. Ashburn was thought to be left out because he was a singles hitter unlike the sluggers from New York. That didn't stop Ashburn supporters from placing bumper stickers on their cars that read "Richie Ashburn: Why the Hall Not?" The efforts of Ashburn and his fans paid off as he was finally elected to the Hall of fame in 1995.

On September 9, 1997, Ashburn finished broadcasting a Phillies – Mets game in New York City. He died of a heart attack later that night in his hotel room. There was a public viewing held in Fairmont Park that drew thousands of his admirers. The baseball fields in the park are named for

This tombstone marks the final resting place of baseball great Richie Ashburn who claimed that he slept with a lot of old bats during his baseball career.

him as is the centerfield entertainment area at Citizen's Bank Park; that area is known as Ashburn's Alley. His uniform number (1) was retired by the Phillies in 1979.

Richie Ashburn is buried in a modest grave in the Gladwyne Methodist Church Cemetery in Montgomery County. In 2005 a book titled *Richie Ashburn Remembered* was published. The book's foreword was penned by Harry Kalas.

"That ball is outta here" was Harry Kalas' home run call, and it has become one of the legendary baseball calls. Harry Kalas was a Hall of Fame broadcaster best known for his role as lead play-by-play announcer for the Philadelphia Phillies. He also was well known as the voice of NFL films from 1975 until his death.

Kalas was born in Naperville, Illinois on March 26, 1936. He graduated from Naperville High School in 1954. He made the University of Iowa his college choice, graduating in 1959. Soon after he left the university, he was drafted into the United States Army. He was stationed in Hawaii where he served until he was discharged in 1961. It was at this point that Harry began his illustrious broadcasting career, calling minor league baseball games for the Hawaii Islanders.

In 1965, he was hired by the Houston Astros to broadcast their games. He remained there until the Phillies hired him in 1971. Initially, his hiring was not met with the approval of a number of Phillies fans. The man he replaced, Bill Campbell, was extremely popular among the team's fan base. Kalas won the fans over quickly. His easy going style that would all of a sudden register great excitement when a Phillie made a great play in the field or delivered a key hit, turned Campbell into a fond memory.

Kalas was the Master of Ceremonies at the opening of Veteran's Stadium. He also called the last game at the "Vet" and the first game at Citizens Bank Park. He was eventually paired up with Hall of Fame player Richie Ashburn and the duo became best friends as well as sports icons in Philadelphia. He and Ashburn broadcast together for 27 seasons until Ashburn's death in 1997.

During his Phillies career Kalas broadcast six no-hitters, six National League Championship Series, and three World Series. He missed broadcasting the 1980 World Series because of a Major League Baseball rule that prohibited local broadcasters from calling the series due to conflict with the networks. As a result of a public outcry the rule was changed. By now, Kalas had clearly made a national name for himself.

Kalas was nicknamed "Harry the K" by Phillies fans and loved the Frank Sinatra song "High Hopes" which he sang on many occasions. The year before his passing, Harry had the opportunity to broadcast the ultimate highlight: calling the game as his beloved Phillies won the World Series and became "the 2008 World Champions of Baseball" He then joined the on-field celebration, grabbing a microphone and belting out "High Hopes."

Tomb of Harry Kalas in Lauel Hill Cemetery

Gravesite of the legendary Phillie and NFL announcer. Note grave goods behind box seats on right side of photo.

To a whole generation of football fans, Kalas was known as the voice of "Inside The NFL." He did the voiceover from 1977 through 2008. In addition to his work with the Phillies and NFL films, Kalas called various sports over the years for the Mutual Broadcasting System, CBS Radio, and Westwood One. This included NFL games, Major league Baseball, college basketball, and Notre Dame football. For many years, he narrated the "Alcoa Fantastic Finishes" in game highlight spots for use during NFL telecasts.

On April 8, 2009, the Philadelphia Phillies honored Kalas by having him throw out the first pitch before a game with the Atlanta Braves. The Phillies received their championship rings as part of the ceremony. It turned out to be the last home game Harry Kalas ever announced. Kalas collapsed in the press box as he was preparing to broadcast a game between the Phillies and Washington Nationals at National's Park. He died on April 13, 2009 at George Washington University Hospital at the age of 73. For the rest of the season, the Phillies wore a patch on their uniforms that bore the initials "HK."

Kalas received the Ford Frick Award from the National Baseball Hall of Fame in 2002. In June 2009, he was inducted into the National Radio Hall of Fame and Museum. He was named Pennsylvania Broadcaster of the Year 18 times.

He is buried in historic Laurel Hill Cemetery overlooking the Schuylkill River. His tombstone is shaped like a giant microphone with the letters "HK" in the middle and a likeness of Kalas' autograph at the microphone's base which sits on top of a raised base shaped like home plate and is flanked on each side by a pair of seats from Veterans Stadium. In 2010, the grave was resurfaced with sod that originally came from Citizens Bank Park. When we visited his grave, visitors had left baseballs there, some autographed, and there were numerous coins as well.

Close-up of grave goods left by visitors to Harry the K's grave.

If You Go:

Richie Ashburn's grave is in the Philadelphia area. Therefore there are many other sites you may wish to visit that we covered in *Volume One* as well as in this volume. After visiting Ashburn, you might want to take in the beautiful grave site of his partner Harry Kalas.

We were both hungry and thirsty after our visit to Ashburn's grave, so we stopped at the Stella Blue and the Star Bar in West Conshohocken. It proved to be a good choice. The bartender was friendly, and the food and drinks hit the spot. The bar has a sleek contemporary décor and an interesting and varied menu and drinks list. It looks like it would be a great spot in the evening, but we were there in the afternoon and had more to do. Hopefully we can make it back there for happy hour on one of our trips.

There are several interesting and famous graves in Laurel Hill Cemetery (See *Volume One*, Chapter 19 on George Meade).

Henry Deringer, who is interred here, was developer of one of the most famous American guns the derringer, designed to be compact and easily concealed. John Wilkes Booth used a derringer to assassinate Abraham Lincoln.

Boies Penrose is also buried nearby. He was a US Senator from 1897-1921. There is a prominent large statue of Penrose on the grounds of the Pennsylvania State Capitol, although it is hard to understand why. The statute shows Penrose with his hand in one pocket. Many from Pennsylvania claim it's not lifelike because Boies never had his hand in his own pocket.

The cemetery itself is located very near the Philadelphia Zoo and the city's art museum. Both deserve a visit. While it is hard to recommend where to stop and dine in Philly (there are so many great places), we had a great lunch at a spot close to the cemetery called the Trolley Car Café on S. Ferry Road. It featured delicious gourmet salads, sandwiches, and soups and offered a patio setting if you wished to move outside.

2

"Babes in the Woods"

NORMA SEDGWICK
ELMO NOAKES
DEWILLA NOAKES
WINIFRED PIERCE
CORDELIA NOAKES

County: Cumberland
Town: Carlisle
Cemetery: Westminster Memorial Gardens
Address: 1159 Newville Road

Sadly, the authors are old enough to have been raised by parents who lived during the Great Depression. I remember hearing lots of stories from my parents and grandparents about how tough times were and how much people suffered during "The Depression." I think I was in high school before I learned that "depression" could be an economic term. Until then, I thought it was called "The Depression" because so many people were depressed emotionally as a result of the hard times. The story of the Babes in the Woods is perhaps illustrative of just how bad things were during that time.

On November 24, 1934, two men were in the woods near Carlisle intending to cut some firewood when they saw a mound covered with a green blanket. Clark Jardine and John Clark thought it was an odd thing to see in the woods and by the looks of it, it hadn't been there very long. They decided to check it out and were horrified at what they found. Under the blanket were the bodies of three young girls. The two men went in search of a telephone and called the police in Carlisle. The police arrived shortly and so did a crowd, some seeking children of their own who had gone missing.

The girls looked like they were almost certainly related to one another. The Carlisle chief of police speculated that they were probably sisters. They were dressed in nice outfits, including coats. No one knew or had any idea who the girls were. A Dickinson College professor analyzed pieces of their hair and corroborated the speculation that they were sisters. The bodies had no wounds or marks on them other than a small mark on the forehead of one girl. This mark launched police on a search for a possible secret society whose symbol might have been marked on the child. This led nowhere. The sad mystery of the three girls swept the nation.

The quest for the girls' identity started a nationwide media frenzy. The photographs of the children lying on a blanket at the site were printed in newspapers across the country. Thousands came to view the bodies in

The bodies of Norma, Dewilla and Cordelia Noakes, collectively known as the "Babes in the Woods," were found Nov. 24, 1934. (Pennsylvania State Police)

hopes of identifying them. Death masks were made before burial to continue the search. The media frenzy led to many false leads for the police.

Five days after the bodies were discovered, a black leather suitcase was found in brush about three miles from the point where the bodies had been located. A man named John Naugle, of New Cumberland, had found the suitcase. It contained clothing similar to that worn by the three small girls, as well as a notebook with the name "Norma" written on it, in what appeared to be a youngster's handwriting.

Shortly after the girls' bodies surfaced, the bodies of a man and woman were found in an abandoned railroad flag stop about 100 miles away in Duncansville, PA, just south of Altoona. The woman had been shot in the heart and the head, and the man had been shot in the head. A few days later a 1929 blue Pontiac sedan was found abandoned in a field near McVeytown, in Mifflin County. The car had no license plates and was out of gas. Its engine number had been intentionally obscured.

The car was traced to a man by the name of Elmo Noakes. The description of the car, the physical features of the bodies and Elmo Noakes' fingerprints from U.S. Marine records led to identification of the bodies as being that of Noakes (31 years old at the time of his death) and Winifred Pierce (age 18), formerly of Roseville, California. Pierce was also identified from pictures and by the fact that she had a deformed left foot.

Elmo Noakes was born on January 8, 1903 in Springville, Utah. He and his brother Robert served in the Marines from 1920 to 1922. In July 1923, he married a woman named Mary Hayford. Mary had a daughter named Norma Sedgwick from a previous marriage. Mary and Elmo had two children together: daughters Dewilla (born May 2, 1924) and Cordelia (born June 2, 1926).

In 1932, Mary died from infection following a self-induced abortion in Salt Lake City, Utah. Subsequently, Elmo moved to Roseville, California, where his three sisters could help care for and raise Norma, Dewilla and Cordelia. He was employed by Pacific Fruit Express, a railroad fruit shipping company.

Winifred "Winnie" Pierce was born on September 1, 1916 in Utah, to father Hugh Pierce and mother Pearl Noakes (Elmo's oldest sister, thus making Elmo Winifred's uncle, and she his niece). Winifred moved to Roseville and attended high school there. After high school, she went to work as a housekeeper for Elmo. How she and Elmo and his three daughters wound up lying dead on Pennsylvania soil would prove to be an interesting challenge for investigators in the Keystone State, who were essentially left with no choice other than to start working backwards in the hopes of piecing together what may have transpired.

Brothers Robert and Elmo Noakes served in the U.S. Marine Corps during World War I.

The girls' bodies were taken to the Ewing Funeral Home on South Hanover Street in Carlisle. An autopsy revealed that the children had had nothing to eat for at least 18 hours prior to their deaths. A pathologist at Harrisburg Hospital, George Moffitt, tested sections of the girls' organs and determined that they had not died of carbon monoxide poisoning, and that they had not been sexually assaulted. Another postmortem exam failed to find any indications of poison in the girls' systems.

If the girls could not be identified, they would be buried in a potter's field. State police asked the PA Board of Education to inquire about missing children of every school in Pennsylvania. Finally, three people came forward who claimed to have seen a man and a woman together with the three children in a restaurant in Philadelphia on November 19. The restaurant was the LaSalle Sandwich Shoppe on North Broad Street. The owner, Louis Ellis, remembered talking to Elmo Noakes about looking for work and Noakes saying he would take anything he could get. He mentioned his family was getting to be a "pretty big burden."

A waitress at the restaurant, Ann Gasparon, seated the party of five at two tables, and remembered that they ordered only one meal to be shared by all of them. A customer sitting nearby with her eight-year-old son heard this and felt sorry for the children. Anna LaFauvre invited the girls to join her and her son for a meal. The youngest Noakes child did, and they had a nice conversation. The girl told Mrs. LaFauvre they were from California and that she was in the third grade.

After the discovery of the bodies, all three adult witnesses from the restaurant were brought to Carlisle to assist in identifying the deceased children. Mrs. LaFauvre identified the bodies and fainted. Ellis and Gasparon also identified the girls as the ones they had seen in the restaurant. They were all driven to view the adult decedents and again recognized the bodies. As a result, the papers printed their identities on November 30, 1934 as:

This sign on a rural Pennsylvania road marks the spot where the bodies of the three young girls were found.

    Cordelia Noakes, age 8
    Dewilla Noakes, age 10
    Norma Sedgwick, age 13
    Elmo Noakes, age 32
    Winifred Pierce, age 18

On December 1, the funeral for the girls was held at Ewing Funeral Home. Hundreds of people attended, despite a heavy rain. The funeral/burial was paid for by the American Legion Post, apparently because Elmo Noakes had been a Marine. Boy scouts and girl scouts served as pallbearers. Presbyterian, Catholic and Episcopal clergy all participated. The burial was in Westminster Cemetery. A stone monument marks their burial spot.

Days later, Elmo Noakes and Winifred Pierce were also buried in Westminster Cemetery, about 100 yards from the girls in separate graves.

The American Legion provided for Elmo's funeral and a bugler played "Taps" over his grave. At that time, his role in the girls' deaths had not been established. Winnie's funeral was paid for by a sister.

Norma Sedgwick's father, Rowland, had tried to gain custody of his daughter after Mary Noakes died. He failed in his efforts and now he could not even afford to have her body transported to Utah where he lived. He was reportedly heartbroken.

In 1968, a group of Pennsylvania highway workers on their own time and initiative erected a blue and yellow keystone-shaped sign along Route 233 where the childrens' bodies were found. It reads:

ON THIS SPOT
WERE FOUND THREE
BABES IN THE WOODS
NOV. - 24 - 1934

We will never know for sure what happened. A State Police investigation concluded that Elmo Noakes left Roseville, California on November 11, 1934, with the three children and Winifred Pierce. Eleven days prior to their departure, on October 31, Noakes had purchased a blue 1929 Pontiac sedan for $46. Police theorized that he ran out of money and without prospects of employment killed the girls on November 21 rather than let them starve. It is generally believed that Noakes killed his daughters by suffocating them while they slept.

Then (the theory goes), after leaving the girls' bodies on blankets in the woods, Noakes and Pierce drove west, abandoned their car when it ran out of gas between McVeytown and Altoona, and hitchhiked to Altoona. On November 23, Pierce sold her coat, which was the couple's last possession except for the clothes they were wearing. Noakes bought a .22-caliber rifle from a second-hand store with the $2.55 Pierce got for her coat, and on November 24 used it to kill Pierce and

This tombstone marks the spot where the babes were laid to rest.

then himself. The weapon was found lying between their bodies. They spent their last night together at the Congress Hotel at 118th Street in Altoona, where the woman who ran the hotel confirmed afterwards that she had indeed rented them a room for all the money they had on them: 48 cents.

By all accounts, Elmo Noakes had a good reputation, a job, loved and cared for the girls, and had a non-violent nature. There are many strange elements to this story—elements on which one can only speculate. For instance, the group left California three days *before* Noakes would have gotten a paycheck for two weeks' work—money that would have come in extremely handy for a group of people about to embark on a cross-country trip. The speculation is that family strife caused them to leave suddenly. News accounts report that Noakes' sisters cared for his daughters at first, that is up until the time Elmo hired his niece, Winnie, to be his housekeeper and take care of the girls. Winnie started by working at Elmo's house in the day and returning to her home at her mother's house in the evening. After about six months however, Winnie quit going home and moved in with Elmo.

Here is the grave of Elmo Knoakes who took his own life after killing his three daughters.

The gossip in the community was that the relationship between uncle and niece had turned romantic, and two of Noakes' sisters strongly objected, even threatening to get the children removed from the household. Soon none of Elmo's sisters would speak to him. There was also acrimony between Winnie's mother, Pearl, and her husband, Hugh, over the situation. After the bodies were found, two of Noakes' sisters were found guilty of disturbing the peace stemming from their harassment of Pearl who they blamed for the deaths. Perhaps the turmoil reached a breaking point and led to impulsive, reckless behavior.

Also puzzling is the fact that—despite Elmo claiming to be looking for work—they traveled very fast across the country, and there were no reports of Noakes or Pierce actually asking for work. Their feeble attempts to avoid identification are also odd. The effacing of the car's VIN number, the discarding of the license plates, the use of aliases at places they stayed, the couples' manner of travel after leaving the bodies—these things all beg for explanations that won't ever be known for certain. Yet even after nearly 80 years, the memory of those beautiful young girls remains as haunting as ever.

If You Go:
Westminster Memorial Gardens is the final resting place for two American heroes:

John W. Minick, who was a staff sergeant in the United States Army when he was killed in action near Hurtgen, Germany, on November 21, 1944. On that day, he voluntarily led a small group of men through a minefield, single-handedly silenced two enemy machine gun emplacements, and engaged a company of German soldiers before he was killed while crossing a second minefield. For his actions he was awarded the Medal of Honor. His citation reads that he killed 22 enemy soldiers and captured 23 more. He was 36 years old.

Randall D. Shughart, who was a Special Forces soldier from Newville, Pennsylvania, and one of two soldiers (the other being Gary Gordon) who died trying to save the life of pilot Michael Durant, the only surviving member of a downed helicopter crew in Somalia on October 3, 1993. Shughart's actions - while costing him his own life - saved Durant's. For those actions, Shughart was awarded the Medal of Honor by President Clinton - the first soldier to be posthumously awarded the Medal of Honor since the Vietnam War. This incident was featured in the book and blockbuster Hollywood film "Black Hawk Down." The movie won two Oscars and was nominated for two more.

Shughart has been memorialized in many ways. A United States Navy ship, a training facility in Fort Polk, Louisiana, and his hometown post office in Newville all bear his name. Twenty years after his death, his modest grave was enhanced with a monument in his memory.

Also in Carlisle is the Old Public Graveyard (South Bedford & East South Streets), where Molly Pitcher and a number of Revolutionary War figures are buried.

A very short distance from Westminster Memorial Gardens is the Rustic Tavern (823 Newville Road). We stopped in for lunch and were hoping the experience would pick up our spirits. It was a cold, gloomy day and the story of the "Babes in the Woods" had proven to be equally cold and gloomy. It worked! The food, service and ambiance were all great. We warmed ourselves by the fire, had a hearty lunch and some spirits, and left determined to live on.

Smedley Butler (left) in Shanghai.

3

"The Fighting Quaker"

SMEDLEY BUTLER

County: Chester
Town: West Chester
Cemetery: Oaklands
Address: 1042 Pottstown Pike

Smedley Darlington Butler, nicknamed "the fighting Quaker" was a Major General in the United States Marine Corps and at the time of his death, the most decorated marine in United States history. Butler was a double-winner of the Congressional Medal of Honor, one of only twenty people to ever be so decorated. He is one of three to be awarded the Marine Corps Brevet Medal and the Medal Of Honor and the only man to be awarded the Brevet Medal and two Medals Of Honor, all for separate actions. During his 34 year career as a Marine, he participated in military actions in the Philippines, China, Central America, the Caribbean, and France in World War I. By the end of his career he had received sixteen medals, five of which were for heroism. Yet his military career is only part of what makes his story so very interesting.

Butler was born in West Chester, Pennsylvania and was the Quaker son of Thomas Stalker Butler who was a lawyer, judge, and for 31 years a Congressman. During the Spanish American War, Butler left high school 38 days prior to his 17th birthday to enlist in the Marine Corps. Although he did not finish all the coursework, he was awarded his high school diploma on June 6, 1898.

In the anti-Spanish war fever of 1898, he lied about his age and received a direct commission as a Marine second Lieutenant. He fought in the Philippine-American war later that year. In 1900, he received a brevet promotion to Captain and the Marine Corps Brevet Medal for his action during the Boxer Rebellion in which he was shot in the thigh and chest. In 1903 he fought to protect the United States Consulate in Honduras from rebels. Between the Honduras campaign and his next assignment, he returned to Philadelphia and on June 30, 1905 married Ethel Conway Peters of Philadelphia. The couple would have three children: a daughter Ethel and two sons Smedley and Thomas.

Butler served in Nicaragua from 1909 to 1912 and then in 1914 he earned his first Medal of Honor for the capture of Veracruz, Mexico during the Mexican Revolution. The citation says he exhibited courage and skill in leading his men.

The following year he was ordered to Haiti when Haitian rebels known as "Cacos" killed the Haitian dictator Vilbrun Sam. The Marines captured the rebel stronghold, Fort Riviere, after engaging in hand-to-hand combat. Butler's performance impressed the Assistant Secretary of the Navy, Franklin D. Roosevelt, who recommended him for his second Medal of Honor which was presented to him in 1917. That made him and Dan Daly the only Marines to receive the Congressional Medal Of Honor twice for separate actions.

During World War I, he was promoted to the rank of Brigadier General and placed in command of Camp Pontanezen at Brest, France, a debark station depot. His performance there earned him the Distinguished Service Medal of both the United States Army and Navy and the French Order of the Black Star.

After World War I, he became the Commanding General of the Marine Barracks at Quantico, Virginia. During a training exercise in 1921 he was told by a local farmer that Stonewall Jackson's arm was buried nearby. Not believing it, he had a squad of Marines dig up the spot and did indeed find Stonewall's arm in a wooden box. He replaced the wooden box with a metal box and reburied the arm. He left a plaque on the granite monument marking the place. The plaque is no longer on the marker but can be viewed at the Chancellorsville Battlefield Visitor's Center.

In 1924 Butler was asked by the Major of Philadelphia W. Freeland Kendrick to become the City's Director of Public Safety. Philadelphia's municipal government was notoriously corrupt, and Butler initially refused. President Coolidge intervened and authorized the necessary leave from the Marines. His major problem was the enforcement of Prohibition and his strong enforcement action earned him both enmity and respect. He left after two years and later stated that "cleaning up Philadelphia was worse than any battle I was ever in."

In 1927 Butler served a tour in China and returned as a Major General in 1929. In 1931 he publicly recounted a story about Benito Mussolini in which Mussolini struck a child with his automobile and refused to stop. This story caused international outrage, and Butler was arrested and court-martialed. The source of the story turned out to be Cornelius Vanderbilt Jr. who years later substantially confirmed the story. Butler was ordered to apologize to Mussolini, but he refused. Secretary of State Stimson issued a formal apology to Mussolini. As a trial approached, the case was settled by Butler receiving a reprimand. He retired on October 1. 1931.

In 1932 he ran for the United States Senate as a proponent of Prohibition but was defeated in the Republican Primary by James Davis. During his campaign, Butler spoke forcefully about the veteran's bonus for service during WW I. He spoke to the famous "Bonus Army" that marched on Washington and made camp nearby and encouraged them in their efforts. On July 28, 1932 army cavalry units led by General Douglas MacArthur dispersed the Bonus Army marchers and their wives and children by riding through Hooverville, as it came to be called, and using tear gas and burning their shelters and belongings. Butler then declared himself a "Hoover for ex-president Republican."

In 1934 Smedley Butler alleged the existence of a political conspiracy of Wall Street interests to overthrow President Roosevelt and that he had been asked to lead it. These allegations became known as the Business Plot. The allegations were never proven, but a Congressional investigation found that such an attempt was actually contemplated. (See *The Plot to Seize The Whitehouse* by Jules Archer.)

Butler became known for his outspoken views against war profiteering. In 1935 he wrote his book *War is a Racket* a condemnation of the profit motive behind warfare. His views are summarized in the following passage from a 1935 issue of the magazine "Common Sense":

"I spent 33 years and four months in active military service and during that period I spent most of my time as a high class thug for Big Business, for Wall Street and the bankers. In short, I was a racketeer, a gangster for capitalism. I helped make Mexico and especially Tampico safe for American oil interests in 1914. I helped make Haiti and Cuba a decent place for the National City Bank boys to collect revenues in. I helped in the raping of half a dozen Central American republics for the benefit of Wall Street. I helped purify Nicaragua for the International Banking house of Brown brothers in 1902-1912. I brought light to the Dominican Republic for the American sugar interests in 1916. I helped make Honduras right for the American fruit companies in 1903. In China in 1927, I helped see to it that Standard Oil went on its way unmolested. Looking back on it, I might have given Al Capone a few hints. The best he could do was to operate his racket in three districts. I operated on three continents."

Butler fought hard to raise awareness of what the real motivating factors of war were. He tried to bring the economic implications of war to the forefront of the public conscience. "War is a racket. It always has been. It is possibly the oldest, easily the most profitable, surely the most vicious" he wrote, noting how proponents typically use God and freedom to explain the mission but never discuss the economic details:

"It is conducted for the benefit of the very few at the expense of the masses. Like all members of the military profession I never had a thought of my own until I left the service. My mental faculties remained in suspended animation while I obeyed the orders of higher-ups."

In June 1940, Butler checked himself into a hospital after becoming sick. His doctor described his illness as an incurable condition of the upper abdominal tract, presumably cancer. He died in the Naval Hospital in Philadelphia on June 21, 1940. He is buried in a modest grave in Oaklands Cemetery in West Chester, Pennsylvania.

The USS Butler was named in his honor in 1942. This destroyer participated in the European and Pacific theaters during WW II. It was later converted to a high speed minesweeper. The Marine base in Okinawa is named in his honor.

Pictured above is the grave of two time Medal of Honor Recipient Smedley Butler who showed courage on the battlefield and beyond.

His books *War Is A Racket* and *The Letters Of A Leatherneck* are still available as are many books about him. There is also a Smedley Butler Society at www.warisaracket.org.

In Soldiers' Grove, behind the Pennsylvania State Capitol Building in Harrisburg, Smedley Butler is memorialized with a headstone in the ground. All of Pennsylvania's Congressional Medal of Honor recipients are honored in this way.

If You Go:
There are a number of other interesting people buried in Oaklands Cemetery. Dewitt Clinton Lewis was a Lieutenant Colonel for the Union army who received the Congressional Medal of Honor for rescuing a private.

William Hollingsworth Whyte Jr., a graduate of Princeton, was author of the 1956 best seller *The Organization Man* and a pioneer in urban planning specifically related to public life and pedestrian behavior.

Joseph Emley Borden was the winning pitcher of the first Major League Baseball game ever played. He pitched for the Boston Red Caps who beat the Philadelphia Athletics 6-5 on April 22, 1876.

Harry Dunn was an artist best known for creating the peacock logo for the NBC television network.

Samuel Barber was a two-time Pulitzer Prize winning composer whose works included symphonies, operas, chamber music and songs. His will stipulated that the burial plot neighboring his should be reserved for his long-time friend and partner Glan Carlo Menotti or at the very least have a stone inscribed "To The Memory of Two Friends." Menotti is buried in Scotland.

4

"Band of Brothers"

DICK WINTERS and JOE TOYE

Counties: Lancaster, Berks
Towns: Ephrata, Laureldale
Cemeteries: Bergstrasse, Gethsemane
Addresses: 9 Hahnstown Road, 3139 Kutztown Road

At a time when the world needed heroes, Dick Winters and Joe Toye served in a Company of Heroes. Their heroics were chronicled first in a book by famous historian Stephen Ambrose and then in an HBO miniseries of the same title: "Band of Brothers."

The story of Dick Winters begins and ends in Ephrata, Pennsylvania. He was born there on January 21, 1918 and moved to Lancaster at the age of eight. He was a reserved, hard-working boy who graduated from Lancaster Boys High School in 1937 and studied economics at Franklin and Marshall College where he graduated in 1941.

Winters enlisted in the Army for what he thought would be one year in August 1941, months before Pearl Harbor. He was disillusioned by what he was experiencing in training camp, and after Pearl Harbor, he took the opportunity to attend Officer Candidate School. He graduated from OCS at Fort Benning Georgia on July 2, 1942. He realized then that he was going to war, and he wanted to serve with the best, so he volunteered for the paratroopers and was assigned to Company E (known as Easy Company), 2nd Battalion, 506th Parachute Infantry Regiment (PIR). The 506th was an experiment in that it was the first to be trained as a unit. The training was very tough. Only 148 officers completed the training out of 500 who volunteered. Out of 5300 enlisted men, only 1800 finished. In June 1943, the 506 PIR became attached to the 101st Airborne.

The first combat for Winters and Easy Company was Operation Overlord, the D-Day Invasion of France. They were dropped behind enemy lines just after midnight on June 6, 1944. The Company Commander was killed before he ever jumped, and Winters was suddenly the man in charge. Winters survived the jump but because of withering anti-aircraft fire from below, they were dropped off target, and Winters had lost his weapon and contact with his men. Somehow he managed to keep his cool, survive through the night, meet up with thirteen other members of Easy Company (including Joe Toye), battle a few patrols and regroup with the main force.

Later that day, he and his thirteen members of Easy Co. were ordered to take out a German artillery bunker that was raining fire on Utah Beach where Allied forces were coming ashore. The bunker was defended by fifty

Dick Winters

German troops and contained four 150 mm heavy guns. Winters divided his squad into two groups. One group laid down covering fire with machine guns while he and a second group attacked the guns one at a time using grenades and TNT to disable them. Winters was shot in the leg, but it didn't stop him from continuing to lead the assault. This action has been called the Brécourt Manor Assault and is still taught at West Point as a textbook case of an assault on a fixed position. As a result of the assault that Winters planned, he and his men saved countless lives. Winters was awarded the Distinguished Service Cross, a promotion to Captain, and a place in American military lore all in his first combat maneuver. Later that afternoon, one of the men found a jug of cider and passed it around. When it came to Winters, he shocked his men by taking a long pull. It was the first alcohol he ever tasted. He thought it might calm him down, he later explained. That night before lying down for some much needed sleep, he made a promise to himself: If he lived through the war, he was going to find an isolated farm somewhere and spend the rest of his life in peace and quiet.

After helping capture the Nazi-infested town of Carentan, Winters and his men were chosen for Operation Market Garden in Holland in September 1944. This involved parachuting deep behind enemy lines, being surrounded, and stopping an attack on the 2nd Battalion's flank. While on patrol, they encountered a large group of Germans at a crossroads where the enemy were firing on American troops. Winters led his thirty-five men in an attack on three hundred Germans and routed them. This experience further sealed the bond between Winters and his men. After this, on October 9, Winters became the battalion executive officer, which was normally held by a major, but Winters filled it while a captain.

As if they hadn't done enough, in December, the 101st airborne was moved by truck to Bastogne, Belgium to defend against a German counter-offensive in what became known as the Battle of the Bulge. They were surrounded but held off elite German forces for a week of non-stop fighting until the U.S. Third Army broke through the German lines and, as the press reported, "rescued" them. No member of the 101st has ever agreed that they needed to be rescued.

Even after being relieved at Bastogne, Winters and his men weren't done. Easy Company led an attack on the town of Foy a few days later. The attack was successful and on March 8, 1945, Winters was promoted to Major. Shortly after he was made acting Battalion Commander.

In May, Easy Co. was ordered to capture Berchtesgaden and Hitler's summer home, "The Eagle's Nest." They were still there when the war ended on May 8, 1945.

On the way to Berchtesgaden, the company discovered a Nazi concentration camp that was part of the Dachau Complex. They saw thousands of prisoners starving in stripped pajamas and hundreds of corpses a little more than skeletons. Winters wrote in his log: "the memory of starved, dazed men who dropped their eyes and heads when we looked at them through the chain-linked fence, in the same manner that a beaten, mistreated dog would cringe, leave feelings that cannot be described and will never be forgotten. The impact of seeing those people behind that fence left me saying, only to myself, 'Now I know why I am here.'"

Winters remained in Europe until the fall of 1945. On November 29, he arrived at Ft. Indiantown Gap, Pennsylvania. In 1948, he met and married his wife Ethel Estoppey. In 1951 they bought a farm in Fredericksburg, Pennsylvania where they settled and raised two children. In 1972, he started his own animal feed business and moved to Hershey, Pennsylvania. He retired in 1997.

Winters led the quiet life he promised himself until he suddenly found himself a celebrity. He met Stephen Ambrose in 1988, and in 1992, Ambrose published "Band of Brothers" which chronicled the experiences of Easy Company. In 2001, it was turned into an HBO mini-series directed by Steven Spielberg and Tom Hanks. English actor Damien Lewis portrayed Winters. The miniseries won six Emmy awards, a Golden Globe, an American Film Institute award, and a Peabody award.

Winters published his own memoir in 2006 with co-writer Colonel Cole Kingseed. It's titled *Band of Brothers: The War Memoirs of Major Dick Winters*. In 2009, Franklin and Marshall College conferred an Honorary Doctorate upon Winters.

Joe Toye

Winters died at an assisted living facility in Campbelltown, Pennsylvania on January 2, 2011. He had been suffering from Parkinson's disease for several years. He is buried in a very modest grave in Bergstrasse Lutheran Church cemetery in Ephrata, Pennsylvania.

Joseph D. Toye was born in Hughestown, Luzerne County on March 14, 1919. His father, Peter, was a coal miner. Joe enlisted in the Army on December 11, 1941 in Wilks-Barre, Pennsylvania, four days after Pearl Harbor. He volunteered for the Paratroopers after basic training and was stationed at Camp Toccoa, Georgia and assigned to Easy Company. He completed the rigorous training and was one of the most respected men in the company. He made his first combat jump on D-Day in France and was one of the few who met up with Winters shortly after hitting the ground. He suffered a severe hand injury on the jump. He helped take out a German patrol on their way to the town of St. Come-du-Monte. He was one of the thirteen with Winters when they took out the guns at Brécourt Manor, and for his valor that day, he was awarded the Silver Star, the third highest combat decoration that can be awarded.

He was with Easy Company in Operation Market Garden where, desperate for information about enemy forces, he left the squad, went out in no-man's land by himself and brought back a live prisoner for interrogation.

On New Year's Day, 1945, the newly promoted Sergeant Toye was hit by shrapnel during a bombing by German planes just outside of Bastogne. This was his third wound; he had been hit in Normandy and again in Holland. He was evacuated to Bastogne for treatment. He could have been evacuated to a rear echelon hospital but asked to be returned to the front. When Major Winters suggested he take it easy for a few days, he answered, "I want to be with my buddies." Two days later, he lost his right leg in a heavy artillery barrage. His buddy, William Guarnere, also lost his right leg while trying to drag Sgt. Toye to safety. Shrapnel also hit Toye in the chest, stomach, and both arms. The shrapnel in his chest was removed in two separate operations, taking it out from the back.

Joe Toye spent about nine months in hospitals and was finally discharged from an Army hospital in Atlantic City, NJ. He had been awarded four Purple Hearts, a Silver Star, and a Bronze Star. It wasn't easy for him to find work with his disability, but he finally found work with Bethlehem Steel in Reading as a drill bit grinder.

He was married twice, the first time while recovering in the hospital. He had three sons and one daughter and seven grandchildren.

Sergeant Joseph Toye died of cancer in Reading on September 3, 1995. Dick Winters delivered his eulogy: "Every man in Company E would tell you that when the chips were down in combat, he would like to have Sgt. Joe Toye protecting his flank," Winters said.

In the HBO miniseries, Joe Toye is portrayed by actor Kirk Acevedo. He is buried in a very modest grave in Gethsemane Cemetery in Laureldale, near Reading, Pennsylvania.

The Emmy-winning HBO miniseries "Band of Brothers" transformed Dick Winters and Joe Toye and all the men of Easy Company into cultural icons. They have become the embodiment of millions of American Servicemen who marched off to war as ordinary men but achieved extraordinary things.

One person who was inspired by the story of Easy Company is Jordan Brown, a young Central Pennsylvania student. He heard of an effort to erect a statue in St. Marie Du-Mont, Normandy, France honoring all the men who served on D-Day. Jordan created olive green wristbands that are inscribed with the expression "Hang Tough" on it. Dick Winters was known for having used the expression often. The wristbands were distributed for a minimum donation of one dollar. Jordan's efforts attracted attention and gained steam and as of March 2012 his mother reported that he raised over $92,000, and the statue was dedicated on June 6th, 2012. Jordan was in attendance.

This tombstone marks the grave of Dick Winters who was certainly one of the greatest in the "Greatest Generation."

Here is the modest grave of four-time Purple Heart recipient Joe Toye a true hero of World War 2.

If You Go:

We found a great place to eat and replenish our vital bodily fluids in West Reading. The 3rd and Spruce Café on 3rd avenue had a great menu of food and drinks, a great atmosphere, terrific service, and an owner who liked our mission so much, he picked up the check. If you go there, be sure to use the restroom and be sure to look up and enjoy the unusual décor.

Also buried in Gethsemane Cemetery is four time all-star third basemen George "Whitey" Kurowski. He played nine seasons (1941-1949) with the St. Louis Cardinals.

Another baseball great is buried a few miles away in Reiffton at the beautiful Forest Hills Memorial Park. Carl Furillo played right field for the Brooklyn Dodgers from 1946-1960. Nicknamed "The Reading Rifle" because of his strong arm, Furillo batted over 300 five times and won the 1953

Here are the authors with the owner of the 3rd and Spruce Café in Reading. He liked us so much he picked up our tab for lunch.

batting title with a 344 average. He also recorded ten or more assists in nine consecutive seasons. He played in seven World Series, six of them against the Yankees, winning in 1955 and 1959 against the White Sox. He was one of Roger Kahn's famed "Boys of Summer" in his 1972 landmark book. When Kahn found him while writing the book, he was installing elevators in the World Trade Center. Furillo died in 1989 of a heart attack at home in Stony Creek Mills, PA at the age of 66.

Charles Evans Cemetery is also in Reading and contains many historical figures and unusual graves, including two prominent Civil War Generals who fought at the Battle Of Gettysburg; General David Gregg and General Alexander Schimmelfennig.

5

"Pennsylvania's Political Kingmaker"

SIMON CAMERON

County: Dauphin
Town: Harrisburg
Cemetery: Harrisburg
Address: 521 North 13th Street

To some, Simon Cameron was a brilliant Pennsylvania politician who built a political machine to advance his friends and himself. Others view him as one of the most corrupt public servants in the history of the Commonwealth. One thing that is certain is that he was one of the most influential Pennsylvanians of his time. Indeed one could argue if not for a man like Simon Cameron, Abraham Lincoln may never have been elected president.

Cameron was born on March 8, 1799, in Maytown, Pennsylvania. Because his parents were poor, he received very little formal education. Cameron's parents both died by the time he was nine, leaving him an orphan. Even as a youth he was driven and ambitious. He became an apprentice to a printer who was the editor of the Northumberland Gazette in order to ready himself to enter the field of journalism. By the time he was 21, his hard work began paying off as he found himself editor of the Bucks County Messenger.

Cameron then secured a position with the printing firm of Gales and Seaton. This firm happened to be the publishers of the Congressional debates. He made the most of this opportunity by making political friends in Washington and learning the art of politics. In 1824, he returned to Harrisburg, married Margaret Brua, and purchased a local newspaper. As the editor of his own paper he issued strong editorials addressing the issues of his day. His influence grew and in 1825 he was made state printer for the Commonwealth of Pennsylvania. Within a year he was also appointed to the position of adjutant general as part of the governor's staff.

One thing we know for sure about Cameron is that the man could identify opportunities. He saw all the internal improvement going on in Pennsylvania and surrounding states. He jumped in, constructing both railroads and canals. To aid in financing these ventures he founded a bank. This was in keeping with what he did his whole life: mixing private business with politics.

Cameron was a strong supporter of Democrats during the administrations of both Andrew Jackson and Martin Van Buren. During this time, he also helped elect James Buchanan to the United States Senate. President Van

Simon Cameron

Buren rewarded Cameron in 1833 by appointing him commissioner in charge of settling Winnebago Indian claims. His term here was tainted by scandal and ultimately led to his dismissal. It seems that Cameron felt it would be a good idea to adjust the claims on notes paid through his own bank. While his political career suffered damage, his ambitions remained and he still was confident in the methods that he had made the choice to employ.

In 1845, Cameron put together a coalition consisting of some Democrats, Whigs, and members of the Native American party and succeeded in his quest to be elected to the United States Senate. He served one term.

When the Republican party began to form Cameron saw, yet again, opportunity. He built up a political machine that returned him to the Senate in 1858 as a Republican. After that election, he attempted to position himself to be the party's nominee for president in 1860.

The Republican convention was held in Chicago, and Cameron arrived with little support outside Pennsylvania. However, the shrewd politician knew he had bargaining power. It was accepted that whoever the eventual nominee was, he was going to need Pennsylvania's support to secure the nomination and head the ticket. On the first ballot, William Seward received 173 and 1/2 votes. Lincoln was second with 102 votes and the other candidates were far back. It would take 233 votes to secure the nomination.

Lincoln had chosen David Davis, who was a long time friend, to represent him at the convention. He gave Davis the explicit instruction not to make deals that would bind him in any way. However, after the initial ballot, Davis was convinced that he needed Cameron's Pennsylvania votes to stop Seward. In order to secure Pennsylvania's support, Davis promised Cameron a cabinet position. Lincoln had received a mere 4 votes from Pennsylvania on the initial ballot but that number increased to 44 on the second. Honest Abe had seized the momentum and on the third ballot he won the nomination.

Lincoln was not happy about the deal that had been made with Cameron. As a matter of fact he made no effort to contact the Pennsylvanian. That did not deter Cameron. He made the trip to Springfield, Illinois to meet with the president-elect. Cameron left this meeting with a letter from Lincoln that promised he would be named either the Secretary of the Treasury or the Secretary of War. Later Lincoln, faced with opposition to the Cameron appointment, attempted to recall the letter. Not only did Cameron not respond to Lincoln's request, he persuaded elements of the Pennsylvania Legislature to pressure Lincoln on his behalf. Finally, Lincoln nominated Cameron to the position of Secretary of War. He did so because he felt Cameron could do less damage there than in the Treasury Department.

Then came the Civil War and the role of the War Department grew in terms of importance. It did not take long for rumors of corruption in the department to begin to grow. When the war began Lincoln made clear to the

Final resting place of one of Pennsylvania's most controversial politicians.

members of his cabinet that the emancipation of the slaves, at this point was not an option. Cameron and some Republican legislators were urging Lincoln to recruit Negro soldiers. Lincoln agreed to use Negroes as laborers in the army but not as soldiers. It was Lincoln's view that arming Negroes would lose the support of southerners still loyal to the union.

Cameron went his own way on the issue. He released his annual report in 1861 and it publicly contradicted the president by taking the position that the Negroes should be freed and be made part of a Negro Army. When word of this report reached Lincoln (Cameron had not run it past the president), he ordered it be withdrawn and rewritten. It turned out to be too late as both versions found their way to the press. The publication of the two reports showed an administration at war against not only the rebels, but against themselves.

During the holiday season between 1861 and 1862 things came to a head. Complaints about irregularities in the War Department had begun to flood Congress. On two occasions Congress demanded that Cameron provide information on contracts awarded since he assumed office. He ignored both requests. In response, the House set up a committee to investigate the War Department. The investigation produced a 1,109 page report that was damning to the administration. Cameron and his "agents" were accused of ignoring the competitive bidding process. It claimed that the department had supplied the army by buying from favored suppliers who were often dishonest. The report alleged that the War Department purchased huge amounts of tainted pork, rotten blankets, knapsacks that couldn't hold up in foul weather, and hundreds of diseased and dying horses at inflated prices. The report also claimed that the department sold condemned Hall carbines cheaply, bought them back for $15.00 apiece, turned around and sold them again for $3.50, and then bought them back at the price of $22.00 a piece.

By early in 1862, Lincoln concluded that Cameron had to go. The president made it easy on him. On January 11, 1862, the president wrote to Cameron, noting that he had requested a change in position. The president said he was pleased to inform Cameron that he was going to nominate him to be minister to Russia. One wonders what Abe may have done had Siberia been an option.

Cameron served in Russia a very short time before returning to Pennsylvania. He regained his Senate seat in 1867 and held it until 1877, when he was sure his son would replace him. Cameron then retired to his farm in the Maytown area where he died on June 26, 1889. He was 90 years old. Perhaps he summed up his public career best when he said, "An honest politician is one who, when he is bought, will stay bought." Simon Cameron is buried in the Harrisburg Cemetery.

If You Go:

Also buried in the Harrisburg Cemetery is Civil War General John Geary (see chapter 10). In addition, the authors urge you to stop at the cemetery office where you can pick up a booklet that provides for a walking tour of the premises. It is a very old and interesting cemetery that includes a section where both Union and Confederate casualties of the Civil War were laid to rest.

You are also very close to the National Civil War Museum, which is located at One Lincoln Circle in Harrisburg's Reservoir Park section - it is definitely worth seeing.

If you choose to dine in Harrisburg, the city offers a "restaurant row" on 2nd Street that provides multiple options. The authors would point out that within about a half mile of the cemetery there is a small Italian place called the Subway Cafe. It is located on Herr Street about a half a block below Cameron Street (yes, *that* Cameron!). The Subway Cafe offers fishbowls of beer and the finest pizza in the land.

6

"The Lattimer Massacre"

MICHAEL CHESLOCK

County: Luzerne
Town: Hazleton
Cemetery: Hazleton
Address: 120 North Vine Street

On September 17, 1897, the *Hazleton Daily Standard* published the following verse:

> If the courts of justice shield you
> And your freedom you should gain,
> Remember that your brows are marked
> With the burning brand of Cain.
> Oh, noble, noble, deputies
> We always will remember
> Your bloody work at Lattimer
> On the 10th day of November.

The verse was a testament to yet another act of violence involving labor and management in the anthracite coal region of Pennsylvania. This incident became known as the Lattimer Massacre.

The coal region is located in northeastern Pennsylvania. It is largely made up six counties: Lackawanna, Luzerne, Columbia, Carbon, Schuylkill and Northumberland. Coal was discovered in the area in 1762. This discovery would have a profound influence on those who chose to settle in the coal region in the 1800's. The coal industry went through a tremendous growth spurt after the civil war. This growth provided tremendous wealth for the few who had the capital to obtain mining rights and the land beneath where the vast deposits of coal could be found. For a minority of people who worked for the mining companies it provided a good job and a decent income. These people were mine bosses, superintendents, and supervisors. The majority of the employees were the actual miners who were faced with extremely dangerous work, harsh conditions and low pay coupled with the fact that they were forced to live in company supplied housing and purchase their goods at company owned stores. Often a miner's wages failed to cover his and his family's expenses, and he went into debt to the company. These conditions led to conflict, sometimes violent, between labor and management (see Chapter 19 titled "The Molly Maguires," p. 119).

Mine workers marching to their slaughter outside of Lattimer, PA, September 10, 1897.

The jobs in the mines were generally filled by the latest groups of immigrants to enter the region. This meant that in the 1890's most of the miners were of Italian or Slavic decent. At this time the company owned town of Lattimer housed an Italian population. Similar company owned towns in the area were largely occupied by Slavic miners and their families. In either case they were renting their homes from mine owner Ariovistus Pardee, who was one of the wealthiest men in America at the time.

As newcomers, these miners were often assigned the most difficult and dangerous jobs available. In addition, they were often subjected to prejudice. For example the Slavic miners were often called "hunkies." They were also angry about the "alien tax" that had been passed by the Pennsylvania General Assembly. This tax required a three-cent levy per day on all immigrant employees. When one considers that the immigrants' earnings were already set lower than their more established counterparts doing the same work, it becomes easy to see the anger that resulted from these conditions. Thus the stage had been set for the latest clash between labor and management in Pennsylvania's Anthracite Coal region.

A number of incidents occurred in the late summer of 1897 that led to the trouble that would eventually take place in Lattimer. In August, Gomer James, who worked for the mine owners in a management position, decided to make a central stable for all of the mules who worked in the mines to save money. Mine owners at this time valued a trained mule more than a miner since it cost about $200 to buy and train the animal. One of the savings was that a single crew could now be given the job of feeding and watering the mules. Another consequence of the decision was that the mules were no longer kept at the mines where they worked and the mule drivers had to travel to the central stable to pick them up. In many cases this added two hours to the workers day as they had to wake an hour early to get to the stable to pick up the mule and then spend an hour after work returning the animal. The workers were angry because they received no compensation for this extra time.

On August 13, 1897, a majority of the mule drivers who worked at the Honeybrook mine went on strike. In addition they formed a human fence

From the New York Evening Journal, 10 March 1898, p. 5

and refused to allow anyone to enter the mine to get to work. When word of this reached Jones, he grabbed a crowbar, rushed to the scene and attacked the nearest striker, hitting him across the shoulders. The other strikers rushed to intervene and soon had Jones on the ground where they began to beat him. The local supervisor, Oliver Welsh, then intervened stopping the beating and promptly firing all the strikers. In breaking up the fight, Welsh suffered a blow to the head from a stone; it took eight stitches to close the wound.

News of what happened at Honeybrook quickly spread across the coal fields. The result was that more miners joined the strike. Within three days more than 800 miners had joined the effort to better their treatment. They demanded a wage hike, the right to shop at stores other than those owned by the company, the freedom to choose their own doctor and an end to the alien tax. The strikers appointed a team of leaders to negotiate with management on their behalf.

The strike ended on a temporary basis when the strikers' leaders negotiated a ten cent pay increase. While the miners were happy with the increase, they remained disturbed that their other issues had not been addressed, and as a result on August 25, 1897, the strike was renewed with a march. Local newspapers reported that anywhere from 300 to 500 miners had taken to the streets to march in protest of their working conditions.

On September 4, 1879, the miners issued a list of demands. These demands included a fifteen cents per day raise for every employee, the right to seek out and pay for the doctor of their choice, they would be paid if they reported to work even if work wasn't possible because machinery was out of order and they would not be compelled to shop in company stores or use the company butcher. The coal companies divided in their response to these demands. By September 6th the men at Coleraine and Milnesville were back at work. The mine owners here agreed that the miners could shop where they wished though the company stores would remain open. That same day, Sheriff Martin of Luzerne County met with supervisors of the Cross Creek Coal Company, and it was decided that none of the strikers' demands would be met. The coal company agreed that it would furnish funds to pay for an armed force of deputies to aid the Coal and Iron Police. Sheriff Martin was dispatched to Hazleton with instructions to raise such a force. Martin had no trouble finding men, and within a day, he deputized approximately eighty volunteers who he armed with new Winchester rifles. Martin also issued a proclamation that he sent to the Wilkes-Barre Times. The proclamation put the striking miners on notice in that it warned against any unlawful assembly or any acts of violence.

On September 9th a group of miners from Lattimer met with their counterparts from Harwood. The Harwood miners were already on strike, and the delegation from Lattimer expressed their desire to join in and close both of Pardee's mines in the area. The largely Slavic miners from Harwood agreed that Pardee would give no concessions unless he was faced with a show of unity from the miners. Therefore, it was decided that the Harwood miners would march to Lattimer the next day where the Lattimer miners would join them in the strike.

September 10, 1897, was a warm and sunny day. Approximately three hundred men appeared at Harwood to join in the march to Lattimer. A few of the men carried American flags to display during the march. The vast majority of the marchers did not speak English nor were they American citizens. Michael Cheslock, who did speak English and had applied for American citizenship, was selected to be one of the leaders of the march. The large group set off for Lattimer; they were unarmed and marched peacefully.

As soon as Sheriff Martin received word of the procession, he mobilized his forces. As the marchers neared Hazleton, they were met by Martin and his posse. Martin pulled his gun pointed it at a marcher and ordered the group to disperse. The miners, who felt they were doing nothing wrong, refused. Around this time a fight broke out, and one deputy grabbed a flag from a marcher and tore it to bits. At this point the chief of the Hazleton police intervened. The fighting stopped when the chief said the march could continue but could not go through Hazleton. The marchers agreed and proceeded on around the city.

Martin ordered his men to trolleys bound for Lattimer. Later some of the trolley passengers would report that tensions were high, and there was talk of a shooting. One deputy was overheard saying "I bet I drop six of them." A reporter notified the Wilkes-Barre Times that serious trouble was coming. Word of what was happening spread through the area. Mothers, in Lattimer, went to the local schoolhouse to remove their children, a wise move in light of what was about to unfold.

FIRING ON THE MINERS. AN ACCURATE VIEW OF THE FIELD WHERE THE TRAGEDY TOOK PLACE
Drawn by an Inquirer Staff Artist.

By a Philadelphia Inquirer staff person, 12 September 1897, front page.

The Lattimer mine shut down. Martin and his men arrived and were joined by coal and iron police. Now in command of an armed force of about 150, Martin assembled his men at the forked entrance to the town of Lattimer.

It was 3:45 that afternoon when the marchers approached Lattimer led by a man carrying the American flag. The miners' ranks had by now swelled to over 400 men. Martin approached the marchers and told them they were participating in an unlawful assembly. He ordered them to disperse. Many of the marchers couldn't understand what the sheriff said and just as many could not hear him. Michael Cheslock and other leaders of the march attempted to talk with Martin, but the sheriff was having none of that. He attempted to grab the American flag from the marcher in front. Failing there, he grabbed a marcher from the second row, and when other marchers came to his defense, a scuffle ensued. Martin pulled his pistol, but it misfired, and at this point someone yelled "fire." Eyewitnesses would claim it was the sheriff, but he would deny the charge. Whoever gave the order, the deputies opened up. Michael Cheslock was shot between the eyes and killed immediately. The marchers, seeing what was happening, turned to run, but the deputies continued to fire. Some ran toward the schoolhouse where the teachers inside soon saw shots piercing the walls and sending wood splinters flying. The shooting went on for at least a minute and a half, and when it was over 19 of the marchers lay dead and another thirty-six were wounded. Some of the deputies walked through the dead and wounded kicking them. Some of the marchers begged for help, and one eyewitness

This monument sits at the site of the massacre.

heard a deputy respond to these pleas by saying, "we'll give you hell, not water, hunkies!" Sheriff Martin surveyed the area around him, and in a classic understatement muttered, "I am not well."

Wagons were called in to move the dead and wounded to local hospitals and undertakers. Many of the dead were taken to Boyle's and Bonin's who, as undertakers, were assigned the responsibility of preparing the bodies for burial.

The grave site of Michael Cheslock who was the first miner killed during the Lattimer Massacre.

Undertaker Boyle would later testify that the bodies left in his care had been shot in the back. Boyle's decedents run a funeral home in Hazleton to this day. The funeral director at present is named Thomas Boyle. Tom and the author went to high school together.

The next few days were bedlam in the coal country. Many of the deputies headed to the Jersey Shore to wait out the events. The Governor of Pennsylvania sent the state militia to Hazleton to preserve order since most expected there would be reprisals. To the surprise of many, the immigrants remained peaceful. Large funerals continued in the days to follow, some drawing crowds of as many as eight thousand people.

The story of the massacre was covered in the press throughout the country. Generally the sheriff and his deputies were found to be at fault. *The Philadelphia Inquirer* said that the massacre was,

> "a human slaughter in which men were mowed down like grain stalks before a scythe, by the deadly bullets which stormed for fully two minutes. An exact list of the dead and wounded is impossible to be obtained tonight, but the Inquirer counted twelve dead men in the field. Two others died at the hospital and a number of others are expected to die at any moment."

Sheriff Martin was being hounded by the press, so he finally told his side of the story. He said he received word of the march from one of his deputies who told him that the miners were heavily armed. In response he gathered his deputies together and told them to remain calm no matter what happened. He said when the marchers arrived in Lattimer, he read them the proclamation but that they paid no attention to him and continued to march. Martin said he told the leader to stop, but that order was also ignored. He said he tried to arrest the leader, but when he did, he was surrounded by the strikers who began kicking him. He then told the reporters,

Here lies 4 of 14 victims of the Massacre who are buried side by side.

"I realized something needed to be done at once or I would be killed. I called to the deputies to discharge their firearms into the air over the heads of the strikers, as it might probably frighten them. It was done at once but it had no effect whatever on the infuriated foreigners, who used me so much the rougher and became fiercer and fiercer, more like wild beasts than human beings."

Martin went on to say that the miners were desperate and did not value human life. He claimed that his deputies were ordered to shoot only to protect their own lives and the property they were there to defend. He said that he felt bad about giving the order to fire but insisted that it was his duty in light of the situation.

Soon after this interview, Martin changed his story. He said the marchers were not on company property; that they were on a public road. When asked if the marchers had done anything that was not peaceful, he said no. He denied giving the order to fire saying; that had been done by someone else. Soon after Martin and his deputies were arrested and charged with murder.

On February 1, 1898, the trial of Martin and his deputies began in Wilkes-Barre. It took over a month to complete and testimony was received from about 200 witnesses. On March 9, 1898 the jury returned with a verdict of "not guilty." News of the verdict sparked outrage not only in the United States but throughout Eastern Europe as well. A Slovak cartoon shows a dead miner laying at the feet of justice. Justice is not depicted as being blind but is seen looking at a bag of money.

In many ways, the martyred miners of Lattimer inspired the working people of America to do something about their working conditions. After the massacre, more than 15,000 workers joined the United Mine Workers of America. In time that union became the most powerful representative of the anthracite workers. At the peak of its power, it represented 150,000 workers in the region.

In 1972 a monument was erected in Lattimer at the site of the massacre. An inscription on the monument reads,

"It was not a battle because they were not aggressive, nor were they defensive because they had no weapons of any kind and were simply shot down like so many worthless objects, each of the licensed life-takers trying to outdo the others in butchery."

Michael Cheslock is buried in the Hazleton Cemetery. His grave is easy to find if you use the Diamond Avenue entrance to the cemetery. As you enter, Cheslock's grave is to your right just a few yards away from your entry point. Cheslock was 39 years old when he was killed.

If You Go:
Also buried in the Hazleton cemetery is Sergeant Robert H. Sinex who fought with the Union during the Civil War. According to one of his death notices, he was a secret service agent who saw Lincoln's assassination and participated in the capture of John Wilkes Booth. If you wish to visit his grave, we suggest a stop at the cemetery office. The Hazleton Cemetery is located on the same side of Hazleton as the Saint Stanislaus's Polish Catholic Cemetery, and a visit to this site is a must. Fourteen of the miners

These 14 tombstones lined up side by side mark the graves of miners shot to death during the massacre.

shot at Lattimer are buried here in a manner to get your attention. The fourteen are lined up side by side against the cemetery wall. Their tombstones are identical and all contain the same information. At the top of the stone is the miners name and inscribed underneath the name on each marker it reads, "Shot September 10, 1897."

This cemetery is located at 652 Carson Street in Hazleton, and the wall you are looking for is the one with the school building right across the street. If you visit Saint Stanislaus's you are right next to the Most Precious Blood cemetery. You may want to stop in here to visit the grave of Jack "the Dandy" Parisi. Parisi was a member of the notorious group Murder Incorporated which accepted and carried out murder contracts from mob bosses throughout the country. A government agent once said of Parisi, "if you hung him up by his thumbs for eight hours he might tell you his name."

If you are in need of refreshments you have plenty of options in Hazleton. We had a pint and the best perogies we have ever tasted at a small pub called the "Battered Mug" located on the corner of South Pine and Beech streets. If you are in Hazleton you are close to many people that we covered within this volume including Jim Thorpe, Black Jack Kehoe of the Molly Maguires, and Mary Jo Kopechne. As it would be very difficult to visit all the sites in one day, we recommend spending the night at the Comfort Inn located in West Hazleton. The hotel is clean, reasonably priced and has a friendly staff. In addition it houses a nice lounge called "Timbers" that offers live entertainment on the weekends.

7

"The Pittsburgh Kid"

BILLY CONN

County: Allegheny
Town: Pittsburgh
Cemetery: Calvary
Address: 718 Hazelwood Avenue

On May 18, 1941, Joe Louis, the undisputed heavyweight champion of the world, stepped into the ring at the Polo Grounds to defend his title for the 18th time. Louis had trained hard for this fight wanting to lose weight and gain speed. At the morning weigh-in, he tipped the scales at just under 200 pounds. Looking across the ring at his opponent, Louis saw a much smaller man. The challenger had weighed in at 169 pounds and was a decided underdog. He had given up his light heavyweight crown in order to earn the right to fight Louis. His name was Billy Conn, the Pittsburgh Kid, and he was about to capture the hearts of the American public.

Conn was born on October 8, 1917 in Pittsburgh, Pennsylvania. The Pittsburgh of that day was far different from the city today. It was the steel city then and with all the black smoke coming from the mills, the streetlights were kept on during the day. H. L. Mencken described it as "so dreadfully hideous, so intolerably bleak and forlorn that it reduced the whole aspiration of a man to a macabre and depressing joke."

Conn's father, Billy Sr., worked in those mills for forty years. He once told his son that one day he would have a job at the plant. The very idea was enough to scare Conn into pursuing another career. Years later he talked about how people always said you had to be crazy to be a fighter. In Conn's words "I was nuts, but it beats working in those mills."

Conn's parents sent him to parochial school at a place called Sacred Heart. He lasted until the 8th grade when one of the nuns suggested that another child could make far better use of the space he was taking up. By this time Conn had already gotten a job in a gym where his primary duty was to clean the place up. The job did provide him with the opportunity to spar and served as his introduction to boxing.

Conn never fought a single fight as an amateur. His manager, Johnny Ray, didn't believe in fighting unless there was a purse at stake. When he was 17, Conn fought professionally for the first time. He went four rounds but lost on a decision to a more experienced opponent. He was paid $1.50 for the bout. He lost a few more fights in 1935 but within a couple of years, he grew as both a fighter and a man. By 1937 he weighed 147 pounds and

Billy Conn

had developed a solid left jab and a hook that Joe Louis would describe as the fastest he had ever seen.

In 1936 Conn won a bout against a future welterweight champ by the name of Fritzie Zivic. Zivic was also from Pittsburgh and the two fighters disliked each other; it was a local rivalry. During round one, Zivac used the laces of his gloves on Conn who responded in round two with a shot to Zivac's groin. The fight went a full ten rounds with Conn emerging the winner by decision. Conn later called Zivac the dirtiest fighter he ever faced. Zivac was one of ten future boxing champions who would lose a fight to the Pittsburgh Kid. This win put Conn on the boxing map from which he would never disappear.

Conn continued to compete against very tough fighters; he never ducked anyone. Once, Pittsburgh Pirate announcer Bob Prince (see Chapter 22, page 151) said on air that Conn had ducked opponents. Conn saw Prince at the Pittsburgh Arena, slammed him into a wall and said he'd beat the hell out of him if he kept up the negative and false reporting. Prince held his tongue, and the two became good friends.

On May 27, 1937 he faced a black boxer by the name of Oscar Rankin. He won his 23rd straight fight that night. It was years later that Joe Louis told Conn that his managers had refused to let him fight Rankin. Louis told Conn, "the people who managed you must not have liked you very much. Nobody would let me fight that sonuvabitch."

By the year 1939, Conn was reaching his prime. He fought Fred Apostoli, who would later become the middleweight champion of the world, twice early in the year with both bouts taking place at Madison Square Garden. Conn won both fights by decision. One of the spectators at the first bout was a beautiful young woman by the name of Mary Louise Smith. Conn first met Mary when she was 15, and he immediately informed her that one day he was going to marry her. Mary's father Jimmy Smith, who played second base for the 1917 World Series Champion New York Giants, didn't approve. In fact he vowed he would never let Conn marry his daughter. A few years later, in 1941, Conn and Mary Louise Smith became man and wife, despite her father's wishes.

On July 13, 1939 Conn met Melio Bettina for the Light Heavyweight Championship of the world. After 15 hard fought rounds, Conn emerged the winner. A rematch was set for September 25, 1939. It took another 15 rounds but Conn successfully defended his title. The number one heavyweight contender at this time was Bob Pastor who had only been defeated once, by Joe Louis, in over 50 fights. On September 6, 1940, Conn fought Pastor in New York City. It was yet another tough fight, but in the 13th round Conn knocked Pastor to the canvas where he was counted out. Conn was now the number one contender for the heavyweight crown. Conn would remain the Light Heavyweight Champion until May of 1941, when he

1946 Joe Louis knocks out Billy Conn.

voluntarily relinquished the title in order to pursue the Heavyweight Championship of the World.

On the night of June 18, 1941, the Pittsburgh Pirates had a night game at home. The Pirates' management knew that everyone in Pittsburgh was going to stay home to listen to the broadcast of the Pittsburgh Kid taking on Joe Louis. In order to draw fans to the ballpark the Pirates announced that once the fight began the game would be halted and the radio broadcast would be played through the stadium's public address system.

Conn entered the ring an enormous underdog. Not only was he much smaller than Louis, but he was facing a man many considered (and many still do) the greatest heavyweight fighter in history. Joe Louis was certainly confident of his place in boxing history as he demonstrated when he appeared on a television show with Muhammad Ali shortly after Ali became champion. Ali asked Louis if he really thought he could have won a fight between the two. Louis responded that when he held the title he went on what people called a "bum of the month" tour as he defended his title on a monthly basis. Ali asked Louis if he was calling him a bum. Louis responded "you woulda been on the tour." But on this night, as Louis was to discover, he wasn't fighting a bum.

The bell rang starting the fight, and Conn as usual started slowly even slipping to the canvas while avoiding a punch from Louis. During round two

Louis was again the aggressor as he attacked his smaller opponent in an effort to wear him out. Then in the third round things began to turn around as Conn got the better of the heavyweight champ. By the end of round nine, a confident Conn told Louis that on this night he was in a fight, and the champ agreed. By the end of round twelve, Conn was clearly in control of the fight. All he had to do was continue to box Louis for the remaining three rounds and the heavyweight championship would be his. In his corner between rounds, Conn predicted he would knock Lois out in the 13th. His handlers responded by telling him to keep boxing and stay away from the champ. In their view the fight had already been won. Across the ring in Louis's corner his people were telling the champ that he needed a knockout to win.

Conn later said that he had promised his mother (who was then lying on her deathbed in Pittsburgh) that he would win this fight by knocking out Louis. Conn answered the bell for round thirteen and went aggressively after Louis. He was playing into the champ's hands, and Louis took advantage rocking Conn with a powerful right hand to the jaw. Conn's legs buckled, but he didn't go down. Louis moved in landing several consecutive punches until Conn did hit the canvas. He was counted out with two seconds left in the round and Louis had retained his title. After the fight Conn said, "What's the sense of being Irish if you can't be dumb?" Years later Conn would ask Louis why he couldn't have just let him be the champion for a few months. Louis responded by telling him he had been champion for twelve rounds but that he couldn't hold the title.

Despite the loss Conn became a nationwide hero. He did tons of radio interviews and was featured in numerous magazines. He even made a movie that was appropriately titled "The Pittsburgh Kid." Many fight fans and ring experts believed the bout to have been the greatest fight in history, and the public wanted a rematch. Louis agreed to fight Conn again, and the two were scheduled to meet in November of 1942. The fight was set even though both men were heading into the military.

Jimmy Smith may have failed at stopping Conn from marrying his daughter, but he was about to play a major role in stopping the Louis–Conn rematch. In May of 1942, Conn was home on leave to attend the baptism of his son Timmy. Timmy's godfather was Art Rooney, the owner of the Pittsburgh Steelers. Rooney arranged a party at Conn's house and invited Jimmy Smith. Rooney told Conn that his father in law was ready to make peace with him. Rooney had miscalculated the bad blood between the two. It began with Smith verbally attacking Conn and it ended in a full-fledged fistfight. During the fight Conn caught Smith on the top of the head with a left; the punch landed but Conn broke his hand. The rematch was called off due to the injury. Conn and Louis did fight again in 1946 but by that time Conn was well past his prime, and Louis took him in eight rounds. Conn retired as a fighter in 1948.

When Conn was 73 years old in 1990, he stepped into a Pittsburgh convenience store where a robbery was underway. The Pittsburgh Kid didn't hesitate as he floored the robber with one punch and then began wrestling him. The robber got away but not before Conn had pulled off his coat which contained the man's name and address and that led to an easy arrest.

Conn passed away in 1993 at the age of 75. He was laid to rest at Calvary Cemetery in Pittsburgh. Conn is remembered as one of the greatest light heavyweights in boxing history. He is a member of both the Ring Boxing Hall of Fame and the International Boxing Hall of Fame.

The gravesite of one the greatest light heavyweight champions in the history of boxing.

If You Go:

There are plenty of other sites in Calvary Cemetery including the great entertainer Frank Gorshin (see Chapter 12, page 77), former Pennsylvania Governor David Lawrence and the quarterback of the four horsemen of Notre Dame Harry Stuhldreher. In addition Pittsburgh is loaded with great eateries and taverns. We would recommend you check out Winghart's located at 5 Market Square in Pittsburgh. We both agreed that this place had the best burgers we had ever tasted. The staff was friendly and the service was great. The city has a great zoo and is home to Kennywood Park.

8

"The First American"

BENJAMIN FRANKLIN

County: Philadelphia
Town: Philadelphia
Cemetery: Christ Church Burial Ground
Address: Corner of 5th and Arch Streets

It is not exaggerating to say that to this day, no Pennsylvanian is as well known or as well respected as Ben Franklin. The man excelled at so many things. He was an author, a political theorist, a scientist, an inventor, a diplomat and politician (though he might disagree), and a revolutionary. He truly earned the title "The First American."

Ben Franklin was born in Boston, Massachusetts on January 17, 1706. His father, Josiah Franklin, was born in England where he married his first wife in 1677. The couple arrived in America in 1683. By that time, they had three children, and after arriving in America, they had four more. Josiah made a living as a soap and candle-maker. After his first wife died, he remarried and had ten more children. Franklin was Josiah's 15th child and his last son.

Franklin's parents wanted a career in the church for him. He was sent to school with the clergy but after two years, his parents could no longer make the payments to allow him to continue. Franklin never graduated, but through his own reading, he continued what would be called a self-education. At the age of twelve he went to work for his brother James, a printer, who taught him the trade. James founded "The New England Courant," the first independent newspaper in the colonies. Franklin began to write letters to the paper under the name of Mrs. Silence Dogwood. The views expressed became the subject of conversation around Boston. When James discovered that Franklin was the popular author, he punished him. In addition to verbal abuse, his brother was known to beat Franklin. Having had enough, Franklin fled his apprenticeship at age seventeen, and according to the laws of the time, became a fugitive.

Franklin arrived in Philadelphia in 1723, seeking a fresh start. With his experience, he was able to find work in printing shops. Pennsylvania's Royal Governor William Keith convinced Franklin to return to England to find the equipment needed to start a new newspaper in Philadelphia. When the Governor failed to provide the backing for the enterprise, Franklin found work in a printer's shop in London. He returned to Philadelphia in 1726, and went to work for a merchant as a clerk, shopkeeper, and a bookkeeper.

Benjamin Franklin

Franklin organized a group of men known as the "Junto" in 1727. The goal of the group was to engage in activities that would improve the members as individuals and at the same time benefit the community. The group created a library. Franklin came up with the idea to form a subscription library, in order to increase the number of books available. This was done by combining the funds of the members to buy additional books that would be available for all to read. Franklin hired the first librarian in 1732.

In 1728, Franklin's employer passed away and Franklin returned to the printing business. The next year, he became the publisher of a newspaper called "The Pennsylvania Gazette." The newspaper provided Franklin with a mechanism to make known his views on the important issues of the time. His observations were well received and his stature continued to grow.

In 1730, Franklin entered into what would be called a common law marriage with Deborah Reed. He could not marry Reed because she already had a husband, though he had abandoned her. One of the reasons that may have led Franklin to make this decision was the fact that he had recently acknowledged that he was the father of an illegitimate son named William, and he wanted to provide his son a family life. William's mother remains unknown. Ben and Deborah had two other children. The first was a son named Francis, who was born in 1732, and died in 1736. The second child, a daughter named Sarah, was born in 1743.

During this time period, Franklin also began a career as an author. In 1733, he began to publish "Poor Richard's Almanac." Franklin seldom published under his own name and in this instance the author was identified as Richard Saunders. Some of his witty adages such as "Fish and visitors stink in three days" are still quoted today. Though published under the name Saunders, it was common knowledge that Franklin was the author. His reputation continued to grow. The almanac itself was a tremendous success, selling about 10,000 copies per year. In today's world, that would translate to about three million copies.

Franklin founded the American Philosophical Society in 1743. The purpose of this organization was to provide a forum where scientific men, like himself, could discuss their projects and discoveries. It was around this time that Franklin began studying electricity. That study would remain a part of his life until the day he died. The story of the kite, the string, and the key is probably a false one. The television show "MythBusters" simulated the supposed experiment and concluded that if Franklin had proceeded as described, he would have been killed.

In addition to his scientific studies, Franklin was also an inventor. Among his more noted inventions are the Franklin stove, the lightning rod, and bifocal lenses. Franklin, viewed his inventions as yet another way that life could be improved for humankind.

In 1747, Franklin decided to get out of the printing business. He formed a partnership whereby David Hall would run the business and the two would share the profits. This provided Franklin with a steady income and also gave him the time to pursue his studies and other interests. His writings, inventions, and discoveries had by now made him well known throughout the colonies and in Europe.

As he grew older, Franklin became more and more interested in public affairs. He was drawn into Philadelphia politics and was soon elected to the post of councilman. In 1749 he became a Justice of the Peace and two years later, he was elected to the Pennsylvania Assembly. In 1753, he was appointed to the post of joint deputy postmaster general of North America. In this role, he worked to reform the postal system. Among his accomplishments was the adoption of the practice to deliver mail on a weekly basis.

During this time, Franklin founded the first hospital in the colonies. Honors continued to come his way. In 1753, both Harvard and Yale awarded him honorary degrees. In 1757, the Pennsylvania Assembly selected Franklin to go to England to oppose the political favoritism that was being shown to the Penn family who were descended from Pennsylvania's founder William Penn. The family was exempt from paying any land taxes and retained the right to veto legislation passed by the Pennsylvania Assembly. Franklin worked on this mission for five years but it ended in failure as the Royal government refused to turn their backs on the Penn family.

During his stay in England, more honors came his way. In 1759, the University of Saint Andrews awarded him an honorary degree. Three years later, Oxford followed suit by awarding Franklin an honorary doctorate for his scientific achievements. It was as a result of this award that he became known as Doctor Franklin. To top it off, he also secured an appointment for his illegitimate son William. The younger Franklin was named Colonial Governor of New Jersey.

When Franklin returned to America, the feud between the Penn's and the Assembly was ongoing. Franklin became leader of the anti-Penn party known as the anti-propriety party. In 1764 he was elected Speaker of the Pennsylvania House. As speaker, Franklin attempted to change Pennsylvania from a propriety to a royal government. The move was not popular with the voting populous who feared that such a change would infringe on their freedoms. As a result, Franklin was defeated in the elections held in October of 1764. After his defeat, the anti-propriety party sent him back to England to try yet again to fight the influence of the Penn family.

While in London, Franklin spoke out in opposition to the Stamp Act of 1765, but the measure passed over his objections. This did not deter him, and he continued to fight the act. His efforts contributed to its eventual repeal. As a result, he became the leading representative for American interests in England.

During his time in Europe, Franklin decided to tour Ireland. This visit would have a profound effect on him. When he witnessed the poverty in Ireland, he became convinced that it was a result of regulations and laws similar to those through which England was governing America. He came to the conclusion that America would suffer a fate similar to Ireland's if England's colonial exploitation continued.

Franklin's common law wife never accompanied him overseas because of her fear of the ocean. While he was on this trip, she implored him to return to America. She claimed she was ill and blamed her condition on his absence. Franklin stayed in England and Deborah Reed died as a result of a stroke in 1774.

Franklin returned to America in May of 1775. By this time the American Revolution had already begun with the battles of Lexington and Concord. Pennsylvania selected him as one of their delegates to the Second Continental Congress. While serving in Congress, he was appointed to the committee chosen to draft the Declaration of Independence. Thomas Jefferson did the bulk of the work on the Declaration, though Franklin did make several minor changes to the draft Jefferson provided to the other members of the committee. As the Declaration was signed, the President of Congress, John Hancock, remarked "We must all hang together." Franklin replied, "Yes, we must, indeed, all hang together, or most assuredly we shall all hang separately."

In July of 1775, the Continental Congress appointed Franklin to the post of United States Postmaster General. He was the country's first postmaster. The appointment made sense based on Franklin's previous postal experience. The postal system that was established then evolved into the United States Postal Service that is still operational today.

In 1776, Franklin was sent to France to represent American interests. He was already well known in that country due to his writings, inventions, and scientific discoveries. His appointment bore fruit. Franklin succeeded in securing a military alliance between the United States and France in 1778. This alliance was of critical importance to the Americans in their struggle against England. There are those who doubt that the American Revolution would have succeeded without the help of France. Franklin also played a key role in negotiating the Treaty of Paris in 1783. This treaty ended the American Revolution and established the United States as an independent country.

Franklin returned to the United States in 1785. His stature as a champion of American independence was exceeded by only one man, that man being George Washington. That same year, he was elected President of Pennsylvania, a post that would be similar to governor today. Franklin served in this position for just over three years.

The authors consider this man to be Mister Pennsylvania and Mister America.

In 1787 he was selected to serve as a Pennsylvania delegate at the Constitutional Convention in Philadelphia. For four months, the delegates met and argued over whether the country should establish a strong federal government. On the day the voting on the proposed constitution was to take place, many of the delegates believed it would be voted down. Prior to the voting, Franklin advised the Convention that he had a few comments to make. At the time he was too frail to deliver the speech himself so he had fellow Pennsylvania delegate James Wilson read it for him. In the speech Franklin spoke of his own misgivings about the Constitution. However in the end he said, "Thus I consent, sir, to this Constitution. The opinions I have of its errors, I sacrifice to the public good." He went on to say, "On the whole, sir, I cannot help expressing a wish that every member of the convention who may still have objections to it would, with me, on this occasion doubt a little of his own infallibility and make manifest our unanimity." When the vote was taken it was close to unanimous. Only three of the forty one delegates refused to sign the document and it was eventually ratified by all thirteen states.

Franklin died in his Philadelphia home on April 17, 1790. He was 84 years old. He is the only founding father who signed all four of the documents central to the establishment of the United States. These are the Declaration of Independence, the Treaty of Paris, the Treaty of Alliance with France, and the United States Constitution. His funeral was attended by an estimated 20,000 people. He was laid to rest in the Christ Church Burial Ground in Philadelphia.

If You Go:

The Christ Church Cemetery charges a modest entry fee. This fee is used to cover the cemeteries maintenance costs. There are a number of other important Americans buried here and maps are available at the cemetery (again for a modest charge) that direct you to their gravesites. If you do make the trip, you are in the midst of Philadelphia's historic district. Both Independence Hall and the Constitution Center are within easy walking distance. In addition, there are many street vendors and numerous restaurants in the area if you desire refreshments. Finally, the Betsy Ross House, which includes her burial site is only about three blocks away.

9

"Smokin' Joe"

JOE WILLIAM FRAZIER

County: Philadelphia
Town: Philadelphia
Cemetery: Ivy Hill
Address: 1201 Easton Road

He was considered one of the greatest heavyweight boxers of all time. His three fights with Muhammad Ali have achieved legendary status. Howard Cosell's repeated cries of "down goes Frazier" during his fight with George Foreman is cemented as one of the greatest sportscasting performances of all time. He was known to boxing fans as "Smokin' Joe" Frazier.

Joseph William Frazier was born on January 12, 1944, in Beaufort, South Carolina. He was the 12th child born to his parents. His early life was lived on the ten acres of farmland owned by his family. In later years Frazier recalled that he was particularly close to his father who would carry him to the still where he made bootleg liquor. Frazier's parents worked the farm which had very poor soil. All they were able to grow was cotton and watermelon.

In the early 1950's Frazier's parents purchased a television. Frazier's family would get together and watch boxing matches. Frazier viewed bouts that featured fighters like Sugar Ray Robinson and Rocky Marciano. During this period one of Frazier's uncles, after taking note of his nephew's sturdy build said, "that boy is going to be another Joe Louis." The next day Frazier constructed his own heavyweight bag that for years he worked on almost every day. It's clear that by this time Frazier's toughness was already in evidence. His classmates would pay him a quarter to walk home with them so the bullies would leave them alone.

At the age of 15 Frazier found work on a farm owned by a white family named Bellamy. One of the Bellamy's was a tough man named Jim. One day a 12 year old black boy accidentally damaged a tractor on the farm. Jim was so angry that he used his belt to whip the boy. Frazier witnessed the beating, and he told other black workers on the farm what he had seen. Later Jim Bellamy confronted Frazier and demanded to know why he told the other workers. Frazier denied he had done so, but Bellamy didn't believe him, and he threatened to take off his belt again. Frazier told Bellamy that he wasn't going to use that belt on him. Bellamy sized up Frazier and decided to settle things by telling Frazier to get off his farm. After this incident Frazier decided he had to leave Beaufort. He took a bus to New York where he lived with one his brothers.

Joe Frazier

Frazier then began his amateur boxing career. In 1962, 1963 and 1964 he won the Golden Gloves Championship in the heavy weight division. In the three years he fought as an amateur, he only suffered one loss and that was to Buster Mathis. In 1964 Frazier attempted to make the United States Olympic Boxing team. He fought his way to the final of the Olympic Trial where he was matched up against none other than Buster Mathis. Frazier was out to revenge his only loss, but at the end of the bout the judges declared Mathis the winner. Frazier disagreed with the judges and remarked, "all that fat boy had done was run like a thief, hit me with a peck and backpedal like crazy." The loss depressed Frazier, and he actually thought about giving up boxing. Fortunately his trainer, Yank Durham, talked him out of it and even convinced Frazier to go as an alternate to Tokyo where the Olympics would be held.

The decision to go to Tokyo turned out to be a good one. Mathis was injured, and Frazier replaced him on the American team. He won his first two fights by knock out. He was the only American boxer left entering the semi-finals. His next opponent was Vadim Yemelyanov from the Soviet Union. Yemelvanov was 6 foot 4 and weighed 230 pounds. Frazier was pounding the Russian and knocked him to the canvas twice in the second round. Late in that round, Frazier landed a left hook and felt a jolt of pain shoot through his arm. He had broken his thumb. Fortunately for Frazier the match was decided in his favor when Yemelvanov's corner men threw in the towel.

Frazier was determined to fight in the final, so he kept the news of his broken thumb to himself. His opponent in the final was Hans Huber who was representing Germany. Frazier relied mainly on his right hand during the bout. He threw very few left hooks, and his punches were not as powerful as they had been in his previous fights. After three rounds it was up to the five judges to decide the winner. Three of them voted for Frazier making him the gold medal winner. Frazier was the only United States boxer to win an Olympic gold medal.

Following the Olympics, Frazier turned professional in 1965. He won his first fight when he knocked out Woody Goss in the first round. After that he won three successive fights, and no opponent lasted longer than three rounds. Then during training Frazier's left eye was badly injured, so badly that he was declared legally blind in that eye. Somehow Frazier continued to pass pre-fight physicals in spite of this condition. Frazier then fought Mike Bruce who actually sent Frazier to the canvas in the first round. Frazier beat the referee's count and knocked Bruce out in the third round.

It was about this time in 1966 that Frazier's trainer, Yancey Durham, convinced Eddie Futch to join Frazier's team as an assistant trainer. Futch was centered in Los Angeles so Frazier went there to train. Frazier fought three times on the west coast winning all three bouts. One of the fights was

Joe Frazier landing one on Muhammad Ali

against George Johnson who went a full ten rounds with Frazier before losing a decision. Ring magazine reported that Johnson bet his entire purse that Frazier would not knock him out.

In 1967 Muhammad Ali was stripped of his heavyweight title when he refused to be inducted into the military. A heavyweight elimination tournament was set up to crown a new champion. At the time Frazier was the number one contender but Fitch convinced him to not participate in the tournament. Fitch was also instrumental in Frazier adopting a bob and weave style which made it more difficult for his opponents to land their punches. At the conclusion of the tournament Jimmy Ellis was crowned Heavyweight Champion.

On February 16, 1970, Frazier fought Ellis at Madison Square Garden for the undisputed heavyweight title. Ellis had never been floored in his career, but Frazier sent him to the canvas twice in the fourth round. When the bell sounded to start round five, Ellis remained in his corner, and Frazier was the new Heavyweight Champion.

In his first bout defending his title Frazier, who had won 26 straight fights, went up against the Light Heavyweight Champion Bob Foster. In the second round, Frazier sent Foster to the floor twice. The second knockdown came as a result of a powerful left hook, and Foster was unable to beat the count. This successful defense set up what would be called the "fight of the century" when Frazier would meet Muhammad Ali who was back in boxing after a three year suspension.

The fight took place in Madison Square Garden on March 8, 1971. Both Ali and Frazier were undefeated, and Ali as usual was predicting a victory. Once again Eddie Futch was a major factor in the outcome of the bout. Futch noticed that Ali had a tendency to drop his right hand prior to using it to deliver a powerful punch, and he instructed Frazier to watch that hand and when he saw it drop to deliver a left hook to Ali's face. Ali won many of the early rounds, but then Frazier began coming on and began pounding Ali to the body. In the 15th round Frazier saw Ali drop his right hand and Frazier, as instructed, delivered a left hook that sent Ali to the canvas. Frazier was declared the winner by unanimous decision. The contest saw both

Beautiful grave site of the great heavyweight champ Smokin' Joe Frazier. (& the reflection of the photographer —Joe Farley)

fighters head to the hospital afterward, and Frazier remained there for a week.

After defeating Ali, Frazier successfully defended his title against Ron Stander and Terry Daniels. Though he had won both fights, many observers felt that he hadn't been as dominant as he had been in previous bouts. In his next title defense Frazier was matched against George Foreman. Although Frazier was the favorite, there were boxing experts, including Howard Cosell on hand to broadcast the event, who were picking Foreman to win. Regardless of predictions nobody expected the fight to unfold the way it did. Frazier came out fast and landed his patented and powerful left hook, but it failed to faze Foreman. It could be that right then Frazier knew he was in trouble. The challenger responded with a combination followed by a right uppercut that sent the champion down. Howard Cosell screamed three times in a row "down goes Frazier." The moment is still remembered as one of Cosell's finest moments.

Frazier rose from the canvas only to be floored again before the round ended. Early in round two Foreman again connected with a right that sent Frazier to the canvas. Cosell described it as target practice for Foreman. Foreman didn't let up, and he floored Frazier three more times. After the 6th knockdown, the referee stopped the fight, and Foreman was the new champion.

Frazier continued to fight winning his next two bouts which set up a rematch with Ali. The fight was considered a letdown based on their earlier bout because there were numerous clinches. After 12 rounds, Ali was declared the winner though many disputed the decision. By the time Frazier and Ali would meet again, Ali would be the champion based on the fact that he knocked out George Foreman in 1974.

It can be argued that the third Ali – Frazier fight was the greatest heavyweight championship bout of all time. It took place on October 1, 1975 in the Philippines and became known as the "Thrilla in Manila." Before the fight Ali consistently referred to Frazier as "The Gorilla." From the beginning, the fight was intense and punishing. Early in the bout Ali said to

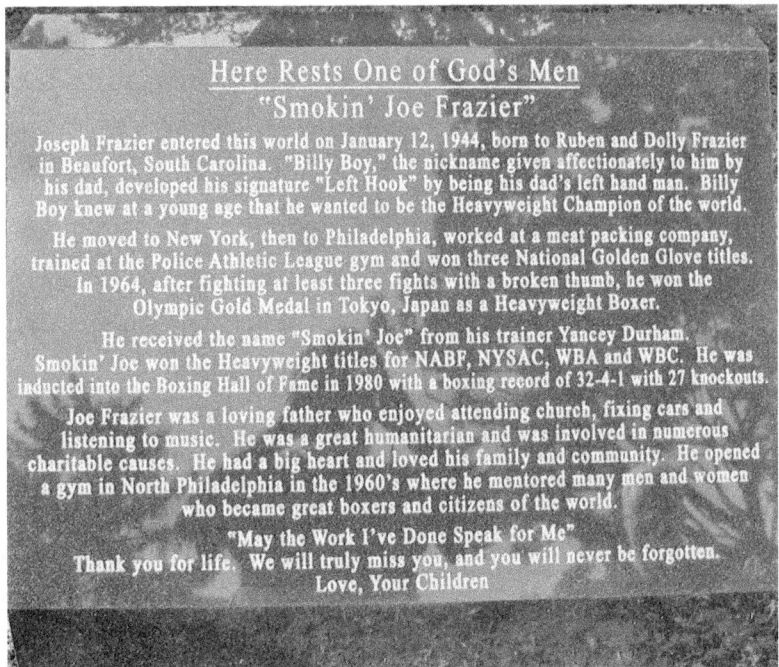

Monument at the grave of Smokin' Joe.

Frazier, "They said you were through Joe." Frazier responded, "They lied, pretty boy." After the 14th round Frazier's eyes were swollen shut, and Eddie Futch refused to let him answer the bell for the final round. Ali emerged the winner, but he commented later that the fight was the "Closet thing to dying that I know of."

Frazier fought a few more bouts before announcing his retirement. He made a brief comeback in 1981 fighting one time before he retired for good. His final record as a professional was 32 wins, 4 losses and 1 draw.

In his later years, Frazier lived in Philadelphia where he owned and managed a boxing gym. He and Ali continued their rivalry. When Ali lit the Olympic flame in 1996, Frazier said that he would have liked to have thrown Ali into the fire. It wasn't until 2009 that Frazier said he no longer had bad feelings about Ali. Frazier was diagnosed with liver cancer in September of 2011. He died on November 7th of that year. Ali was among those who attended his funeral.

If You Go:
Others buried in Ivy Hill Cemetery include Willie Anderson, Franklin Gowen and Bill Tilden. Anderson was the first golfer to win four U.S. Open Championships (see *Volume One*, Chapter 2). Gowen was famous for leading the prosecution, some would say persecution, of the Molly Maguires in the 1870s (see Chapter 19). Tilden was a tennis great who dominated that sport in the 1920s and 30s (see *Keystone Tombstones Volume 1*, Chapter 27). Both Harold Melvin of Harold Melvin and the Blue Notes and Marion Williams the famed gospel singer are also buried at Ivy Hill, but they are in unmarked graves. You can still visit their gravesites as the folks working in the cemetery office will be glad to provide you with their locations. In addition if you are at Ivy Hill, you are about a mile away from Holy Sepulcher Cemetery. Frank Rizzo and Connie Mack are buried there. Rizzo was a colorful and controversial Mayor of Philadelphia (see Chapter 23). Mack was a legendary major league baseball manager (see *Keystone Tombstones Volume 1* Chapter 16).

10

"An American Success Story Few Have Heard"

JOHN WHITE GEARY

County: Dauphin
Town: Harrisburg
Cemetery: Harrisburg
Address: 521 North 13th Street

John Geary has a county in Kansas named for him. Kansas also has a Geary State Park. There is a Geary Boulevard in San Francisco, California named in his honor. There is a Geary street in both New Cumberland (where he owned a home) and Harrisburg, Pennsylvania. Not to be left out, there is a Geary Street in South Philadelphia as well. There is a monument honoring Geary in Mount Pleasant, Pennsylvania. There is a dorm building at the Pennsylvania State University named Geary Hall. Finally, on August 11, 2007, a statue was unveiled on Culp's Hill, which is part of the Gettysburg Battlefield. It was erected to honor Geary. Clearly, the subject of this chapter was a man who got around.

Geary was born on December 30, 1819 in what is today the greater Pittsburgh metropolitan area. His father, Richard Geary, was considered a well educated man. Richard took on the task of educating his two sons. After being prepared by his father, Geary became a student of law and engineering at Jefferson College in Canonsburg, Pennsylvania. Prior to his graduation, his father passed away and he was forced to leave school. He found work in Kentucky as a surveyor. While in Kentucky, he also tried his hand at land speculation. He was successful enough to earn the money he needed to return to college, and he graduated in 1841. Upon graduation, he worked at a number of professions including the mercantile trade and civil engineering. He also studied law and was admitted to the state bar.

In 1843, Geary married Margaret Ann Logan. In 1846, his first son Edward was born. During this time, Geary was employed by the Allegheny Portage Rail Road as an engineer. He was instrumental in creating the rail line that traversed the Allegheny mountains. His ideas would later be used in the construction of the famed horseshoe curve.

Geary was already a high ranking officer in the Pennsylvania militia when the Mexican War began in 1846. He formed a company he called the "American Highlanders", all volunteers and all from Cambria County. This unit was joined with a company from Pittsburgh and Geary was elected second in command.

John White Geary (by Mathew Brady)

The combined unit sailed for Mexico, but encountered delays due to both weather and disease. As they approached the Gulf of Mexico, a few cases of smallpox appeared and the ship was sent to be quarantined. Finally, all signs of the disease disappeared and on April 12, 1847, Geary and the rest of the company arrived in Vera Cruz. By this time that city had already been taken by the Americans, so he had to wait for the Battle at Chapultepec to lead his men into an actual engagement with the enemy. He performed heroically, and was wounded multiple times during the battle. Considering that he stood at six foot six inches tall and weighed 260 pounds, he must have made for an inviting target. At the war's conclusion, Geary had earned the rank of colonel and returned to the United States a hero of the Mexican War.

After the war, President Polk appointed Geary postmaster of San Francisco. Geary embarked for the west coast with his three year old son, his pregnant wife, and thousands of pieces of mail. He and his family arrived in 1849 at the height of the gold rush. He quickly dove into his duties establishing post offices, mail routes, and appointing postmasters. His management skill earned him the admiration of the local citizens. Despite his success in this office, President Taylor, who succeeded Polk, replaced Geary as postmaster.

It appears that the people of San Francisco did not agree with the new president. In 1850, Geary was easily elected the first mayor of the city. He remains the youngest mayor in San Francisco's history. By this time, due to his wife's failing health, Geary had sent her and his two sons back to Pennsylvania. He remained in California where he governed capably. He worked hard to get the city's finances in order and was successful. At the same time, he added to his own fortune by selling city lots he acquired at little cost to him. In 1852, he returned to Pennsylvania to be with his family and care for his wife. It was to no avail as she passed away in 1853. Geary would remarry in 1858.

At this point in his life, Geary was determined to devout himself to farming and his various business pursuits. This was not to be. His reputation as a war hero and capable administrator led to President Pierce offering him the governorship of the Kansas territory in 1856. At the time "Bleeding Kansas", as it was called, was a battleground between pro and anti slavery forces. Geary was not eager to accept the position but acquiesced when Pierce appealed to his patriotic spirit.

In this instance Geary's initial reluctance may have been correct. His predecessor as governor remarked, "that to govern Kansas in 1855 and 1856, you might as well have attempted to govern the devil in hell." Bleak were the conditions Geary inherited when he arrived in Kansas on September 9, 1856. The Kansas territory was practically a war zone over the issue of slavery. The new governor pledged to be impartial and fair in

Geary's monument stands where he fought, atop Culp's Hill on the Gettysburg battlefield.

dealing with the opposition factions in the territory. This policy resulted in the further alienation of both sides.

Geary's problems in Kansas were complicated by the fact that many of President Pierce's appointees in the territory were solidly pro slavery. These officials resisted Geary's efforts to enforce the law, and bring peace to Kansas. Geary wrote to the president requesting the removal of multiple judges, and the replacement of the Federal Marshall, the Secretary of State, and the Attorney General. With a presidential campaign in progress, Pierce determined that the best course was to let his successor handle the problem. James Buchanan of Pennsylvania, who had no record on the issues in Kansas, won the election. Geary clearly lacked confidence in the new president, and he tendered his resignation on March 4, 1857. It was the very day Buchanan was inaugurated. Later in recalling his Kansas experience, Geary wrote, "I have learned more about the depravity of my fellow man than I ever knew before."

After his time in Kansas Geary returned to Pennsylvania where he met Mary Church Henderson of Carlisle. Soon, the two were married. In a short time, they welcomed their first child, a girl who they named Mary.

Although Geary was a staunch Democrat, he was also firmly anti-slavery. As soon as Geary received word that rebel forces had fired on Fort Sumter, he began recruiting troops. He set up recruiting stations in Philadelphia and elsewhere. Based on his reputation, he had little trouble securing volunteers. Sixty-six companies from all over the Commonwealth requested to be put under his command. In the end, Geary formed a 15 company regiment. He and his men saw their first action in October 1861, near Harpers Ferry. In 1862, he led his men across the Potomac and captured the rebel town of Leesburg, Virginia. As a result, Geary was promoted to Brigadier General.

Later that year, Geary faced rebel forces under the command of Stonewall Jackson during the Battle of Cedar Mountain. Geary was wounded in both the arm and the leg during the fighting. The wound to the arm was so severe that amputation was considered. While amputation was avoided, Geary was forced to return home to rest and recover.

When Geary returned to the army, he was put in command of the Second Division of the twelfth Corps under General Slocum. Geary would remain in charge of this division until the war's end. Geary's men saw plenty of action performing heroically at both Chancellorsville and Gettysburg. It was at Gettysburg atop Culp's Hill that Geary and his men repulsed repeated confederate assaults and succeeded in holding the union's right flank. The action on Culp's hill cemented Geary's reputation as a civil war hero. However, the man was not one to rest on his laurels.

In September of 1863, Geary's division was sent to Tennessee to join the forces of Generals Grant and Sherman. On October 27, 1863, Geary's forces were attacked by a superior force of confederates. In an intense battle

Geary's grave in the Harrisburg Cemetery is the only one topped by a statue. The monument was erected by the Commonwealth of Pennsylvania.

known as the Battle of Wauhatchie, the union forces turned back repeated confederate assaults. During the fighting, Geary's son Eddie was mortally wounded. He died in his father's arms, but Geary and his men held their ground.

Geary's division went on to fight in the Battle of Lookout Mountain, the Atlanta campaign, and Sherman's march to the sea. He led the union forces into Savannah where he was appointed military governor of the city. He ended his army career by serving on the military tribunal that tried Major Henry Wirtz, who had served as commandant of the Andersonville prisoner of war camp. Wirtz was found guilty of war crimes and was hanged in December of 1865.

Geary now returned to Pennsylvania. Though he had always been a Democrat, powerful elements of the Republican party began looking at him as a potential candidate for governor. Supported by the former Secretary of War, Simon Cameron, Geary was selected to head the Republican ticket in Pennsylvania. He won the election by 17,000 votes and was inaugurated governor in Harrisburg on January 15, 1867.

Geary served two successful terms as governor. He championed education and was a big supporter of Penn State University. He also worked against the influence of the railroads, and for improvements in mine safety. His policies resulted in a reduced public debt and an increase in revenues. He left the state in a far better condition than he had found it when he left the governor's office in 1873.

No sooner than Geary left office, rumors began to circulate that he was considering a run for president. That was not to be. Less than three weeks after leaving the office of govenor, on February 8, 1873, Geary suffered a massive heart attack and died while preparing breakfast at his home. He was 54 years old.

Geary was given a state funeral that included speeches from the political leaders of the Commonwealth. The funeral was followed by a large procession to the Harrisburg cemetery where he was laid to rest. His grave is marked by a monument that is topped by a statue of the great man. It is the only statue in the cemetery and was erected by the Commonwealth of Pennsylvania.

If You Go:
See the "If You Go" section of Simon Cameron, (p. 34).

"The Black Babe Ruth"

JOSH GIBSON

County: Allegheny
Town: Pittsburgh
Cemetery: Allegheny Cemetery
Address: 4734 Butler Street

Josh Gibson is generally considered the greatest hitter in the history of black baseball. An almost mythical figure, Gibson was often referred to as the "Black Babe Ruth" due to his tremendous power at the plate. Those who followed Negro league baseball regularly preferred to think of Ruth as the "White Josh Gibson." Statistical validation for Negro league players is difficult, but Gibson reportedly won nine home run titles and four batting championships during a seventeen-year career that began in 1930 and ended in 1946. The Baseball Hall of Fame claims he hit "almost 800" homers in that span against Negro League and independent baseball opposition. They report his lifetime batting average to be .359, and he has been credited with as many as 84 homers in one season. Belting home runs of more than 500 feet was not unusual for Gibson. One homer in Monessen, Pennsylvania was measured at 575 feet, and one in a Negro League game in Yankee Stadium measured 580 feet. Although never proven, infielder Jack Marshall of the Chicago American Giants and others claimed they saw Gibson hit a fair ball out of Yankee Stadium. If so, it would be the only fair ball ever hit out of the House that Ruth Built.

Born in Buena Vista, Georgia on December 21, 1911, Joshua Gibson moved to Pittsburgh in 1923 after his father found work at a Pittsburgh Steel Company. He initially planned to become an electrician and attended two vocational schools. However, he began to entertain thoughts of a baseball career at the age of sixteen after a job as an elevator operator at Gimbels department store led to a spot on an amateur team sponsored by Gimbels. His professional career began at the age of 18 under unusual circumstances. The Homestead Grays were playing the Kansas City Monarchs in Pittsburgh on July 31, 1930, and the Grays Catcher injured his hand and was unable to continue. The Grays manager Julius "Judy" Johnson knew of Gibson's reputation as a semi-pro player for the Pittsburgh Crawfords and had seen him in the crowd. Johnson went into the stands, found Gibson, and asked if he wanted to catch. He said, "Yes, sir." They held up the game while he put on a uniform. He played so well they signed him the next day.

In 1928, Josh Gibson met Helen Mason and the two married in March 1929. Helen was pregnant when Gibson made his debut with the Grays. A

Josh Gibson

few days later, on August 11, Helen went into premature labor and died while giving birth to twins, a son Joshua and a daughter named Helen.

Gibson played for the Grays the rest of that season and in 1931, before jumping to the Crawfords from 1932 to 1936. He caught Satchel Paige in 1936 to form the most popular battery in African-American history. He returned to the Grays from 1937 to 1939 and from 1942-1946. He started 1937 in the Dominican Republic and played in Mexico from 1940 to 1941.

The thing that makes his statistics so difficult to analyze is that Negro League statistics are extremely sketchy and the level of their reliability is further compromised by the fact that they are generally intermingled with figures compiled in games played against other levels of competition. The Negro Leagues generally found it more profitable to schedule relatively few league games, allowing the teams to earn extra money through barnstorming against semi-pro and other non-league teams.

Splitting the majority of his career between the Negro Leagues' two most dominant teams, the Homestead Grays and the Pittsburgh Crawfords, Gibson is estimated to have hit close to 800 home runs over his seventeen year playing career. His lifetime batting average was somewhere between .359 and .384 and he batted over .400 at least twice.

He hit .351 in 56 at-bats in exhibition games played against white major leaguers.

Satchel Paige called him "the greatest hitter who ever lived and Monte Irvin, who played against Gibson in the Negro Leagues and later with Willie Mays on the New York Giants said, "I played with Willie Mays and against Hank Aaron. They were tremendous players, but they were no Josh Gibson. He had an eye like Ted Williams and the power of Babe Ruth."

This modest tombstone pays tribute to the man many consider to be the greatest hitter in the history of baseball.

While Gibson certainly could have helped any major league team, the unwritten rules of baseball kept him out of the majors his entire career.

In early 1943, Josh Gibson fell into a coma and was diagnosed with a brain tumor. He came out of the coma but refused the option of surgical removal. He lived and played the next four years with recurring headaches. He died of a stroke in 1947 at the age of 35, just three months before Jackie Robinson became the first black player in modern major league history. He was buried in the Allegheny Cemetery where he lay in an unmarked grave for nearly thirty years. His teammate Ted Page started a movement in 1975 to obtain a marker for Josh Gibson. Pirates legend Willie Stargell donated the first $100 and Bowie Kuhn, then Major League Baseball Commissioner, donated most of the rest. It reads "Josh Gibson, 1911-1947, Legendary Baseball Player."

In 1972, Gibson and teammate Buck Leonard were the second and third players, behind Satchel Paige, to be inducted into the Baseball Hall of Fame for their performance in the Negro leagues.

There are many stories about Josh Gibson's baseball feats, but one of the most popular is told in Robert W. Peterson's book *Only the Ball was White*...

"One day during the 1930s the Pittsburgh Crawfords were playing at Forbes Field in Pittsburgh, where their young catcher, Josh Gibson, hit the ball so high and so far that no one saw it come down. After scanning the sky carefully for a few minutes, the umpire deliberated and ruled it a home run. The next day the Crawfords were playing in Philadelphia, when suddenly a ball dropped out of the heavens and was caught by the startled center fielder on the opposing club. The umpire made the only possible ruling. Pointing to Gibson he shouted, 'Yer out—yesterday in Pittsburgh!'"

If You Go:
Allegheny Cemetery is a well-maintained, large, historical cemetery with a great number of interesting graves. Near Josh Gibson's grave is the grave of colorful, controversial William "Gus" Greenlee. Greenlee migrated to Pittsburgh from North Carolina in 1916. He established a bootlegging business that he operated from his taxi and he and a friend are credited with introducing the numbers racket to Pittsburgh in 1926. He and William Harris turned it into one of the largest and most complex gambling networks of the period. He opened a nightclub called The Crawford Grill and attracted numerous jazz greats including Louis Armstrong, Dizzy Gillespie, and Miles Davis. "The Grill" was a center of black life in Pittsburgh's Hill District. He was very involved in boxing as a manager and was known for his many charitable acts and contributions. He was perhaps best known, however, as the owner of the Pittsburgh Crawfords baseball team from 1931 to 1939. The 1935 squad may have been the best ever to play in the Negro League, as it fielded five Baseball Hall of Fame players including Josh Gibson, Satchel Paige, Oscar Charleston, Judy Johnson, and Cool Papa Bell. He was also president of the Negro National League for five years and helped institute the famous East-West Game, an all-star baseball game played in Chicago. He died of a stroke in 1952.

Two of Josh Gibson's teammates, Harold Tinker and Theodore "Ted" Page are also buried in Allegheny Cemetery as is Albert "Rosey" Roswell, a broadcaster and "voice of the Pittsburgh Pirates" for nineteen seasons. He was one of the first broadcasters to enthusiastically and unabashedly cheer on the air. His famous trademark was his home run call, "Raise the Window, Aunt Minnie!" followed by his partner dropping a tray filled with nuts and bolts, simulating the sound of broken glass.

Also buried there are Stephen Foster (See *Volume Two,* Chapter 8), Lillian Russell, Harry Thaw (See *Volume Two,* Chapter 25) General John Neville of Whiskey Rebellion fame, two Congressional Medal of Honor recipients (See chapter on Stephen Foster) and many other historical figures.

12

"What Does it All Mean?"

FRANK GORSHIN

County: Allegheny
Town: Pittsburgh
Cemetery: Calvary
Address: 718 Hazelwood Avenue

Riddle me this. A famous actor, both stage and screen, a fantastic impressionist, a well known nightclub performer, and a featured guest star on numerous variety television shows who is best known for his role in the campy television series "Batman." If you answered Frank Gorshin, you solved the riddle. To this day he is most closely associated with his role as the Riddler.

Frank Gorshin was born in Pittsburgh, Pennsylvania on April 5, 1933. He was born during the Great Depression and both his parents worked. His mother was a seamstress and his father was employed by the railroad. When he was 15, Frank found employment himself, working as an usher at the Sheridan Square Movie Theatre in Pittsburgh. While watching the movies, he began to impersonate his favorite stars. Soon he was doing Jimmy Cagney, Cary Grant, Burt Lancaster, and Edward G. Robinson among others. At the age of 17 he won a local talent contest. First prize was a one week engagement at a New York nightclub, the Carousel. His parents said he should do the show, and he did, even though his 15 year old brother had been hit by a car and killed just two days earlier. While his entertainment career was underway, he also attended school at the Carnegie-Mellon Tech School of Drama where he acted in plays while at the same time performing in Pittsburgh nightclubs.

In 1953, Gorshin was drafted into the United States Army. He served two years in the Armed Forces. His primary job in the army was to entertain the troops. He did, however, meet a man by the name of Maurice Bergman while he was there. At the completion of Frank's tour, Bergman, introduced him to Paul Kohner, a Hollywood agent.

It was at this point that Gorshin's career took off. He landed a film role in "The Proud and the Profane." He also began appearing in television dramas. He was at home in Pittsburgh in 1957, when his agent called and said he had a screen test set up for him for the movie "Run Silent Run Deep." He decided to drive back to Hollywood, but after 39 straight hours, he fell asleep at the wheel and crashed. He suffered a fractured skull in the accident and was in a coma for four days. One Los Angeles newspaper

Actor Frank Gorshin

mistakenly reported that he had died in the crash. He lost the part to Don Rickles.

After he recovered from the accident, Gorshin appeared in a string of B-movies from 1956 through 1960. These movies included "Dragstrip Girl," "Invasion of the Saucer Men," and "Hot Rod Girl." He also married Christina

Randazzo in 1957, and though they eventually separated, they were never divorced. In 1960, he landed a role in a mainstream movie titled "Bells Are Ringing" which starred Dean Martin and Judy Holiday. Gorshin would later make numerous appearances on Martin's TV variety show. In 1961, he appeared in the movie "The Great Imposter" that starred Tony Curtis.

In early 1964, Gorshin made his first appearance (there would be twelve in all) on The Ed Sullivan Show. Among the other acts making their first appearance on the show that night was a musical group called The Beatles and a young fellow by the name of Davy Jones who later became part of the made for TV musical group The Monkees.

In 1966, Gorshin was offered the role of the Riddler on the TV show Batman. He told the story himself: "When I was first approached to play the Riddler, I thought it was a joke. Then I discovered the show had a good script and I agreed to do the role..." We think it's good to remember at this point that Gorshin had agreed to do 'Invasion of the Saucer Men'. He continued with, "Now I am in love with the character. I developed the Riddler's fiendish laugh at Hollywood parties. I listened to myself laugh and discovered that the funniest jokes brought out the high-pitched giggle I use on the show. With further study, I came to realize that it wasn't so much how I laughed as what I laughed at that created the sense of menace." Whatever it was, it worked. Gorshin was nominated for an Emmy award for Outstanding Performance by an Actor in a Supporting Role in a Comedy. Gorshin was the only person who appeared in the series to receive a nomination. Later, he recalled that he "could feel the impact overnight." He gained recognition nationwide and soon became a headliner in Vegas. In 1969, he received another Emmy nomination this time for his performance as Commissioner Bele in a Star Trek episode called "Let That Be Your Last Battlefield."

Gorshin also appeared on Broadway. In 1970, he starred in the play "Jimmy" based on New York's flamboyant Mayor Jimmy Walker. He received fantastic reviews. In 1971, he appeared in "Guys and Dolls." His final appearance on the Broadway stage was in a one man play titled "Say Goodnight Gracie" in 2002. He portrayed the legendary comedian George Burns in the production.

He stayed active in his final years. His last job was a guest appearance on the season finale of CSI: Crime Investigation in an episode titled "Grave Danger." Quenton Tarantino was the director. Some find it ironic that the man so well known for his impressions played himself in this episode. It aired two days after he died and was dedicated to his memory.

Gorshin died on May 17, 2005, at the age of 72. He had taken a flight to Los Angeles and upon landing was rushed to a hospital. He died from lung cancer, emphysema, and pneumonia. He is buried in his family's plot in Calvary Cemetery in Pittsburgh.

Batman's arch enemy "the Riddler" lies beneath this stone. Though in our view his talents exceeded anything he did on that TV show. ("Ghost" of the co-author in reflection!)

If You Go:
We would strongly suggest you visit the cemetery office to obtain directions to the graves you might want to visit at Calvary. It's a very large cemetery and without guidance you could be there for days. For more information on who is buried in Calvary and what you can do in Pittsburgh (see chapter 7 on Billy Conn).

13

"Hancock the Superb"

WINFIELD SCOTT HANCOCK

County: Montgomery
Town: Norristown
Cemetery: Montgomery
Address: 1 Hartranft Avenue

Winfield Scott Hancock was an American hero named after an American hero and given an appropriate and well-earned nickname, "Hancock the Superb." He was a career U.S. Army Officer, a hero in the Civil War, a commanding general at the Battle of Gettysburg, and the Democratic nominee for president in 1880.

Winfield Scott Hancock was born in Montgomery County, Pennsylvania on Valentine's Day in 1824. He was named after General Winfield Scott, a hero in the War of 1812. Hancock was born with an identical twin brother named Hilary Booker Hancock. Hancock was educated at Norristown Academy at first but transferred to public schools in the late 1830's. In 1840, he was nominated to West Point by Congressman Joseph Fornance. He graduated in 1844 ranked eighteenth of twenty-five. He was commissioned a second lieutenant and assigned to the infantry.

When the Mexican War broke out in 1846, he was initially assigned to recruiting in Kentucky. He worked hard to get assigned to the front, but he was so successful as a recruiter, they were reluctant to let him go. He finally did get assigned to the front in July of 1847 in a regiment that made up part of the army led by General Winfield Scott. He was promoted to 1st Lieutenant for "gallant and meritorious conduct" at the Battle of Churubasco where he was wounded in the knee and developed a fever. The fever kept him from participating in the final breakthrough at Mexico City much to his regret. He remained in Mexico until the peace treaty was signed in 1848.

After the Mexican War he served in the West, in Florida, and elsewhere. It was while serving in St. Louis that he met Almira (Allie) Russell whom he married in 1850. The couple had two children, Russell (1850-1884) and Ada (1857-1875). In 1855, he was promoted to Captain and in November 1858, he was stationed in Southern California and joined by Almira and the children. There, Hancock became friends with several officers from the South and became especially close to Lewis Armistead of Virginia. At the outbreak of the Civil War, Armistead and other Southerners were leaving to join the Confederate Army, while Hancock was remaining in the U.S Army.

Winfield Scott Hancock

On June 15, 1861, Hancock and Almira hosted a party for their friends who were scattering because of the war. The party has become legend and is recounted in Michael Shaara's "The Killer Angels" and in the movie "Gettysburg." Armistead, who was widowed twice, had grown very close to the Hancock's and shed tears when it became time to end the party and depart. He gave some personal effects to Almira for safe keeping and promised he would not take arms against his friend "Winnie." Almira said later that at the Battle of Gettysburg, Hancock's men killed three of the six Confederates who attended that party.

Hancock headed east to assume quartermaster duties for a rapidly growing army but on September 23, 1861 was promoted to brigadier general and given command of an infantry brigade in the Amy of the Potomac. He took part in the Peninsula Campaign and at the Battle of Williamsburg on May 5, 1862 he handled his troop so well that General George McClellan reported "Hancock was Superb." The epithet seemed to stick to him afterwards and "Hancock the Superb" was born.

This monument marks the spot on the Gettysburg where Hancock was wounded. The bullet that was removed from Hancock is preserved by the Montgomery County Historical Society.

He played a significant role at the Battle of Antietam and shortly afterwards was promoted to Major General of Volunteers in November 1862. He led his division in the disastrous attack on Marye's Heights in the Battle of Fredericksburg the following month, where he was wounded in the abdomen. He was wounded again at the Battle of Chancellorsville covering General Hooker's withdrawal. On that day, General Darius Couch asked to be transferred out of the Army of the Potomac in protest of the actions of General Hooker. As a result, Hancock assumed command of 11 corps, which he would lead until shortly before the war's end (General Couch had a long distinguished military career and has the remains of a fortification built to defend Harrisburg named after him in Lemoyne, PA).

Hancock's most famous service was at the Battle of Gettysburg during July 1-3 1863. On the first day, after his friend Maj. Gen. John Reynolds (see *Keystone Tombstones – Susquehanna Valley Region*, p. 134) was killed, Gen. George Meade (see *Keystone Tombstones – Philadelphia Region*, p. 281), the new commander of the Army of the Potomac, sent Hancock ahead to take command and to decide whether to continue to fight there or to fall back. He decided to stay, rallied his troops, and held Cemetery Ridge until the arrival of the main body of the Federal Army. During the second day's battle, he commanded the left center and, after General Sickles had been wounded, the whole left wing. On the third day, he commanded the left center and thus bore the brunt of Pickett's Charge. Hancock was shot in the groin while rallying and commanding his troops on horseback. Although severely wounded, he refused to be evacuated to the rear until the battle was resolved. During the battle, his old friend General Lewis Armistead was mortally wounded. As he lay wounded and dying, he asked to see Hancock. When told that Hancock could not come to see him because he had been wounded himself, Armistead asked that Hancock be told that he was sorry. Armistead died two days later while Hancock took six months to recover enough to return to command. There is a monument on the Gettysburg battlefield commemorating their friendship and another marking the spot where Armistead fell. Hancock was considered by many to have made the most impact by a general at Gettysburg. His courage in the face of fire and leadership played a huge role in the Union victory.

This is the Friend to Friend monument in the Gettysburg National Cemetery. The monument portrays the final moments in the life of Confederate General Lewis Armistead who died at Gettysburg and was close friends with General Hancock.

Hancock suffered from the effects of his Gettysburg wound for the rest of the war. After recuperating in Norristown, he returned in March to the front and led his old corps under

This monument on the Gettysburg battlefield marks the spot where Confederate General Lewis Armistead fell mortally wounded.

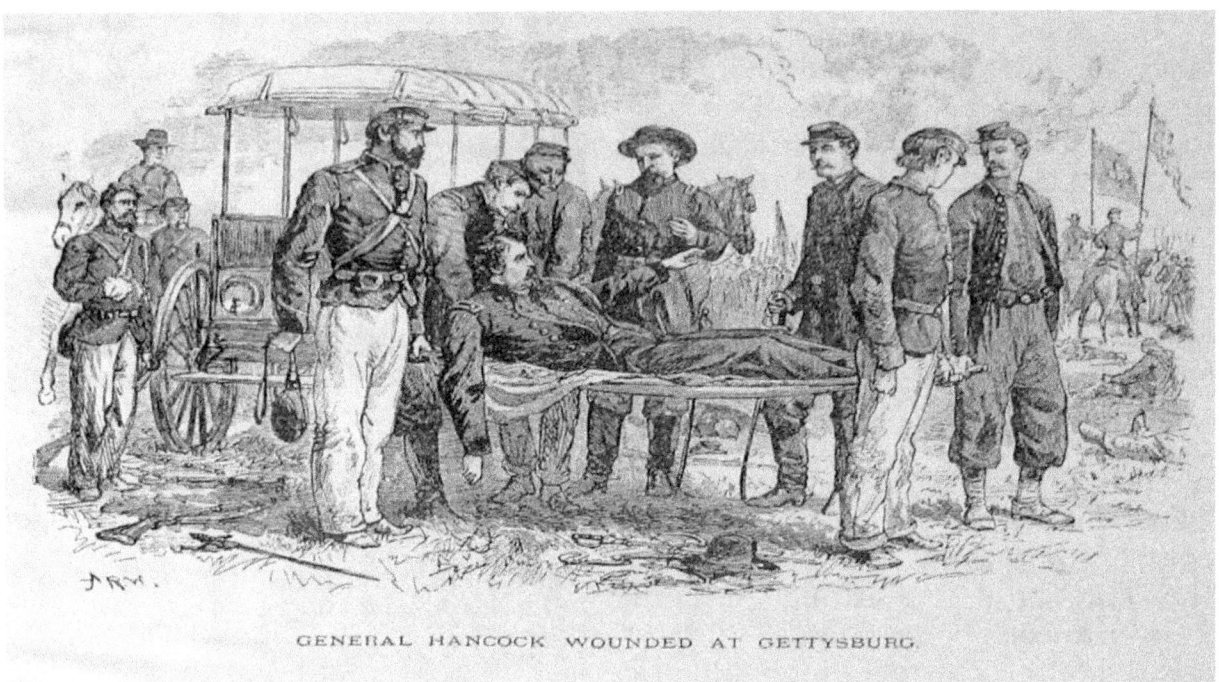

This drawing of a wounded Hancock at Gettysburg is in the office at the Montgomery Cemetery.

General Ulysses S. Grant in the 1864 Overland Campaign but was never quite his old self. He performed well at the Battle of the Wilderness, which began in May, and continued to fight at Yellow Tavern, North Anna, Old Church, Cold Harbor, Trevilian Station, and finally the siege of Petersburg. In June, his Gettysburg wound reopened but he soon resumed command, sometimes travelling by ambulance. After his corps participated in the assaults at Deep Bottom, Hancock was promoted to Brigadier General in the Regular Army, effective August 12, 1864.

In Grant's campaign against Lee, Hancock and his famed 11 Corps were repeatedly called upon to plunge into the very worst of the fighting, and the casualties were terrible. The losses and lingering effects of his Gettysburg wound caused Hancock to give up field command in November 1864. He left the 11 Corps after a year in which it had suffered over 40,000 casualties but had achieved significant military victories. He was again promoted in March 1865 to Brevet Major General in the Regular Army.

After the assassination of Abraham Lincoln in April, Hancock was placed in charge of Washington D.C. and it was under his command that John Wilkes Booth's accomplices were tried and executed. Hancock was reluctant to execute some of the less-culpable conspirators, especially Mary Surratt. He hoped Surratt would receive a pardon from President Johnson. He was so hopeful that he posted messengers from the Arsenal, where the hangings took place, to the White House, ready to relay the news of a pardon to him, but no pardon was forthcoming. Afterwards, he wrote that "every soldier was bound to act as I did under similar circumstances."

Hancock remained in the postwar army, and in 1866 Grant had him promoted to Major General in the Regular Army, and he served at that rank for the rest of his life. He served briefly in the west and then was named military governor of Louisiana during reconstruction. His policies there angered Republicans and Grant but made him popular among Democrats. When Grant won the presidency in 1868, Hancock found himself transferred to the Department of Dakota, which covered Minnesota, Montana, and the Dakotas. It was during this tour that Hancock contributed to the creation of Yellowstone National Park and had a summit (Mt. Hancock) at the southern boundary named in his honor.

Here is the grave of one of the greatest Union Civil War Generals.

With the death of General George Meade in 1872, Hancock became the senior major general in the U.S. Army and was assigned to take Meade's place as commander of the Division of the Atlantic at Governor's Island in New York Harbor.

Hancock had been considered as a presidential nominee by the Democrats as early as 1864. In 1880, he was finally chosen at the convention in Cincinnati along with William Hayden English of Indiana as his running mate. They ran against James Garfield and Chester Arthur in an election that was very close in the popular vote, but not so close in the electoral. Garfield won by less than 10,000 votes, but won the electoral vote 214 to 155. Garfield was assassinated in September 1881.

Hancock finished his life as Commander of the Division of the Atlantic and died at Governor's Island from an infected Carbuncle complicated by diabetes on February 9, 1886.After a funeral in New York City, General Hancock's remains were taken to his boyhood home of Norristown, PA and placed with his daughter Ada in a mausoleum that he had designed.

Winfield Scott Hancock is memorialized three times at Gettysburg: once in a statue on Cemetery Hill, once on a statue as part of the Pennsylvania Memorial, and as a sculpture on the New York State Monument. There are statues in Washington DC at Pennsylvania Avenue and 7th street N.W. and in Fairmont Park in Philadelphia and a bronze bust in Hancock Square, New York City. His portrait adorns U.S. currency on the $2 Silver Certificate series of 1886 and is quite valuable today.

Here are the Joes at Brother Paul's at 3300 Ridge Pike, Eagleville, PA, refreshing themselves after visiting Montgomery Cemetery. They hope to get back to visit the brothers in the future.

Hancock was portrayed by actor Brian Mallon in two films about the Civil War: *Gettysburg* (1993) and *Gods and Generals* (2003). He is portrayed very favorably in both films. There are numerous books about Hancock, the most notable is *Winfield Scott Hancock: A Soldier's Life* written by David M. Jordan and published in 1998.

If You Go:
There are a few other interesting graves in Montgomery Cemetery. The most notable is the grave of John Frederick Hartranft (see *Keystone Tombstones Volume 3* chapter 13).

Also buried in Montgomery Cemetery with Hancock is Brigadier General Samuel Kosciuszko Zook (see *Keystone Tombstones Civil War* chapter 23) who fought with him at Gettysburg and was fatally wounded on the second day of the battle.

You may also want to visit the grave of Brigadier General Adam Jacoby Slemmer, who steadfastly refused to surrender Fort Pickens in Pensacola Harbor to the Alabama and Florida authorities during the early days of secession. He had moved his forces from Fort Barrancas to Fort Pickens, which was more easily defended. Fort Pickens remained under Federal control for the duration of the war and ensured Union control of the Gulf of Mexico. Slemmer was assigned to General Don Carlos Buell's command later in the year and took part in the Corinth Campaign and the relief of Nashville. He was wounded in the Battle of Stones River, Tennessee, receiving a wound that incapacitated him for the rest of the war. He died on October 7, 1868 at the age of forty, from typhoid fever that he had contracted during the war. At the time of his death he was in command of Fort Laramie, Wyoming.

"The Chocolate King"

MILTON S. HERSHEY

County: Dauphin
Town: Hershey
Cemetery: Hershey
Address: 325 Laudermilch Road

Milton Hershey endured years of failure before introducing milk chocolate to the world, and then used his fortune to help those less fortunate. He went on to become one of the wealthiest individuals in America whose products are known all over the world. He built a town, which bears his name, and his generosity continues to touch the lives of thousands.

Milton Snavely Hershey was born on a central Pennsylvania farm in Derry Township on September 13, 1857. His education was haphazard and ended after the fourth grade when his father decided he should become an apprentice to a printer in Lancaster. He hated it and was fired. His mother found him a second apprenticeship with a confectioner named Joseph Royer, which he found much more appealing.

After four years, at the age of nineteen, he established his own candy making business in Philadelphia. It was 1876, and he hoped to take advantage of the Great Centennial Exposition celebrating the 100th anniversary of the Declaration of Independence. He kept it going for six years, but the strain of making taffy and caramels all night and selling them from a pushcart all day eventually wore him down, and he closed up shop in 1882.

He moved to Denver and worked for a candy maker and then tried to establish his own candy business in Chicago and then New York, both of which failed.

He returned to Lancaster in 1883 and set up yet another candy manufacturing business which specialized in producing caramel. He concentrated on making fine caramels using fresh ingredients, and it worked. Soon his Lancaster Caramel Company was shipping all over the U.S. and Europe and employed 1400 people.

In 1893, Milton Hershey attended the World's Fair in Chicago, which was officially known as The World's Columbian Exposition. He was so impressed with chocolate making machinery from a German exhibitor that he purchased the machinery and began to make chocolate and chocolate covered caramel products and Cocoas as an arm of the Lancaster Caramel Company. At that time, milk chocolate was considered a luxury imported item, but Hershey was fascinated with making chocolate. In 1900 he sold Lancaster Caramel and acquired 200 acres in Derry Township where he

Milton Hershey

Milton and Kitty Hershey at the Great Pyramid in Egypt.

built what was to become the world's largest chocolate making plant. He created his own formula for milk chocolate and, being surrounded by dairy farms, was able to use fresh milk to mass-produce quality milk chocolate.

The Hershey Chocolate Company thrived, and Hershey believed that his company and the community were intertwined and that he had a responsibility to his employees and the community. He directed the development of a town with nice homes, parks, transportation, and recreational facilities, like Hersheypark, which opened in 1907. The town of Hershey now promotes itself as the "sweetest place on Earth."

In 1898 Hershey married Catherine "Kitty" Sweeney, a beautiful Irish Catholic girl from New York. They were very happy together but saddened that they had no children. To fill this void, they founded the Hershey Industrial School, now known as Milton Hershey School, for orphaned boys in 1909. Kitty died in 1915, and Hershey never remarried. Shortly after her death, he donated his entire fortune to the school and expanded it to serve children of both sexes from Kindergarten through high school.

The Hershey's were to travel on the ill-fated luxury liner the Titanic in 1912 but canceled because Mrs. Hershey became ill. The Hershey museum displays a copy of the check Hershey wrote as a deposit for a stateroom on the Titanic.

During the Great Depression, Hershey embarked on a building project that included a hotel, a high school, community building, a sports arena, and a new office building. The Hotel Hershey incorporated his favorite details from hotels worldwide. Mr. Hershey would later boast proudly that none of his workers were ever laid off during the Depression. In fact, he hired 600 additional laborers.

Here is the grave of the America's chocolate king who was lucky enough to miss his passage on the Titanic.

Hershey Chocolate supplied the U.S. Military with chocolate bars during World War II. They developed an unmeltable, four-ounce bar with extra calories and vitamins, which could be used as emergency provisions. Over three billion of the "Field Ration D" bars and "Tropical Bars" were produced and distributed to military personnel throughout the world. The U.S. Government gave Hershey the Army/Navy E award for his civilian contribution to the war effort.

Milton Hershey died in Hershey, Pennsylvania on October 13, 1945, one year after his retirement as Chairman of the board. He was 88 years old. He is buried in a beautiful grave in Hershey Cemetery.

In 1995, Milton Hershey was honored again by being pictured on a postage stamp commemorating him a part of the U.S. Postal Service's Great American's series.

In 2011, the Hershey Company topped six billion dollars in sales. That's a lot of chocolate!

This is the memorial to children who passed away while attending the Milton Hershey School.

If You Go:
Rival candy maker, Harry Reese, is buried near Milton Hershey in Hershey Cemetery. Reese founded H.B. Reese Candy Company around 1917. During the mid-twenties, he started to make an item called the Peanut Butter Cup. Reese died in 1956 and six years later, the company was sold to Hershey Chocolate for $235 million.

Hershey has an abundance of great places to eat and drink and we have visited many of them, some numerous times. The Majestic Hershey Hotel and grounds is itself a sight to see. We recommend the Iberian Lounge as a place to relax and unwind. Expertly prepared cocktails (yes, even a chocolate martini), plush seating, and a roaring fireplace make you feel special.

Devon Seafood Grill offers premium seafood and drinks in an upscale casual atmosphere and is in the same building (the Hershey Press Building on Chocolate Ave) as the always fun and reliable Houlihan's Restaurant and Bar.

A few blocks away on Cocoa Avenue is another fun place with a great menu, Fire Alley. It's a casual, fun atmosphere with booths and tables and even bench seating at the bars. We love it. We also love Overtime Sports Bar at 312 Mill St. Plenty of TV's, a great bar menu, and friendly neighborhood atmosphere.

Also about twenty minutes from Hershey in Mechanicsburg at 6108 Carlisle Pike is a great place called Black N Bleu. The theme is "Black Tie or Bleu Collar, come as you are." A great menu (had a hard time deciding) and a nice selection of beers and wines served by an attentive friendly staff make this an experience we want to have again and again.

15

"An Act of God?"

JOHNSTOWN FLOOD VICTIMS

County: Cambria
Town: Johnstown
Cemetery: Grandview
Address: 801 Millcreek Road

Heavy rainfall caused water to rise in the streets of Johnstown, Pennsylvania in late May 1889. That seemed normal and didn't raise any alarms. Being built on the fork of Little Conemaugh and Stony Creek rivers, flooding had been a problem since its founding. On June 1, 1889, Americans woke to the news that Johnstown had been devastated by the worst flood in the nation's history. A neglected dam and phenomenal storm led to a catastrophe in which 2209 people died. It's a story of great tragedy and when the full story came to light, many believed that if it was a "natural" disaster, then surely man was an accomplice.

The Little Conemaugh and the Stony Creek rivers meet in Johnstown and form the Conemaugh River. In 1889, Johnstown was a town of Welsh and German immigrants with a population of about 30,000 including surrounding towns. High above the city, the South Fork Dam was built by the Commonwealth of Pennsylvania between 1838 and 1853 as part of a cross-state canal system. The reservoir behind the dam, Lake Conemaugh, supplied water to the city.

As railroads replaced canal barge transportation, the canal was abandoned by the Commonwealth and sold to the Pennsylvania Railroad. The dam and the lake were subsequently sold to private interests. One of the private interests was a group led by Henry Clay Frick, chairman of Carnegie Brothers Company, who had made a fortune selling coke. Their intent was to modify the lake and convert it into a private resort for the wealthy of Pittsburgh. They formed the South Fork Fishing and Hunting Club and bought it in 1879. The purpose of the club was to provide the members and their families an opportunity to escape the noise, heat, and dirt of Pittsburgh. There were sixty-one members at that time including Andrew Carnegie, Henry Clay Frick, Andrew Mellon, Philander Chase Knox (who served as US Attorney General, US Senator, and Secretary of State), and Benjamin Thaw, the uncle of Harry Thaw. They built a 47-room clubhouse with a huge dining room and 16 houses along the lake's shores. The club's boat fleet included a pair of steam yachts, many sailboats, and canoes and the boathouses to house them. The club did engage in some periodic maintenance of the dam, but also made some harmful

Detail of The Great Conemaugh Valley Disaster—Flood & Fire at Johnstown, Pa., subtitled Hundreds Roasted Alive at the Railroad Bridge. Reproduced from a lithograph print published by Kurz & Allison Art Publishers, 76 & 78 Wabash Avenue, Chicago, Illinois.

modifications to it. They lowered the dam to make its top wide enough to hold a road, and they installed fish screens across the spillway to keep expensive game fish from escaping, which had the unfortunate effect of capturing debris keeping the spillway from draining the lake's overflow.

On May 30th, 1889, unusually heavy rains hit the area. The U.S. Army Signal Corps estimated 6 to 10 inches of rain fell in 24 hours. At around 3:10 PM, the South Fork Dam burst. The collapse sent twenty million tons of water roaring downstream toward Johnstown. On its way it picked up debris, such as trees, rocks, houses, and animals. When it hit Johnstown, it was about 40 feet high and a half-mile wide and traveling about 40 miles an hour. Just outside of East Conemaugh, a locomotive engineer, John Hess, was sitting in his locomotive. He heard the rumbling of the approaching flood and, correctly assuming what it was, tried to warn people by blowing the train whistle and racing toward the town riding backwards. His warning saved many people who were able to get to high ground. Hess himself miraculously survived despite the locomotive being picked up and tossed aside by the wall of water and debris. At 4:07 PM, the wall of water hit Johnstown. At first, it sounded like a low rumble that grew to a roar like thunder.

It was over in ten minutes, but for some, the worst was still yet to come. Darkness fell, thousands were huddled in attics, others floating on the debris, while many more had been swept downstream to the old Stone

Bridge at the junction of the rivers. There, much of the debris piled up against the arches and caught fire, killing eighty people who had survived the initial flood wave. The fire burned for three days. The pile of debris reached seventy feet in height and took three months to remove because of the masses of steel wire from an ironworks factory binding it. Dynamite was eventually used to clean it.

Many bodies were never identified, hundreds of the missing never found. The official death toll registered 2209 people killed or presumed lost. Among the dead were 99 entire families, 396 children under the age of ten, and 777 unidentified victims.

Emergency morgues and hospitals were set up, and commissaries distributed food and clothing. Across the country and around the world, people responded with a spontaneous outpouring of time, money, food, clothing, and medical assistance. A total of $3.7 million was collected from the U.S. and eighteen foreign countries.

The American Red Cross, which was formed in 1881 by Clara Barton, arrived in Johnstown on June 5, five days after the disaster. This was the group's first major disaster relief effort, and Clara Barton herself was to lead the relief efforts. She and many other volunteers worked tirelessly and didn't leave for more than five months.

Debris being removed from the railroad bridge.

The media response to the disaster was immediate. Over 100 newspapers and magazines sent writers and illustrators to Johnstown. The Johnstown Flood was the biggest news story since the Civil War. The dead were lined up in morgues throughout the city and in communities further down the river until some survivor in search of a loved one came to identify them. The living set up tents, often near the place their homes had been located, and began the task of cleaning up and starting life again. Although not noted for their accuracy, the reports touched the hearts of readers. Residents of Johnstown and Americans in general began to turn their wrath on the members of the South Fork Fishing and Hunting Club. Newspapers all across the country denounced the sportsmen's lake. *The Chicago Herald's* editorial on the disaster was entitled "Manslaughter or Murder?" On June 9, the *Herald* carried a cartoon that showed the members of the club drinking champagne on the porch of the clubhouse while, in the valley beneath them, the Flood is destroying Johnstown. A *New York World* headline on June 7 declared, "The Club is Guilty."

In the immediate aftermath of the tragedy, the club contributed 1000 blankets to the relief effort. A few of the club members served on relief committees. Only about half the club members contributed to the disaster relief effort, including Andrew Carnegie whose company gave $10,000 and

Debris on Main Street.

who later rebuilt Johnstown's library. However, no club member ever expressed a sense of personal responsibility for the disaster.

The club had very few assets aside from the clubhouse, but a few lawsuits were brought against the club anyway. Legal action against individual club members was difficult as it would have been necessary to prove personal negligence —and the power and influence of the club members is hard to overestimate. Despite the accusations and the evidence, they were successfully defended by the firm of Knox and Reed, both partners of which were club members (Philander Knox and James Reed). The Club was never held legally responsible for the disaster. The court held the dam break to have been an Act of God and granted the survivors no legal compensation.

Memorial to 777 unidentified victims of the Johnstown flood.

Many bodies were never identified and hundreds of the missing never found. The cleanup operation took years with bodies being found months later and, in a few cases, years after the flood. In 1989, on the 100th Anniversary of the flood, 106 year-old survivor Elsie Frum was interviewed by news organizations. Her father was alerted by John Hess's train whistle and had gotten his family to safety, thus saving young Elsie's life. Frank Shomo, reportedly the last survivor of the Johnstown Flood, died in 1997 at the age of 108.

There is a large, beautiful memorial marking the resting place of 777 flood victims who could not be identified in Grandview Cemetery in Johnstown. The State Flood Commission purchased the plot, called "The Unknown Plot," for burying the unidentified and bought markers for each grave. It was dedicated on May 31, 1892, exactly three years after the flood.

The Johnstown Flood Museum is located on Washington Street in Johnstown in a large beautiful brick building that was built for the city, as the new library, by Andrew Carnegie. The museum provides exhibits and artifacts that tell the story of the flood

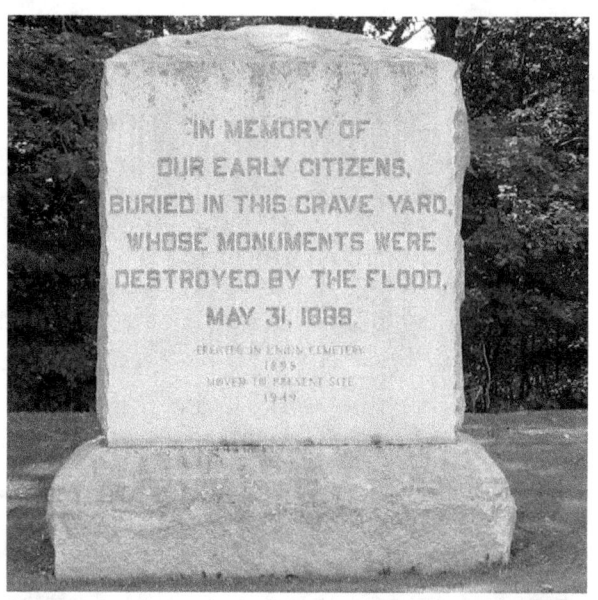
Memorial to those who had their graves destroyed by the Johnstown flood.

and the film "The Johnstown Flood," winner of the 1989 Academy Award for Best Documentary Short Subject, is shown each hour at the museum's theater. The Johnstown Flood National Memorial is located about ten miles northeast of Johnstown. The park preserves the remains of the South Fork Dam. The visitor center features multi-media exhibits including a fiber optic map, which describes the path of the flood.

If You Go:
Grandview Cemetery is the final resting place of Congressional Medal of Honor Recipient George W. Reed. Reed was awarded his medal for his bravery in action at the Second Battle of Weldon Railroad, Virginia during the siege of Petersburg in the Civil War in 1864.

There is also an impressive grave marking the remains of Boyd "Buzz" Wagner, the World War II fighter ace. Wagner rose to Lieutenant Colonel in the Army Air Corps during World War II. He shot down eight Japanese planes and earned the title as America's first fighter ace. He was a recipient of the Purple Heart and the Distinguished Flying Cross. John McCrory, the founder of the McCrory Five and Ten Cent, store chain is also buried there in the family mausoleum above whose entrance is inscribed "McCrorey" the original spelling of the family name. His hundreds of stores would come to be known as the second of the great five-and-dime chain stores following Woolworks and preceding Kresge.

Pete Duranko, the Notre Dame All American from the 1966 national championship team and eight year NFL veteran, is also buried in Grandview Cemetery, as is Congressman John Murtha. Murtha represented Pennsylvania in Congress for 36 years and was the first Vietnam Veteran elected to the U.S. House of Representatives.

16

"What If?"

MARY JO KOPECHNE

County: Luzerne
Town: Larksville
Cemetery: Saint Vincents
Address: Washington Avenue

The subject of this chapter is different than anyone else appearing in this volume. Mary Jo Kopechne is famous as a result of the way she died. Virtually everyone else in the book gained their fame through the things they accomplished while living. It is a fact that nobody can say how different America, and for that matter, world history might have been had Kopechne lived.

Mary Jo Kopechne was born in Wilkes-Barre, Pennsylvania on July 26, 1940. While she was still an infant, her family relocated to New Jersey. In terms of her education through High School, she was a product of the parochial school system. When it came time to choose a college Mary Jo decided on the Caldwell College for Women which is also located in New Jersey. She graduated in 1962 with a degree in business administration.

After graduation, Kopechne's first job was teaching at the Mission of Saint Jude in Montgomery, Alabama. In 1963, she moved to Washington, D. C., to work for Florida Senator George Smathers. Smathers was a close friend of John F. Kennedy, and he may have assisted Mary Jo in moving to Robert Kennedy's staff when he was elected Senator by the people of New York in 1964.

Kopechne was a loyal Robert Kennedy employee right up until the time of his death. When Kennedy decided to run for president in 1968 she went to work on his campaign. She worked with a group of women that became known as the "Boiler Room Girls", a nickname the six women earned because the office they worked in was hot and had no windows. Among their duties was tracking democratic delegates and how they intended to vote. One of the states that fell under Kopechne's responsibility was Pennsylvania.

On June 5, 1968, Robert Kennedy was assassinated. Kopechne was devastated and, at first, claimed she couldn't return to Washington. However, in December 1968, she was hired by Matt Reese Associates, a political consulting firm based in Washington. Through her work for the firm she soon found that she was on her way to a successful career.

By this time, Robert Kennedy's younger brother and senator from Massachusetts, Edward Moore Kennedy was already being mentioned as a potential candidate for president in either 1972 or 1976. Edward was

Mary Jo Kopechne, far left during 1967 staff meeting with RFK.

commonly known as Ted or Teddy Kennedy and he had already turned down the chance to be a vice-presidential candidate in 1968. Many political pundits held the opinion that it was just a matter of time until the youngest of the Kennedy brothers would be elected president.

On July 18, 1969, Ted Kennedy hosted a party on Chappaquiddick Island, just off the Massachusetts coast to honor the Boiler Room Girls. It is impossible to say with any certainty what happened that night and in the early morning hours of the next day. According to Kennedy, at about 11:15 p.m. he indicated he was going to leave the party. He said that Kopechne asked him if he could drop her off at her hotel. Kennedy then obtained the car keys from his chauffeur. When asked why he didn't have the chauffer drive them both he said that the chauffeur was finishing his meal and he didn't see a reason to disturb him. Kennedy and Kopechne left the party. Mary Jo did not inform her friends she was leaving and she failed to take either her purse or her hotel key with her. Kennedy said he was driving the car, a 1967 Oldsmobile, when he took a wrong turn onto Dike Road. He said he was driving at about twenty miles an hour when he came to a wooden bridge known as Dike Bridge that had no guardrails. Immediately before reaching the bridge Kennedy hit his brakes and then drove off the side of the structure. His car ended up upside down underwater in Poucha Pond. Kennedy said he escaped the vehicle, though he could not remember how. He called out for Kopechne and getting no response he claimed he repeatedly dove into the water but that his attempts to reach the vehicle were unsuccessful. He then said that he rested for a time before returning on foot to the Lawrence Cottage, where the party was being held.

According to his testimony, Kennedy denied seeing any houses with their lights on as he walked back to the party. According to others, he would have passed four houses on his way back to the party. The first of these residences was known as "Dike's House." It was 150 yards from the bridge. Sylvia Malm, who was living there at the time stated that she had left lights on in the house when she retired for the evening and that she had a working telephone. There was also a working telephone in the Lawrence Cottage.

The men at the party included Kennedy cousin, Joseph Gargan, and a friend of Gargan's named Paul Markham. According to Kennedy, he, Gargan, and Markham returned to the scene of the accident. Again attempts by all three men to reach the vehicle were unsuccessful. Gargan and Markham then drove Kennedy to the ferry landing though the last ferry had left for the evening. Both told Kennedy he needed to report the accident. Reportedly Kennedy responded, "You two take care of the girls, and I will take care of the accident." He then dove into the water, swam across the 500-foot channel, and returned to his hotel room. Gargan and Markham later took the position that they did not report the accident because they assumed Kennedy was going to do it.

At 8 a.m. the following day Gargan and Markham arrived at Kennedy's hotel room. According to his testimony, Kennedy said the two asked him why he had not reported the accident. He claimed that as he swam the channel he began to believe that somehow it would be found out that Mary Jo had survived. The three men then took the ferry back to Chappaquiddick where Kennedy made calls to friends, from a pay phone, requesting advice. The accident remained unreported.

That morning, fishermen spotted the automobile submerged in the water. They went to a nearby cottage and the residents notified the authorities. It was about 8:20 a.m. The Edgartown Police Chief James Arena, responded arriving in about 15 minutes. When his attempts to examine the interior of the vehicle were unsuccessful, he called a diver and a truck with towing capability. The diver, a man named Jim Farrar, arrived dressed in his scuba gear and recovered Mary Jo's body in about 10 minutes. He also checked the license plate and found that it was registered to Kennedy.

Shortly, the news reached Kennedy that the car and Mary Jo's body had been discovered. At this point, he took the ferry back to Edgartown and went to the police station to report the accident. When he arrived at the station, he made a few more phone calls before submitting a statement to the police. The statement, much of which has been covered above, created more questions than it answered.

Seven days after the incident, Ted Kennedy pleaded guilty to leaving the scene of an accident after causing injury. Judge James Boyle sentenced Kennedy to two months in jail but he promptly suspended the sentence, citing Kennedy's unblemished record. In his remarks, the judge noted that Kennedy "would continue to be punished beyond anything this court could impose." No one knows whether the judge was referring to the guilt Kennedy would be required to carry, or to the damage done to his political career.

There are many unanswered questions from the incident. John Farrar, the diver who recovered Mary Jo's body, claimed that her death was caused by suffocation and not by drowning. He said Kopechne had positioned her body to take advantage of an air pocket in the vehicle. It was his belief that if he had been called to the scene in a timely manner Mary Jo would have survived.

There is yet another interesting possibility as to what took place that night. A deputy sheriff by the name of Christopher "Huck" Look was working as a special officer that night due to the various celebrations related to the Edgartown Regatta. He was driving home at about 12:40 a.m. when he saw a parked car containing a man and a woman stopped on a private road. Thinking the couple might be lost he went to offer assistance. He stopped his vehicle and at a distance of twenty to thirty feet began walking toward the car. The car started up and moved by him quickly. Look later recalled that the license plate contained an "L" and two "7"s a description that matched Kennedy's vehicle.

There are those that have put forth the theory that after eluding the deputy sheriff, Kennedy left the car and walked back to the party. Meanwhile, Kopechne, being unfamiliar with the area, drove off the bridge instead of returning to the party. The proponents of this theory argue that it accounts for Kennedy's lack of concern until the vehicle was discovered.

Whatever actually happened, it altered Kennedy's political life forever. While the people of the Bay State never turned on him, many of those outside Massachusetts never really trusted him again. He did not run for the presidency in 1972 or 1976. When he did run in 1980 against an incumbent president who was a member of his own party, he failed. In running against Kennedy, President Jimmy Carter often repeated that "he had never panicked in a crisis." For the remainder of his life Ted Kennedy remained the senior senator from Massachusetts. By all accounts he served his state well and was well respected by his fellow senators.

Mary Jo Kopechne died when she was just shy of her 29th birthday. She is buried in Saint Vincent's Cemetery in Larksville, Pennsylvania. As you enter the cemetery, you will notice a main section that makes its way up a

modest hill. Mary Jo is about a quarter of the way up right in the middle of the main section.

If You Go:

You are close to the final resting places of two people covered in *Keystone Tombstones Volume 1*; Congressman Dan Flood (chapter 7) and Jim Crowley in chapter 6 titled "Half the Horseman."

17

"The Blond Bombshell"

JAYNE MANSFIELD

County: Northampton
Town: Pen Argyl
Cemetery: Fairview
Address: South Main Street

Jayne Mansfield was an American actress who worked on both the Broadway stage and in Hollywood movies. She was born on April 19, 1933 in Bryn Mawr, Pennsylvania. Her name at birth was Vera Jayne Palmer. Early in her childhood, her family moved to Dallas, Texas. It was in Dallas that she spent her formative years. She studied at the University of Dallas and the University of Texas. She spoke five languages and reportedly had a very high IQ. She claimed it was 163. In addition, she was classically trained on both the piano and violin.

While in Dallas, she began to study acting. She was a student of Baruch Lumet, the father of the famed Hollywood director Sidney Lumet. She was also busy winning beauty contests having been named "Miss Photoflash", "Miss Fire Prevention Week," and "Miss Magnesium Lamp."

In the early 1950's, she was working at the Pasadena Playhouse. A Warner Brothers talent scout discovered her and signed her to a contract. Her movie career began with bit parts. Her appearance in movies and her pictorial as the Playboy Playmate of the month in February 1955 turned her into one of the leading sex symbols of her era.

Mansfield's first movie role was in "Female Jungle," a 1954 production. She appeared in a film starring Jack Webb Titled "Pete Kelly's Blues" in 1955. That same year, she returned to Broadway, appearing in the successful play "Will Success Spoil Rock Hunter?" By the next year, she was back in Hollywood starring in "The Girl Can't Help It." This film included performances from early rock stars such as Eddie Cochrane, Fats Domino, and Little Richard. I think we can all agree that a meeting between Mansfield and Little Richard would have been worth seeing.

In 1957, she reprised her Broadway role for the film "Will Success Spoil Rock Hunter?" The film was a success. As a matter of fact, "The Girl Can't Help It" and "Will Success..." are now considered classics. That same year she appeared in the film "The Wayward Bus" with Dan Dailey and Joan Collins. For her performance, she earned the Golden Globe award as New Star of the Year in the actress category. Natalie Wood was among the other nominees. Unfortunately for Mansfield, she also appeared in "Kiss Them for Me" with Gary Grant that same year. The film was soundly panned by the

Actress Jayne Mansfield

critics and, as it turned out, was her final starring role for a well known Hollywood studio.

After that, quality roles in quality films were not offered to Mansfield. In 1963, she appeared in "Promises, Promises" where she became the first well known mainstream American actress to appear nude on film. The city of Cleveland banned the movie, though it did enjoy box office success elsewhere.

Though her Hollywood career was floundering she continued to have success in other venues. She appeared on stage in Vegas in a show titled "The House of Love." For her efforts there, she earned $35,000 per week. Even without making films, she was earning anywhere from $8,000 to $25,000 a week for her night club act. She also made a few recordings. In 1965 she released, "As the Clouds Drift By" with "Suey" on the flip side. One of the backing musicians on the recordings was Jimi Hendrix.

At that point in her career, she was also doing television variety shows. She did the popular Ed Sullivan Show and also appeared with Jack Benny, Steve Allen, and Jackie Gleason. She entertained the troops with Bob Hope when he did his tours entertaining the boys overseas. While her film career was over, she was making a great living in the entertainment business.

Mansfield was married three times. Two of her marriages ended in divorce. There were rumors of numerous sexual affairs that included liaisons with men such as John F. Kennedy. She was the mother of five children. One of her children, Mariska Hargitay, is known for her role in the television series "Law and Order: Special Victims Unit."

On June 28, 1967, Mansfield was performing in Biloxi, Mississippi at the Gus Stevens Supper Club. After the performance, she, a male friend, their driver Ronnie Harrison, and three of Mansfield's children who were in the back seat, headed for New Orleans. The party needed to get there that night because Mansfield was scheduled to do a television interview the following morning. At about 2:25 a.m. on June 29th the car carrying Mansfield and her passengers crashed into the rear of a tractor trailer. All three adults died instantly; the children escaped with minor injuries. Word spread that Mansfield had been decapitated. This was untrue; she died from fatal head trauma.

Jayne Mansfield is buried beneath a beautiful heart shaped headstone in Fairview Cemetery in Pen Argyl Pennsylvania. As evidenced by the grave goods (in her case coins) we found on her tombstone, Mansfield has not been forgotten. In 1980 the "Jayne Mansfield Story" aired on CBS. It starred Loni Anderson and Arnold Schwarzenegger. It was nominated for three Emmy awards.

If You Go:

While there are no other cemeteries of note in the vicinity of Fairview, you are within a half hour of Allentown. Right in downtown Allentown, behind the old Pennsylvania Power and Light building (you can't miss it as it is by far the tallest structure in the city) lies an old cemetery. Within this cemetery lie the remains of many veterans of the American Revolution and the War of 1812.

The authors admit they were perplexed as to how Jayne Mansfield came to be buried in Pen Argyl. As it turns out, we stopped to have lunch in a small diner just outside of Pen Argyl in the town of Gap. We quizzed our waitress but she had no idea who Jayne Mansfield was. She did tell us that there was a gentleman named Charlie in the diner who knew all the local

The sex symbol form the 50's and 60's lies beneath this beautiful tombstone. Note the grave goods (coins) left for her after all these years. Some guys never forget.

history, and she offered to direct him to our table. We immediately accepted the offer.

Charlie arrived in a flash. We later guessed him to be in his late 70's or early 80's, but he was still in great physical condition, and he appeared to be sharp as a tack. After introducing ourselves we asked about Mansfield. Charlie advised us that Mansfield's mother had settled in Pen Argyl and that she had arranged to have the body shipped there for burial. He also said that Mansfield had other relatives in the area. He then told us he used to have drinks with one of her cousins all the time at the local Legion, until he (Charlie) was banned from the club due to his fondness for foul language.

Charlie asked us why we were interested in Jayne Mansfield and we explained the basis of the book to him. He immediately said, "You boys are doing Mary Jo Kopechne, right?" We had to admit she wasn't on our list, but agreed she should be (See Chapter 16). Our thanks go out to Charlie for the information on Mansfield and for bringing Mary Jo to our attention.

"The Mysterious Case of Mary Pinchot Meyer"

MARY PINCHOT MEYER

County: Pike
Town: Milford
Cemetery: Milford
Address: Route 209

She was born on October 14, 1920, in New York City, to a wealthy and politically connected family. Her father was a lawyer active in the Progressive party who contributed funding to the socialist magazine "The Masses." Her mother was a journalist who wrote for magazines such as "The Nation" and "The New Republic." Her uncle Gifford Pinchot was a two time Governor of Pennsylvania (see *Keystone Tombstones – Anthracite Region*, p. 80). She would eventually marry Cord Meyer who would go on to work for the Central Intelligence Agency. She would become a friend and lover of President John F. Kennedy. She was murdered in the fall of 1964, and many believe her death was related to her interest in the assassination of President Kennedy. Her name was Mary Pinchot Meyer.

Meyer grew up at the Pinchot family home named Grey Towers in Milford. As a child she met a number of left leaning intellectuals through her parents including Louis Brandeis and Harold Ickes. She was educated at Brearley School and Vassar College. It was during these years that she developed an interest in communism. This did not bother her father at all. He wrote a letter to his brother where he states, "Vassar seems to be very interested in communism. And a great deal of warm debating is going on among the students of Mary's class, which I think is an excellent thing. People of that age ought to be radical anyhow." It was during this period that she first met John F. Kennedy when she attended a dance at Choate Rosemary Hall.

After she graduated from Vassar, Meyer began working as a journalist for United Press. By this time she had joined the American Labor Party. Joining that party resulted in the Federal Bureau of Investigation opening a file on her political activities. Like her parents, Meyer was a pacifist. In 1944 she met Cord Meyer. Meyer was a marine who had suffered serious combat injuries that resulted in him losing an eye. At the time the two had similar political views and on April 19, 1945, they were married. Shortly after their marriage the couple attended the conference held in San Francisco that resulted in the establishment of the United Nations. Cord Meyer went as an

Mary Pinchot Meyer was found shot and killed near her Georgetown home.

aide to Harold Stassen while his wife covered the conference for the North American Newspaper Alliance.

During this time period the Meyer's started a family. Their first son Quentin was born in 1945, followed by Michael in 1947. The couple had a third son named mark who was born in 1950. With three small children, Meyer settled into the role of being a housewife.

The couple at this time supported the idea of world government. However in 1950 after the family moved to Cambridge, Cord Meyer lost his enthusiasm for the idea. It was also around this time that he began working secretly for the Central Intelligence Agency (CIA). In 1951 he officially became an employee of the agency where he became a key player in "Operation Mockingbird" a covert operation designed to move the American media toward the positions supported by the CIA.

The Meyer family now moved to Washington D.C. and settled in Georgetown. The couple was very visible in Georgetown social circles that included people like Katherine Graham, Clark Clifford and the high ranking CIA official by the name of Richard M. Bissell. In 1953 Senator Joe McCarthy accused Cord Meyer of being a communist. Allen Dulles was successful in defending Meyer, and he was able to keep his position with the CIA. In the summer of 1954 John F. Kennedy and his wife Jackie purchased Hickory Hill a house close to that of the Meyers. Mary Meyer and Jackie Kennedy became good friends and often went on walks together. As the Meyer's political views grew apart, it put a strain on their relationship. In 1956 their son Michael was killed after being hit by a car close to the family home. In 1958 Mary Meyer filed for a divorce. In the filing she alleged "extreme cruelty, mental in nature, which seriously injured her health, destroyed her happiness, rendered further cohabitation unendurable and compelled the parties to separate."

After the divorce Meyer and her two surviving sons remained in the family home. She began painting in a garage at the home of her sister who was married to the *Washington Post's* Ben Bradlee. In her book *A Very Private Woman* Nina Burleigh, who knew Meyer personally, wrote that during this period Meyer "was out looking for fun and getting in trouble along the way."

During this period Meyer began running into John Kennedy at social functions and parties. Many were aware that he was very much attracted to her, but Meyer knew about his womanizing and for a time that put her off. In addition Kennedy's plans to make a run for the presidency were, by this time well known, and she thought his womanizing was reckless.

After Kennedy's election Meyer evidently changed her mind. Beginning in October 1961, she became a frequent visitor to the White House. The general consensus is that once their relationship became intimate Kennedy and Meyer got together at least 30 times. In addition it is generally believed that on her visits to the White House Meyer brought with her marijuana and in some cases LSD. Meyer during this period told some friends she was keeping a diary.

How close was the relationship between Kennedy and Meyer? In an interview with Nina Burleigh, Kennedy aide Myer Feldman responded to a question with the following, "I think he might have thought more of her than some of the other women and discussed things that were on his mind not just social gossip." Burleigh wrote that "Mary might actually have been a force for peace during some of the most frightening years of the cold war."

In 1976 Ron Rosenbaum and Phillip Nobile wrote an article titled, "The Curious Aftermath of JFK's Best and Brightest Affair." They refer to Mary in the article as the "secret lady Ottoline of Camelot." They claimed to have been granted an interview with a source who did not wish to be identified but was in a unique position to comment on the couple's relationship. The interview went as follows:

"How could a woman so admired for her integrity as Mary Meyer traduce her friendship with Jackie Kennedy?"

"They weren't friends" was the curt response.

"Did JFK actually love Mary Meyer?"

"I think so."

"Then why would he carry on an affair simultaneously with Judith Exner?"

"My friend there's a difference between sex and love."

"But why Mary Meyer over all other women?"

"He was an unusual man. He wanted the best."

In 1983 former Harvard professor Timothy Leary claimed that Meyer visited him and said that she was involved in a plan to avert nuclear war by convincing powerful men in Washington to take mind altering drugs with a goal of having them reach the conclusion that the Cold War was meaningless. According to Leary the purpose of her visit was to find out how to conduct LSD sessions with these men. When Leary suggested that Mary bring the men here so he could conduct the session she responded by saying that was impossible since the man she was involved with was much too powerful.

In her book Burleigh confirms Meyer's own use of LSD and her involvement with Leary which occurred at the same time she was involved with Kennedy. While Burleigh draws no conclusions as to whether Kennedy participated in any LSD sessions she does note that the timing of her visits to Leary coincided with Meyer's known meetings with Kennedy. During a 1990 interview Leary was asked point blank whether he had any doubt that Kennedy was using LSD in the White House with Meyer. He responded by saying, "I can't say that." He pointed out that it was his assumption that Meyer had proposed to take LSD with Kennedy but that he had no proof it had actually happened. Pressed, Leary agreed, that it was possible, even likely, that Kennedy had taken LSD, but he would go no further than that.

On September 24, 1963, Kennedy went with both Meyer and her sister Tony for a visit to the family's Grey Tower estate in Milford, Pennsylvania.

The purpose of the President's visit was to dedicate a gift from the Pinchot family to the United States Forest Service. The gift included a large piece of land and the Pinchot mansion which had served as the home of Meyer's uncle and former Pennsylvania Governor Gifford Pinchot. As documented by Peter Janney in his excellent book *Mary's Mosaic* Tony had no idea about the affair between her sister and the President. She said, "I always felt he liked me as much as Mary. You could say there was a little rivalry." Ironically on the same day as the dedication, the United States Senate ratified Kennedy's Limited Nuclear Test Ban Treaty with the Soviet Union and the United Kingdom.

Two months later, after Kennedy was assassinated, Leary said he received a phone call from Meyer who sobbed and said "They couldn't control him anymore. He was changing too fast ... They've covered everything up. I gotta come see you. I'm afraid."

There is no way to document where Meyer was when she got word of the assassination. She spent the night at a friend's house in Georgetown. The friend recalled that Meyer was very sad and that they both cried but said very little.

As detailed in Janney's book Meyer spent the next year trying to solve the mystery surrounding Kennedy's death. From the first she was sure it had been a conspiracy, and one of the first people Meyer questioned was Kennedy aide Kenneth O'Donnell. O'Donnell respected Meyer largely because he was aware of the role she had played in the president's life. During one interview O'Donnell said he, "feared she had a hold on Jack."

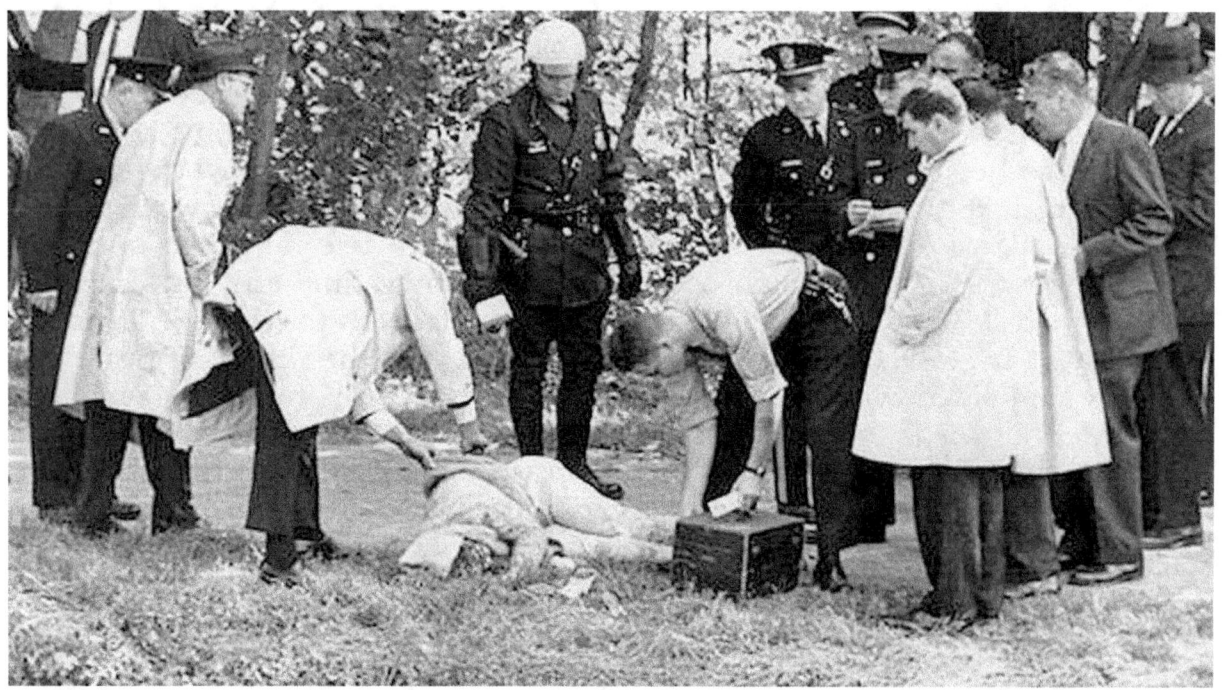

Mary Pinchot Meyer's murder scene

O'Donnell and another Kennedy aide by the name of Dave Powers were riding in the car directly behind Kennedy in the motorcade. Both were combat veterans of World War II. O'Donnell told Meyer about what he and Powers had witnessed that day, the smell of gunpowder and the fact that at least two shots were fired from behind the fence on what has become known as the grassy knoll. Twenty-five years later his account was confirmed by Speaker of the House Tip O'Neill. O'Neill recalled a conversation he had at a dinner with O'Donnell and Powers five years after the assassination. The two told O'Neill that two shots had come from behind the fence. When O'Neill responded, "That's not what you told the Warren Commission." O'Donnell readily agreed saying that the FBI told him it couldn't have happened that way so he testified the way "they wanted me to" because I didn't want to cause more pain or trouble for the family.

Dave Powers was interviewed on the radio in 1991 where he basically told the same story. It was around the time that Oliver Stone's film JFK had been released. After the broadcast Woody Woodland, who had done the interview, was walking Powers to his car when he asked Powers if he had seen the film. He replied that he had. Woodland then asked, "What did you think of it?" Powers responded, "I think they got it right." "Really?" was the reply from a surprised Woodland. "Yes,' said Powers, "we were riding into an ambush. They were shooting from behind the fence." Woodland pointed out that was different from what Powers told the Warren Commission. Powers also admitted that that was true but added he had been told not to say that by the FBI.

Meyer began collecting information on the assassination. One of the people she sought out with regard to the assassination was William Walton, a gay man who had been her escort to many White House social affairs. Walton met Kennedy after World War II, and the two developed a close friendship. Kennedy's wife Jackie enjoyed Walton's company as well and when Kennedy was elected president, Walton enjoyed an almost unchecked access to the White House, and soon he became a close friend of Bobby Kennedy's as well. When Walton met Mary he found her to be distraught with grief. He told her that Bobby suspected something far deeper than Lee Harvey Oswald when it came to the death of his brother. He said Bobby had a plan to take back the presidency, but that it would be years before he could do anything about his brother's death. Despite this information Meyer continued her quest to learn more about Kennedy's death.

In the summer of 1964, Meyer began telling friends that she believed someone had been in her house while she was away. She told another friend that on one occasion she saw someone leaving the house as she was entering. Her friends confirmed that Meyer was frightened by these incidents. By this time Meyer had told a friend, Ann Truitt, that she had kept a diary that detailed her relationship with Kennedy. She asked Truitt to retrieve the diary should anything happen to her.

On October 12, 1964, Meyer was taking her daily walk on the Chesapeake and Ohio towpath in Georgetown. Henry Wiggins a car mechanic was working on a car on Canal Road when he heard a woman scream, "Someone help me, someone help me." Almost immediately he heard two gunshots. Wiggins ran to the edge of a wall overlooking the towpath where he saw a black man wearing a light jacket, dark pants and a dark cap standing over the body of a white woman. Wiggins would later tell police that the man was between 5 feet 8 inches to 5 feet 10 inches and weighed about 185 pounds. According to Wiggins the man turned and looked at him for a few seconds and after shoving something in his pocket turned and walked away disappearing down an embankment.

Meyer's body was taken to the Washington D. C. morgue where an autopsy was performed by Deputy Coroner Doctor Linwood L. Rayford, a man who, by this time, performed more than 400 such procedures on gunshot victims. He found that Meyer had been shot twice: once in the head and once in the back. He concluded that both shots were fired at close range. According to the doctor Meyer probably survived the first shot to the head though it would have rendered her unconscious. He noted that the second shot was fired with remarkable precision. That bullet severed the aorta and death would have been instantaneous. That bothered Rayford because he felt that it indicated that whoever killed Meyer was a professional.

Meanwhile the police had arrested a black man, Ray Crump, who was found in the area of the shooting and who stood 5 foot 4 inches tall. They conducted tests to show that he had fired the gun that killed Meyer but found no nitrates on either his hands or his clothes. They conducted an extensive search for two days that included the use of scuba divers and actually draining the canal near the scene of the murder. No gun could be found. Crump was eventually acquitted (for a detailed account of that story the authors strongly recommend Janney's book *Mary's Mosaic*).

Ann Truitt was in Tokyo when Meyer was killed. She called Meyer's brother-in-law Ben Bradlee and told him about the diary. The next day Bradlee and his wife went to the Meyer home when they arrived it was locked and when they entered they found James Angleton, the CIA

This modest tombstone marks the final resting place of a woman who refused to believe the conclusions reached by the Warren Commission.

counterintelligence chief already searching for the diary. There are various reports of what happened to it. Some believe Angleton burned it while others believe it remains in someone's possession.

In February of 2001, a writer asked Cord Meyer about Mary Meyer. He responded by saying it had been a bad time because his father had died that same year. Getting back to Mary Meyer the writer asked who could have committed such a heinous crime. Cord Meyer responded, "The same sons of bitches that killed John F. Kennedy."

Mary Pinchot Meyer was laid to rest in the Pinchot family plot in the Milford, Pennsylvania cemetery. She lies next to her son Michael.

If You Go:
Meyer's uncle and former Governor of Pennsylvania Gifford Pinchot (see *Keystone Tombstones Volume 1*) is housed in a large mausoleum in the Milford Cemetery. Just across the road from his gravesite is the grave of Charles Henry Van Wyck. He was a New York Congressman, a Senator from Nebraska and a Brigadier general in the Civil War (See *Keystone Tombstones Civil War*, chapter 30)

On February 22, 1861, Van Wyck survived an assassination attempt in Washington. The attempt took place on the same night that an attempt was made to assassinate President-Elect Lincoln in Baltimore. The attack on Van Wyck was apparently motivated by a harsh anti-slavery speech he delivered on the floor of the house. In the speech he denounced the southern states for the "crime against the laws of God and nature." He fought off the attack and survived only because a book and papers that he carried in his breast pocket blocked the thrust of a Bowie knife.

Also buried in the Milford Cemetery is General Daniel Brodhead. He fought with George Washington on Long Island and wintered with the Continental Army at Valley Forge in 1777-1778.

General Daniel Brodhead3

John "Black Jack" Kehoe, "King of the Mollies," soon before his execution in 1878.

"The Molly Maguires"

BLACK JACK KEHOE and FRANKLIN GOWEN

Counties: Schuylkill, Philadelphia
Towns: Tamaqua, Philadelphia
Cemeteries: Old Saint Jerome's, Ivy Hill
Addresses: Corner of High and Nescopeck Streets, 1201 Easton Road

In Pennsylvanian history, there are few groups as interesting or as controversial as the Molly Maguires. Some historians view them as an Irish Catholic terrorist organization, while to others, they are no more than an organized labor movement created as a response to the persecution of Irish coal miners. Still, there are some who argue that the organization never existed. Undeniable, however, is the fact that between June 21, 1877, and October 9, 1879, twenty Irish catholic men were hanged for murder and accused of belonging to a secret society known as the Molly Maguires. Ten of these men were hanged on June 21, 1877, a day that would become known as "Black Thursday" or "The Day of the Rope."

The Molly Maguire story began in the early 1860's and ended in 1879 when the last hanging took place. The center of action was the anthracite coal region in northeastern Pennsylvania. The alleged Mollies were most active in two counties Carbon and Schuylkill.

As a result of the potato famine in the late 1840's, many Irish immigrants landed in America. Those who settled in the Pennsylvania coal region found that the only jobs available to them were in the mines. The work was difficult and dangerous. In addition, the miners were forced to live in coal company provided housing and could only shop at the company store where prices were so inflated that it was not unusual for a miner to find himself in debt to the company as his wages could not cover his rent and other expenses. These conditions led to the beatings and murder of mine owners, foreman and superintendents. The mine owners and newspapers believed these beatings and killings were part of an organized conspiracy headed by Irishmen who called themselves the Molly Maguires.

During the Molly era, the miners were forming a union under the leadership of John Siney. The union was known as the Workingmen's Benevolent Association and through Siney, and the leadership of the organization as a whole, they sought to seek concessions through negotiations. At times, they used strikes as a tool. In December of 1874, what was called the long strike began in the coalfields. The strike lasted for

The tombstones in this old cemetery have been destroyed due to vandalism. Two alleged Molly Maguires are buried here including Alec Campbell. Almost all historians agree that one of the two interned here, placed their handprint on his cell wall prior to his execution. The print remains to this day as a sign of his innocence.

just under six months and when the miners broke they were forced to return for lower wages than they had previously earned. The person responsible for this settlement was Franklin B. Gowen, the President of the Philadelphia and Reading Coal and Iron Company.

Gowen was born in Mount Airy, Pennsylvania on February 9, 1836. He was the fifth child of an Irish Protestant immigrant who made his living as a grocer. Franklin attended a boarding school, John Beck's Boys Academy, starting at age 9 and ending when he was 13. After serving an apprenticeship to a Lancaster merchant, he decided to study law and worked under an attorney in Pottsville, Pennsylvania which happened to be the county seat of Schuylkill County. In 1860 he was admitted to the County Bar and in 1862 he was elected District Attorney of Schuylkill County. He held this position until 1864 when he resigned in order to pursue a private practice. Among his clients was the Philadelphia and Reading Railroad. He soon left private practice to head that company's legal department. It proved to be a wise move for in 1869, Gowen was appointed acting President of the company.

By this time, Gowen already had the Molly Maguires in his sights. In 1873, he hired the Pinkerton Detective Agency for the purpose of infiltrating the Mollies. Several Pinkerton operatives were sent into the coalfields, including James McParlan, who arrived in Schuylkill County on October 27,1873, using the alias of James McKenna. In April of 1874, McParlan was initiated into the Ancient Order of Hibernians (AOH), a legal Irish Catholic organization. It was Gowen's belief that the Molly Maguires operated within this organization. It is worth noting that violence on both management's and labor's side increased once the Pinkertons arrived in the area.

The Pinkertons were not the only weapon used by Gowen in his attacks on the Mollies. He had his own private police force known as the Coal and Iron police. An 1868 act of the legislature authorized the creation of this private army. A deputy commissioner for Pennsylvania's Bureau of Labor Statistics held the opinion that the coal operators were their own personal government in the middle of a republic. There was no limit to the number of Coal and Iron policemen that could be hired by the Reading Coal and Iron Company, nor were there any background checks on those who applied to join the force. This police force patrolled the coal region unmolested by local authorities. In May of 1875, Pinkerton sent Captain Robert Linden to the coal fields. He immediately received an appointment as a Coal and Iron policeman. The power of this police force was absolute. They were more powerful than the civil authorities. Linden was instrumental in investigating the crimes that led to the arrests of the alleged Molly Maguires.

One of the most important murders in the Molly Maguire story took place in Tamaqua during the evening hours on July 5, 1875. The Tamaqua police force consisted of two men: Barney McCarron and Benjamin Yost. Yost had a history of running into trouble with an Irish minor named James Kerrigan.

Yost had arrested Kerrigan on several occasions for public drunkenness, and in at least one instance subdued Kerrigan with his billy club.

One of the duties of the Tamaqua police force was to extinguish the gas street lights. As Yost was climbing a ladder to shut off one of the light, shots rang out, and Yost fell to the ground. McCarron Turned towards the sound of the shots and saw two forms running away. McCarron gave chase but the assailants escaped. Yost died several hours later and word spread that the murder had been carried out by the Molly Maguires.

The first Mollies that ended up on the gallows were arrested in September of 1875 for the murder of mine superintendent John P. Jones. Jones was shot and killed at a railroad station in Lansford while on his way to work by two men who quickly left the scene. A witness to the murder quickly made the trip to Tamaqua and spread the news. In addition, this man claimed to have seen a man waving something white in the woods outside Tamaqua an apparent signal that brought two other men to him. A posse was formed to investigate. The three men arrested for the crime were found in those same woods having a meal. The men were identified as Edward Kelly, Michael Doyle, and Jimmy Kerrigan. Both Kelly and Doyle carried documents that identified them as members of the AOH. The three were taken to the Carbon County jail in Mauch Chunk, now known as Jim Thorpe.

These initial arrests provided the break the Pinkertons were waiting for, and they quickly took advantage of it. The accused men requested separate trials, and Michael Doyle was the first to be tried. Meanwhile Kerrigan and Kelly were kept in solitary confinement in the county jail.

This initial trial set the tone for the ones that would follow. The jury would have no Irish or catholic members and would be made up largely of Germans, including some who spoke little or no English. The District Attorney, while present, did not try the case. This duty fell to attorneys who worked for the railroad and coal companies. In the Doyle trial the prosecution was headed by General Charles Albright who worked for the Lehigh and Wilkes-Barre Coal Company. The general wore his civil war uniform, including his sword, throughout the trial. One has to wonder how he would have gotten past security today.

The prosecution called more than 100 witnesses that established that Doyle was seen in Lansford on the day of the murder. While no one testified that they had seen Doyle murder Jones, he was described as walking quickly toward the murder site and observed running away with a pistol in hand. The defense did not call a single witness in the case. In their summation the defense conceded that Doyle was in Lansford that day, but he was simply looking for work.

The prosecution case was at its weakest when it came to providing a motive for the murder. Detective McParlan's reports to his superiors laid out a scenario that would have provided a motive. According to the detective, Kerrigan (the head of the Mollies in Tamaqua) had been beaten by the

On June 21, 1877, within the walls of the Schuylkill County prison (pictured above) in Pottsville six alleged Molly Maguires were executed by hanging.

policeman Yost. Another Molly, Hugh McGehan, had been blacklisted by the mine foreman, Jones. Kerrigan initiated contact with James Roarity, the head of the Mollies in Coaldale, in order to exact revenge for these perceived wrongdoings. Kerrigan and Roarity decided that McGehan and a man by the name of James Boyle would murder Yost with the assistance of Kerrigan. Doyle and Kelly, again with Kerrigan's help, would take care of Jones.

The only way the prosecution could introduce this evidence would be to call McParlan as a witness. Because McParlan was still gathering information and the use of his testimony would have exposed his identity as a detective, the prosecution went on without him. It didn't matter. On February 1, 1876, the jury pronounced Doyle guilty and on the 23rd he was sentenced to be hanged.

At later trials, McParlan claimed that it was a common practice among the Mollies to trade jobs. This was done to make it difficult for the townspeople to recognize the out of town assailants.

Something of greater importance to the Molly Maguire story took place during the trial. Jimmy Kerrigan confessed. In fact, he produced a 210 page confession and agreed to testify against his fellow Irishmen in return for immunity. This action earned "Powder Keg" Kerrigan a new nickname, he would henceforth be known as "Squealer" Kerrigan.

Based on McParlan's reports and information supplied by Kerrigan, a unit of the Coal and Iron Police led by Captain Linden made a series of arrests. On February 4th this group set out and arrested James Carroll, James Roarity, Thomas Duffy, Hugh McGehan, James Boyle and Alexander Campbell for the murders of Yost and Jones. Six days later the Coal and Iron Police arrested Thomas Munley as a suspect in the murders of Thomas Sanger and William Uren. Another alleged Molly, Dennis Donnelly, would be arrested later for his part in the murders.

Sanger and Uren were shot and killed on September 1, 1875. On that morning Sanger, who was a mine boss, left for work accompanied by Uren who worked for him. While on the road, the duo was attacked by five heavily armed men who shot and killed them both. Sanger had been targeted for evicting Irishmen. Uren was simply in the wrong place at the wrong time.

Following these murders, a one page handbill titled "Strictly Confidential" began circulating in the coalfields. The paper claimed to present facts to be considered by the Vigilance Committee of the Anthracite Coal Region. The document goes on to list a number of murders that had occurred in the region and named the murderers and their residences. In terms of the Sanger and Uren case the handbill states, "On September 1st, 1875 at about 7 A.M. Thomas Sanger, a mining boss, and William Uren, a miner of Raven Run, were shot and fatally wounded by James O'Donnell, alias "Friday," and Thomas Munley, as the unsuspecting victims were on their way to work. Charles O'Donnell, Charles McAllister, and Mike Doyle were present, and accessories to this murder." The information in the handbill was almost certainly based on reports from Detective McParlan, and it is just as probable that it was distributed by the Pinkerton's.

The handbill began circulating in the fall of 1875, on December 10th of that year it would bear fruit. At about 3 in the morning of the 10th Charles and Ellen McAllister were asleep in their home in Wiggans patch. A small child lay between them and Ellen was pregnant. Ellen's mother was also in the house along with her unmarried sons James "Friday" O'Donnell and Charles O'Donnell. Four borders were also asleep in the house including James McAllister who was the brother of Charles.

Charles McAllister was awakened by a crashing noise: the kitchen door being smashed in. He told his wife to stay in bed and ran to the cellar where he made his way to his neighbor's through a door that connected the residences. His wife did not obey; she got up and opened a door that led to the kitchen and was shot and killed. Now pairs of men began searching every bedroom in the house. They brought James McAllister down the stairs into the yard where he freed himself and ran. Shots were fired, and he was hit in the arm but escaped. James O' Donnell also managed to escape.

Charles O'Donnell was not so lucky; he was taken outside, and when he struggled free, he was downed by gunshots. Men gathered around his fallen body and emptied their pistols. The shots were fired so close to the body that they burned the flesh. The next day a note was found on the property that stated "You are the killers of Sanger and Uren." Black Jack Kehoe, the man Gowen considered to be the King of the Mollies, was the brother-in-law of both Charles McAllister and Ellen McAllister.

To this day no one knows who the men were who participated in what became known as the Wiggans Patch massacre. What we do know is that Detective McParlan felt responsible. Upon hearing of the killings, he sent a letter of resignation to the Pinkerton office in New York City. In the letter he states, "Now I wake up this morning to find that I am the murderer of Mrs. McAllister." His resignation was not accepted.

Events moved quickly as a series of Molly Maguire trials commenced. The second trial, that of Edward Kelly, began on March 29th. Again, there were no Irish on the jury and the prosecution team was the same. The jury returned a guilty verdict on April 6th, and six days later Kelly was sentenced to be hanged.

After these first two convictions, the Pottsville Courthouse in Schuylkill County was the scene of the next trial. Leading the prosecution in this case would be Franklin Gowen, President of the Philadelphia and Reading Coal and Iron Company. Gowen was well acquainted with the Pottsville Courthouse. As stated previously, he had served as Schuylkill County's District Attorney. The trial started on May 4 and involved the killing of the Tamaqua police officer Benjamin Yost. James Boyle, James Roarity, Hugh McGehan, Thomas Duffy and James Carroll stood accused of the murder.

This trial marked the first appearance of the detective James McParlan as a witness for the prosecution. The informer, Jimmy Kerrigan, would also testify. Just as the trial was getting underway, news spread that the coal and iron police had arrested ten more Mollies in Schuylkill County. Among the ten was Black Jack Kehoe. Kehoe was a respected man active in community affairs who had written to local newspapers denying the existence of an organization known as the Molly Maguires. He was also active in the leadership of the Hibernians. In addition, he had worked his way out of the mines and had much to lose if his leadership of such a group as the Mollies could be proven.

Detective McParlan was the main witness at this trial, and through his testimony, the prosecution was able to leave the impression that the AOH and the Molly Maguires were one and the same. McParlan detailed secret signs and sayings that members used to identify each other. He stated that the chief purpose of the organization was to protect, and, when necessary, seek revenge for members who felt they had been wronged in some manner. In this way he tied the murders and beatings of the mine owners and bosses to the organization. Jimmy Kerrigan also testified and supported McParlan's account.

The defense did call several witnesses in this case including Mrs. Kerrigan who testified that her husband told her he had murdered Yost. She also condemned him for allowing innocent men to take the blame for his crime. While she was being cross examined, one of the jurors became ill. On May 18th the trial was suspended pending his recovery, however his condition did not improve and on May 25th he died of pneumonia. All the work that had gone into the case was lost. The jury was dismissed, and the prisoners returned to the county jail to await a new trial.

Before the second Yost trial began, Alexander Campbell was brought before the court in Mauch Chunk for the murder of John P. Jones.

Joe Farrell stands in front of Jack Kehoe's grave holding the key supplied by a local resident which allowed us entrance to the aged cemetery. Kehoe has been called the "King of the Mollies" but he was almost surely innocent of the crime that sent him to the gallows.

Campbell, like many of the accused Mollies, was born in Ireland. He arrived in Pennsylvania in 1868 where he opened a saloon in Tamaqua. He later moved to the Lansford area where he operated another saloon, the Columbia house. Campbell was viewed by many to be the leader of the Mollies in Carbon County. What made the Campbell trial important was that all agreed he was not present when Jones was killed. He was charged as an accessory before the fact, accused of being involved in the planning of the murder. The prosecution alleged that Kelly, Doyle and Kerrigan spent the night before the killing at Campbell's tavern. The defense countered with several witnesses who said they had been at Campbell's that night and had not seen the three men. After an eleven day trial the jury quickly returned with a guilty verdict and on August 28th Campbell was sentenced to be hanged. Clearly, an Irishman owning a public tavern was a dangerous business to be involved in at the time.

Before Campbell's trial was over, another had begun in Pottsville where Thomas Munley was tried for the murders of Thomas Sanger and William Uren. The prosecution case rested entirely on the testimony of McParlan. Several of Munley's family members testified that he was at home on the day of the murder. Despite this testimony, Munley was found guilty and sentenced to death.

By then, the second Yost trial was underway with the accused being Boyle, Carroll, McGehen and Roarity. Thomas Duffy had requested and was granted a separate trial. McParlan and Kerrigan repeated their testimony and all four men were found guilty. They too were sentenced to be hanged. In addition, the separate trial did not help Duffy as he was also found guilty and received the same sentence.

The Pinkertons continued to investigate past murders including that of mine boss Morgan Powell who had been killed in 1871. Three men, John Donahue, Thomas Fisher and Alec Campbell, were arrested and tried for this murder. All three were convicted and sentenced to death. This was Campbell's second conviction.

The first ten executions took place on June 21, 1877, Black Thursday, or the Day of the Rope as it was referred to by locals. Four of the convicted Irishmen would be hanged in the Mauch Chunk jail. The other six would face the hangman in Pottsville.

The Mauch Chunk hangings occurred first. The gallows had been constructed so that all four men could be hanged at the same time. At around 10:30 in the morning, Alexander Campbell took his place on the gallows. In his final statement, he forgave his executioners. Michael Doyle was next, and he took his spot on the gallows. He said that he had come to this point because of his failure to follow the advice of his church on secret societies. John Donahue took his place and declined comment. Edward Kelly was the last to take his place and, led by his priest, forgave everyone and added that if he had listened to his priests, he would not have found

Here is Jack Kehoe's Hibernian House looking much as it did the day he was arrested. It is still in operation and run by Kehoe's great-grandson.

himself on the gallows. The men were then readied for execution and at approximately 10:45, the trap was sprung and the four hurtled to their death. After the bodies were cut down and their hoods removed, the sheriff invited the spectators present to inspect the bodies.

In Pottsville, the authorities had decided to hang the prisoners two at a time. Between 8 and 10 AM, those with official passes were allowed into the prison where they scurried to find the best spots to watch the executions. Meanwhile, the area around the prison, including the hills, were packed with people.

Around 11 AM, the first two prisoners, James Boyle and Hugh McGehan emerged from the jail and made their way to the gallows. Both asked for forgiveness, and Boyle pardoned those who were about to hang him. Ten minutes later, the two were dead. The pair to follow were James Carroll and James Roarity. The latter had been convicted primarily based on the testimony of Jimmy Kerrigan who claimed that Roarity had paid him to have Yost killed. On the gallows, Roarity insisted that this was not so, and he added that Thomas Duffy had nothing to do with the Yost murder. Carroll simply stated that he was an innocent man. Both men were hung at around 12:20. Thomas Duffy and Thomas Munley were the last to the gallows. Neither said much beyond that it was no use and at 1:20, both were sent falling to their death.

At this point the Mollies, if they ever existed, were finished as a power in the coal region. Ten more would be hanged, and others would serve long prison terms. This was not enough to satisfy Franklin Gowen. He wouldn't be happy until he saw Jack Kehoe, who was already serving a seven year prison term, at the end of a rope.

Kehoe was a man who worked his way out of the mines. By 1873, he opened a tavern and rooming house in Girardville called the Hibernian House. He ran this business for three years and during this time became active in local politics. He was elected to the post of Constable in Girardville and was also named Schuylkill County delegate in the AOH. When local newspapers, based on information supplied by the Pinkertons, began linking the Hibernians to the Molly Maguires Kehoe publicly denied such charges. It was Kehoe's view that the Mollies were the fictional invention of the mine owners. Based on information supplied by Detective McParlan, Kehoe was arrested in 1876 and charged with conspiracy to commit murder. This charge did not carry a death sentence, but Gowen resurrected a murder that occurred in 1862 and named Kehoe one of the killers.

Frank Langdon was a mining boss in Audenried where Kehoe lived and worked. On June 14, 1862, he was assaulted by at least three men. He was able to return home, but he died three days later as a result of the beating. In January of 1877, Kehoe was tried for his murder. The evidence presented at the trial was murky at best. Kehoe was said to have threatened Langdon weeks before he was beaten, but other witnesses claimed to have seen

On the Day of the rope four alleged Mollies were hanged together at the same time in the old jail in Jim Thorpe. The gallows were built in the middle of the cell block so the condemned men were able to hear the construction prior to their execution. x

Kehoe on a hotel porch at the time Langdon was assaulted. In his summation, Gowen described Kehoe as a man who made money by his traffic in the souls of his fellow men. Despite the lack of evidence, Kehoe was found guilty and sentenced to death.

Kehoe's lawyers fought the conviction to the State Supreme Court which denied the appeal. Next they petitioned the Board of Pardons where they produced sworn statements from John Campbell and Neil Dougherty (both of whom had been convicted of second degree murder in the matter) admitting their participation in the beating and swearing that Kehoe was not present. In September 1878, the Board voted 2-2 on the petition. A tie vote meant the conviction was upheld.

On December 18, 1878, Kehoe waited in his cell with one of his lawyers, Martin L'Velle. He told L'Velle that he was prepared to die. Shortly thereafter, Kehoe took his place on the gallows in Pottsville. Given the opportunity to speak, he proclaimed his innocence, adding that he had not even seen the crime being committed. After making his statement, Kehoe nodded to the sheriff signifying that he was ready. He was quickly shackled and strapped, and at 10:27 a.m., the trap door was sprung. Four other men would be hanged as Mollies after Kehoe, but public interest in the story and in the hangings was never the same. In September of 1978, the Governor of Pennsylvania, Milton Shapp, released a statement that included the

Final resting place of Franklin Gowen who was the man most responsible for the hangings of 20 alleged Molly Maguires during the 1870's.

following; "It was Jack Kehoe's popularity among the workingmen that led Franklin Gowen to fear, despise, and ultimately destroy him." On January 12, 1979, Shapp signed a posthumous pardon for Jack Kehoe. This is the only posthumous pardon issued in the history of Pennsylvania.

Kehoe is buried in the old Saint Jerome's Catholic Cemetery in Tamaqua. The two victims of the Wiggans Patch massacre, Ellen McAllister and her brother, Charles O'Donnell, were also laid to rest here. The cemetery is located on the corner of High and Nescopeck streets, and it is fenced in and locked. A neighbor who lives on that corner has a key that he is happy to share with visitors. When we were looking for a way in, he appeared and asked "You here to see Kehoe?" That's how we found our way into the cemetery. Two other alleged Mollies, Thomas Duffy and Jack Donahue, are also buried there in unmarked graves. Another place worth visiting in relation to Kehoe is his Hibernian House in Girardville, which is now run by his great grandson. Among the artifacts that can be viewed at this location is Kehoe's cell door from the Pottsville prison.

Alec Campbell is buried in Saint Joseph's Catholic cemetery on Ludlow Street in Summit Hill. There are no grave markers in this cemetery due to acts of vandalism. A mock trial of Campbell was held in Jim Thorpe recently using the transcripts from his trial. A relative portrayed Campbell, and he was found innocent. Another alleged Molly, Thomas Fisher, lies there as well.

The Schuylkill County jail in Pottsville where many of the hangings took place is still in operation, but aside from plaques noting what happened, there is little to see. There is one interesting plaque that is on the wall at the jail's main entrance. The plaque notes that the largest mass execution in Pennsylvania history took place inside this prison. It also references the four executions that took place in Mauch Chunk that same day. What is striking is it ends by stating that the pardon of Jack Kehoe reflects "the judgment of many historians that the trials and executions were part of a repression directed against the fledgling mine workers union of that historic period."

The Carbon County jail, however, is now a museum where regular tours are conducted. A replica of the gallows stands where the original one once stood. In addition, visitors can view the mysterious handprint in cell 17. According to legend, as one of the Mollies (either Alec Campbell or Thomas Fisher) was about to be taken to the gallows, he put his handprint on the wall of his cell saying that it would remain forever as a sign of his innocence. Despite efforts to remove the print, it remains to this day.

Things went well for one of the other main characters in the Molly story. James McParlan was named manager of the Pinkertons' office in Denver Colorado. He passed away in Denver in 1919.

Franklin Gowen eventually lost his leadership position in the Philadelphia and Reading Coal and Iron Company. He returned to private practice. On December 13, 1889, according to the coroner who investigated the death, Gowen shot himself while staying in a hotel in Washington D.C. Many of Gowen's family and friends believed he was murdered. In 2002, a book written by Patrick Campbell (a descendant of Alec Campbell) entitled "Who Killed Franklin Gowen," concludes that Gowen was a homicide victim. Gowen is buried in the Ivy Hill Cemetery just outside Philadelphia.

In 1969, a highly fictionalized major motion picture called "The Molly Maguires" was released. It was filmed largely in Pennsylvania including several scenes that take place in Jim Thorpe. Much of the movie was filmed in Eckley, not far from Hazleton. Eckley in now a museum and visitors are most welcome. In the movie, Richard Harris plays Detective McParlan and Sean Connery stars as Black Jack Kehoe. It's worth a look.

If You Go:
In the center of downtown Jim Thorpe, you can always visit the Molly Maguire Pub where one can find good food and drink at reasonable prices. The pub has a large outdoor deck that is open weather permitting. That same section of Jim Thorpe is home to many antique and specialty shops that you might want to check out.

In addition, the town is quite close to the Pocono's, so white water rafting is available as well as skiing depending on the season. Finally, you can visit the Jim Thorpe Memorial which is the final resting place for that great athlete (see Chapter 28).

"America's Answer to the Ripper"

HERMAN WEBSTER MUDGETT
aka Dr. Henry H. Holmes

County: Delaware
Town: Yeadon
Cemetery: Holy Cross
Address: 626 Baily Road

One can reasonably argue that the most famous serial killer in history is Jack the Ripper. There have been numerous books written and films made about the Ripper. The actual Ripper was never found, and to this day there are numerous theories as to who he was and the suspects include members of the Royal Family. The Ripper murders began in the Whitechapel district of London in 1888, and some believe they continued until 1891. However most who have studied the case believe the Ripper was responsible for only five of the ten murders in that time frame and that his last victim was killed November 9, 1888. In contrast, America's answer to the Ripper may have tortured and killed as many as 200 people, mostly young women. He was born Herman Webster Mudgett on May 16, 1861, in New Hampshire. However, during his killing spree, he went by the name Doctor Henry H. Holmes, and that is how we shall refer to him in this chapter.

Holmes was known as a bright boy with strange tendencies. His father was a violent alcoholic, and his mother a Methodist who would read the bible to the young boy. Holmes was bullied at school, and he went through several traumatic experiences as a child. He and one of his few close friends explored a deserted house one day, and Holmes watched his friend fall to his death from a landing in the home. In addition bullies dragged him into a doctor's office and forced him into the arms of a medical skeleton. The bullies' goal was to scare him. Instead he became obsessed with death.

As he hit his teens, his fascination with death manifested itself in the killing and dissection of animals. Holmes claimed his purpose in these mutilations was medical examination. Academically he continued to do well, and in 1884 he graduated with a medical degree from the University of Michigan in Ann Arbor. While at the university, he began an unusual business pursuit that would provide funds for him throughout his life. He began taking life insurance policies out on corpses in the medical school. He would steal the corpses and mutilate them in a manner to show they had died in an accident. Then he would make his claim to the insurance company.

Herman Webster Mudgett

Holmes married his first wife in 1878. She bore him a son named Robert Lovering Mudgett who would go on to serve as city manager in Orlando, Florida. Holmes would marry two more times during his life without ever getting divorced. In addition he used his charm to prey on countless young women who fell for him and later died at his hands.

In 1886 Holmes moved to Chicago where he found work as a drugstore assistant. E. S. Holton, the owner of the store, was dying of cancer and his wife spent most of her time caring for her ailing husband. Holmes saw his opportunity, and he took it. When Holton died, Holmes persuaded Mrs. Horton to sell him the store. When the deal was complete, he murdered her and told those who asked about her that she had moved to California. In 1888 Holmes travelled to London where he sold skeletons to medical schools. He returned to the states in December of that same year, a time frame that becomes important later in his story.

The infamous Murder Castle: Holmes Motel at 63rd & Wallace on Chicago's south side.

Now that he owned a drug store that was making a good profit, Holmes began putting his plan into place. He purchased a vacant lot across the street from his store where he intended to build his "Castle." It was a three story hotel that Holmes personally designed. The ground floor featured Holmes's drugstore. The second and third floors made up the hotel and featured secret passages, concealed chambers, staircases that led to brick walls and soundproofed rooms with peepholes in the doors. In addition several of the rooms had been fitted with gas pipes that would allow Holmes to inject lethal gases into the area at the moment of his choosing. The basement was an addition to this house of horrors. It contained a dissection chamber and pits of lime and acid as well as cremation furnaces. Holmes constructed the "Castle" by using multiple contractors. Once part of the building was complete he would either fire or refuse payment to a contractor and hire another. As a result no one could piece together what Holmes planned to do in what would become known later as "the killing house."

The building was completed in time to take advantage of the many visitors to the 1893 Chicago's World Fair. The fair itself was a tremendous success and attracted visitors from all over the country. The fair marked the appearance of the first Ferris wheel which was a gigantic machine compared to what we have today. For example, each of the 36 cars on the wheel could hold as many as sixty people. The cars were 24 feet long and 13 feet wide and weighed 26,000 pounds. The fair itself, whose buildings reflected the big dreams of the era, was known as the "White City" and even received praise from that great critic of the "Gilded Age" Mark Twain. The owner of the new hotel, which he called the World's Fair Hotel, was eager to offer housing, and in many cases more, to those who chose to visit the fair.

Holmes didn't wait for the fair to open to begin more killings. In 1890 a man named Ned Connor went to work for Holmes as a watchmaker and jeweler. He and his very attractive wife named Julia and their daughter Pearl moved into an apartment above the drugstore. Holmes gave Julia a job as a bookkeeper and then seduced her. Ned Connor found out about the affair and left his wife and daughter. By this time in 1891 Holmes was living in the "Castle." He took out life insurance policies on Julia and Pearl that named him as the beneficiary. Around this time, Holmes began a relationship with a woman named Minnie Williams. Julia became angered by this turn of events especially in light of the fact that she was carrying Holmes's child. Holmes convinced Julia to have an abortion that he would perform. He led her to the basement where he aborted the child and killed Julia. He then killed Pearl using chloroform.

With his hotel now open, Holmes put his killing machine to work. Not only hotel staff but guests turned up missing. Holmes particularly enjoyed killing young women that he found attractive. Hotel staff were required to take out life insurance policies naming Holmes as the beneficiary. Holmes murdered his victims in a number of ways. He gassed some in their rooms, he tortured some on a stretching rack he kept in the basement, he dissected a few victims while they were still alive and he also had some fireproof rooms so he could fill the room with gases, ignite the vapors and burn the victim to death. The bodies were disposed of in his vats of acid or crematoriums. With some of his victims, he would remove the flesh and sell the skeletons to medical institutions. It is impossible to tell how many people he killed, but estimates range from 50 to 200.

When the World's Fair ended, the depression of 1893 was in full swing. With business way down at the hotel and his creditors on his back, Holmes left Chicago. He headed for Texas where he had inherited property from two sisters one of which he promised to marry. He never married her, but he did kill both sisters. He had hoped to build another Castle here, but he found that law enforcement officers were more aggressive in Texas than in Chicago so he headed back east.

In 1894, he and an associate named Benjamin Pitezel made a deal. Pitezel would take out a $10,000 life insurance policy, Holmes would find and disfigure a dead body claim that it was Pitezel and the two would split the money. Instead Holmes murdered Pitezel in Philadelphia by burning him alive to support the story of a laboratory accident. He then collected the money himself.

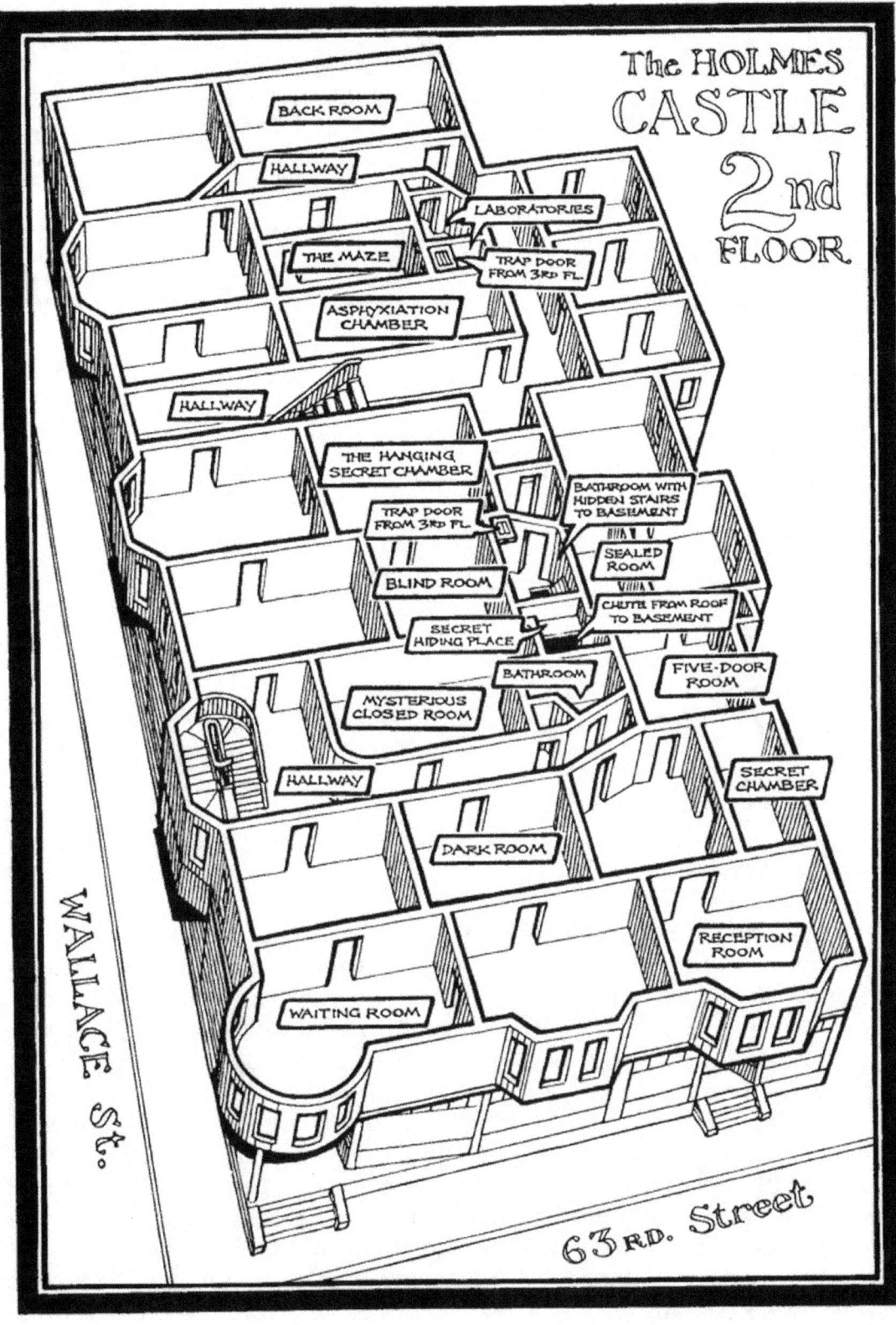

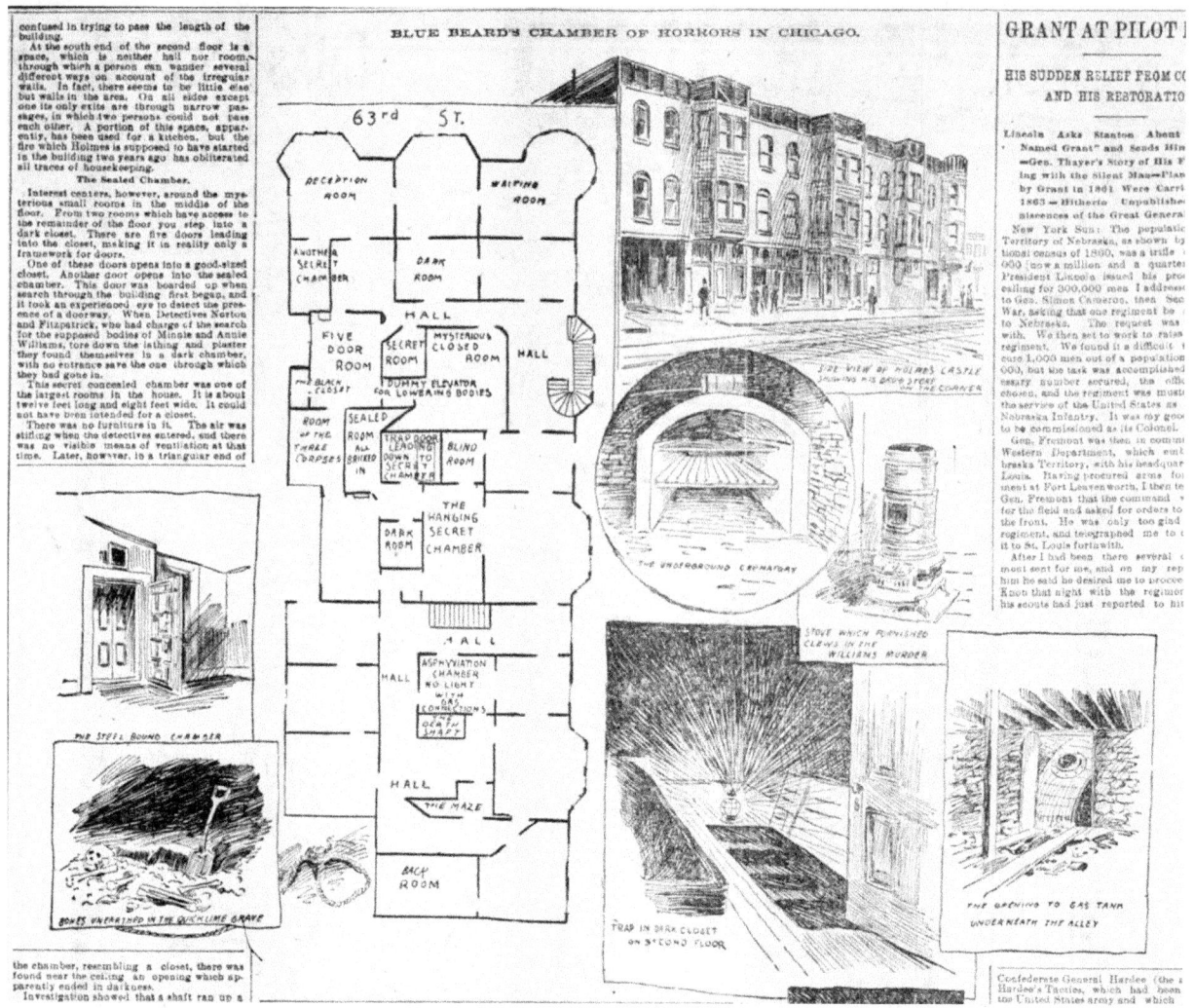

The Chicago Tribune of Sunday, August 18, 1895.

Pitezel had three of his five children with him at the time and Holmes took the three, a boy and two girls, through the northern United States into Canada. On the way in Indianapolis he killed the boy, cut up the body and burned it. In Toronto he put the girls into a trunk and gassed them to death. He then buried their bodies in the cellar of the house where he was staying.

Holmes had been jailed for a brief time for his involvement in a horseracing scam prior to his trip to Canada. While in jail, he told a cellmate about the plan he and Pitezel put together and he offered the cellmate $500 if he could find a lawyer that would assist Holmes with any legal questions should they arise. The cellmate found the attorney, but Holmes never paid him the $500 and as a result the cellmate told the police about the Pitezel scam. Holmes was arrested in Boston on November 17, 1894.

Following his arrest, the Chicago police searched the "Castle." In the basement they found the remains of some of Holmes's victims. They also found evidence that murders had been committed in other rooms in the hotel. Meanwhile a detective by the name of Frank Geyer was investigating the Pitezel case. He would eventually find the remains of the three children Holmes had killed during his trip to Canada. The public was satisfied that Holmes was a monster.

Holmes was put on trial in Philadelphia for the murder of Pitezel. He was convicted and sentenced to death. After his conviction he confessed to 30 murders. The Hearst newspapers paid him $7,500 (over $200,000 in today's dollars) for his confession. Holmes went to the gallows on May 7, 1896. The assistant superintendent, a man named Richardson, appeared more nervous than Holmes as he prepared the noose. Holmes turned to him and said, "Take your time, old man." Holmes neck did not snap, and as a result he died slowly. He was pronounced dead twenty minutes after the trap had been sprung.

Here is the final resting place of America's first serial killer.

Holmes was buried based on instructions he left behind. First cement was poured into the coffin and then Holmes's body was put in which was then covered with more cement. His body was then taken to Holy Cross Cemetery just outside of Philadelphia. The grave was dug and the coffin placed inside. Workers then filled the grave with cement. The grave was left unmarked. Holmes wanted to make sure that neither medical researchers nor relatives of his victims could get to his body.

During his stay in prison, Holmes claimed that he was possessed by the devil. Events that occurred after his execution caused some to believe it. Detective Geyer became seriously ill. The warden at the Philadelphia prison where Holmes was held and executed committed suicide. An accidental electrocution took the life of the foreman of the jury that convicted Holmes. The priest who delivered the last rites to Holmes was found dead on church grounds. Finally a fire destroyed the office of the Chicago district attorney leaving only a picture of Holmes untouched.

Recently Jeff Mudgett, Holmes's great-great grandson, has written a book about his ancestor titled *Bloodstains*. The book provides evidence that Holmes may have been Jack the Ripper. Mudgett notes that there exist records documenting Holmes travelling to London in 1888 to sell skeletons to medical schools. He was not in Chicago when the five murders credited to the Ripper took place. When Holmes returned to Chicago in December of 1888, the Ripper murders stopped. Many believe that the Ripper possessed surgical skills which Holmes certainly had. Finally Mudgett had scientists at the University of Buffalo analyze letters written by Jack the Ripper and those written by Holmes while he was in prison. They reached the conclusion that the classifier performance number (97.95%) indicate that the writings of both men are similar in style. Was America's answer to the Ripper actually the Ripper himself?

When we visited Holy Cross Cemetery to photograph Holmes final resting place we had the section, range and lot number of the location of the grave. To be sure that our information was accurate we went to the cemetery office to verify it. The cemetery employee we spoke to told us, "We are not allowed to talk about that grave."

If you go:
See the "If You Go" section of the "Philadelphia Sinners" in *Volume Two*, chapter 18.

"JoePa"

JOE PATERNO

County: Centre
Town: State College
Cemetery: Spring Creek Presbyterian
Address: Country Club Road

It's probably hard to find an adult in Pennsylvania who hasn't heard of Joe Paterno. "JoePa," as he was commonly known, was the College Football Hall-of-Fame coach of the Pennsylvania State University Nittany Lions from 1966 until 2011.

Joseph Vincent Paterno was born in Brooklyn, New York on December 21, 1926. His parents, Florence and Angelo Paterno, stressed hard work and the importance of education. Angelo embodied this belief as he worked to support his family while attending law school. He got his law degree when he was 40 years old. Apparently the drive and determination rubbed off on Joe.

Joe attended St. Edmond's Grammar School and Brooklyn Prep High School, where he was a very good student. In the Flatbush section of Brooklyn, the Paterno family was known for its spirited arguments and debates over dinner which were encouraged by the parents.

As a senior at Brooklyn Prep, Joe and his younger brother, George (a junior), gained notoriety throughout the New York metropolitan area for their exploits on the football field (not to mention the basketball court). Asked years later to describe Joe's football abilities, a high school teammate of Paterno's stated, "He couldn't run, he couldn't kick, he couldn't pass." The teammate quickly added however, "All he could do was win." The Paterno-led Brooklyn Prep football team headed into its final game of the 1943 season undefeated, and considered by many to be one of the best teams on the American eastern seaboard. Their opponent in that final game? St. Cecilia's, a Roman Catholic high school in Englewood, New Jersey. The coach of St. Cecilia? A 30-year-old fellow Brooklynite named Vince Lombardi. To motivate his players before the game, Lombardi read letters that were sent to him by friends in Brooklyn, telling Lombardi how great Paterno was and how Brooklyn Prep was going to destroy St. Cecilia's that day. Tired of hearing about the kid from Brooklyn, the St. Cecilia players came out extra riled up. (As it turned out, the letters hadn't come from anyone in Brooklyn; Lombardi himself had written the letters.)

Paterno hurt his left (throwing) shoulder in the first half of the game, and was briefly replaced by his backup. At halftime, he got a shot of Novocain so he could play in the second half, continuing the game essentially one-armed.

Joe Paterno

In the second half, Lombardi employed a four-man defensive line, something which Brooklyn Prep had never seen before let alone been trained to deal with. After the game, Paterno and his teammates were stunned they had lost. Lombardi's St. Cecilia's squad was recognized as the top football team in the nation that year, in large part based on their victory over Brooklyn Prep.

Paterno graduated from Brooklyn Prep in 1944 and was quickly drafted into the Army. He was still in training stateside when World War II ended. He was discharged in time to matriculate at the start the 1946 school year. He decided to attend Brown University, where he would play quarterback and cornerback. His tuition was paid by wealthy Brown alumnus Everett "Busy" Arnold, a publisher and owner of Quality Comics. Quality Comics was a comic book company that was very successful in the 1930's and 1940's.

Truth be told, Paterno was not an outstanding football player. He didn't have loads of "raw talent." He wasn't terribly "fast." He wasn't exceptionally "strong," mostly due to the fact that he didn't possess a great deal of "size." But Joe was extremely intelligent, and boy could he inspire his teammates. In 1949, he led the Brown Bears to an 8-1 record. He snagged 14 interceptions during his Brown career, a school record which he shares to this day. He also returned kicks and played two seasons of basketball for Brown, where in his freshman year he was coached by Weeb Ewbank (who went on to be a Hall-of-Fame football coach, winning NFL titles with Baltimore and the New York Jets).

After graduating from Brown in 1950, Paterno fully expected to enter Boston University Law School. But fate intervened. His Brown Coach, "Rip" Engle, had just accepted the job as head coach at Penn State. Having admired Paterno's cerebral play as his coach at Brown (Engle said in 1949 that having Paterno at quarterback was "like having another coach on the field"), Engle offered Paterno a job to join him as his assistant at the small agricultural school in the middle of Pennsylvania. Figuring he could postpone law school and save up some money, Paterno accepted Rip's offer.

He must have liked it, considering he stayed a Penn State football coach for the next 62 years, turning down a number of NFL opportunities! He was promoted to the top assistant spot in 1964 and when Engle announced his retirement in February 1966, Paterno was named his successor the next day.

In the meantime, Joe planted roots amidst the agricultural setting State College provided. He married Suzanne Pohland of Latrobe, Pennsylvania in 1962. Between 1963 and 1972, the couple had five children, all of whom would go on to attend Penn State.

Penn State went 5-5 in Paterno's first year, but in his second year they compiled an 8-2-1 record and a Gator Bowl appearance. In this third (1968) and fourth (1969) years, Penn State recorded undefeated seasons en route to a 31-game unbeaten streak. In 1968, they were ranked number 2 in the final national poll, and finished in that same spot again in 1969 after beating Missouri in the Orange Bowl. The 1969 experience was particularly upsetting to Paterno. Both Texas and Arkansas were undefeated and playing each other in early December. President Nixon declared that the winner of that game would be the national champion. Texas won and Nixon presented the mythical "national championship plaque" to the Longhorns. A few years later, while speaking at Penn State's Spring 1973 commencement, Paterno would ask "How could Nixon know so little about Watergate in 1973 and so much about football in 1969?"

That autumn the Nittany Lions continued their outstanding play, led by running back John Capelletti (who would become the first Penn State player to win the Heisman Trophy). As in 1968 and 1969, Penn State was once again undefeated and untied (11-0) heading into its bowl game: the January 1, 1974 Orange Bowl against LSU. Penn State won, and afterwards Paterno told reporters:

"I had my own poll, the Paterno Poll. And the vote was unanimous. Penn State is number 1. I took the vote a few minutes ago."

Unfortunately for Penn State and its fans, the polls did not agree with JoePa. Penn State was ranked 5th in the final poll, behind #1 Notre Dame (11-0), #2 Ohio State (10-0-1), #3 Oklahoma (10-0-1), and #4 Alabama (11-1). Paterno paid to have championship rings made for every player on the team.

Ironically, when Penn State *was* voted as number one at the end of the 1982 season, they were *not* undefeated. They had lost a mid-season game to Alabama, but won seven straight games after that, including a win over Georgia in the Sugar Bowl.

Another shot at finishing the season ranked No. 1 came in 1986 after an 11-0 season. The only thing standing between #2-ranked Penn State and another championship? A Fiesta Bowl showdown with the undefeated, #1-ranked Miami Hurricanes.

The Jimmy Johnson-led Hurricanes had a firm grasp on the #1 ranking for most of that season. The team's star quarterback was Vinny Testaverde, the 1986 Heisman Trophy winner. Miami also featured All-Americans Jerome Brown and Bennie Blades on defense, future NFL Hall-of-Famer Michael Irvin at wide receiver, and running back Alonzo Highsmith. The Penn State defense harassed Testaverde into five interceptions and the underdog Nittany Lions won 14-10. Years later, Johnson would describe that year's Miami team as the most talented he had ever coached, and said that losing the Fiesta Bowl to Penn State remains the one loss in his entire career that still haunts him.

By this time, JoePa had become well-known for doing things his way. He expected his athletes to get an education. The graduation rate of his players was consistently above the national average. He refused to modernize the team's uniforms, refused to put players' names on the back of their jerseys, and was known for his gameday image—thick glasses, rolled up pants, white socks and Brooklyn accent.

Paterno statue before it was removed (courtesy of Bob And Holly Frymoyer)

He was also renowned for his charitable contributions to academics at Penn State. The Paternos have given the university over $4 million towards various departments and scholarships. After they helped raise $13.5 million for the 1997 expansion of the library, it was named after them. Paterno often joked that Penn State was the only campus that had a library named after a football coach and a sports arena (the Bryce Jordan Center) named after a former university president.

After earning the number one ranking at the end of the 1982 season, Paterno attended a meeting of the Board of Trustees where he urged them to raise entrance requirements and spend more money on the library. According to a story in *Sports Illustrated*, "it may go down as the only time in history that a coach yearned for a school the football team could be proud of." He called this meeting of athletics and academics a "Grand Experiment." Sue Paterno played a role too, often tutoring players at the team's study hall or even sometimes at their home.

Penn State had five undefeated, untied seasons under Paterno, winning a major bowl at the end of each of those seasons. Four of those teams (1968, 1969, 1973 and 1994) were not awarded a national championship—the lone exception being 1986.

Heading into the 1994 for what would turn out to be Penn State's final undefeated season under Paterno, Penn State had joined the Big Ten Conference. Its 38-20 victory over #12 Oregon in the Rose Bowl on January 2, 1995 capped a perfect 12-0 season. Yet once again, the polls denied them the number one spot. Penn State finished second, behind Tom Osbourne's 13-0 Nebraska team, led by quarterback Tommy Frazier. The previous season had seen the Cornhuskers fall just short of their first national title under Osborne with a controversial Orange Bowl loss to Florida State 18–16. The 1994 offseason was dubbed "Unfinished Business" by the Huskers, in their quest to secure a national championship for the coming season.

The AP poll heading in to their respective October 29, 1994 games had Penn State ranked #1 and Nebraska #3. That day both teams won at home: Penn State defeated #21 Ohio State 63-14 at Beaver Stadium, while Nebraska beat visiting #2 Colorado 24-7. In the ensuing AP poll, not only did Nebraska supplant Colorado as expected, but it also leapfrogged over Penn State to claim the #1 spot (Penn State "slipped" to #2). The two teams would remain locked in those positions the rest of the way, each winning out the remainder of their respective regular season schedules and bowl games (Nebraska defeated #3 Miami in the Orange Bowl 24-17 on January 1, 1995).

Under JoePa's reign, Penn State made a record 37 bowl appearances and won a record 24 times. He is the only coach to win the Rose, Orange, Fiesta, Sugar and Cotton Bowl games at least once. His teams finished in the top 10 in national rankings 29 times. In 2001, Penn State honored Paterno with a statue outside Beaver Stadium—a stadium that underwent six capacity expansions during his tenure, increasing from 46,284 seats in 1966 to 106,572 in 2001. He was named the American Football Coaches' Association Coach of the Year Award five times (1968, 1978, 1982, 1986 and 2005) and received dozens of other coaching and sportsman awards. In May 2006, Paterno was elected to the College Football Hall of Fame. He even had an award named after him in 2010: the Maxwell Football Club of Philadelphia established the Joseph V. Paterno Award, to be awarded annually to the coach who has made a positive impact on his university, his players and his community.

At the time of his death in 2012, Paterno had accumulated 409 wins, the most ever by a major college coach. Paterno offered up many pearls of wisdom during that legendary 1973 commencement speech, including this statement, which has since been often repeated: "Success without honor is an unseasoned dish; it will satisfy your hunger, but it won't taste good."

If only the story ended here!

On November 5, 2011, a former Penn State defensive coordinator, Jerry Sandusky, was arrested and charged with 52 counts of sexual abuse of young boys over a 15-year period. Sandusky had served as an assistant coach under Joe Paterno for almost 30 years. In 1977, Sandusky founded The Second Mile, a non-profit charity serving Pennsylvania's underprivileged and at-risk youth. Now Sandusky was accused of meeting his victims through The Second Mile, and many of the incidents were alleged to have taken place in Penn State facilities, including the Penn State football locker room.

A grand jury investigation reported that then-graduate assistant Mike McQueary had told Paterno in 2002 that he witnessed Sandusky abusing a 10-year-old boy in the football team's shower facilities. Paterno reported it to his boss, the Athletic Director, and did nothing more. Reports indicate that no one ever contacted the police.

The news rocked the sports world and beyond. While prosecutors did not accuse Paterno of any wrongdoing, he was criticized for his failure to follow up on McQueary's report. Sandusky continued to have unrestricted and unsupervised access to the University's facilities and affiliation with the football program until his arrest on November 5, 2011.

On November 9, as a result of the growing outrage and swirling controversy, Paterno announced he would retire at the end of the season. Later that evening however, the Penn State Board of Trustees decided to reject Paterno's offer to resign, instead voting to relieve him of coaching duties effective immediately. The Board notified him of their decision over the phone. At the same meeting, the University President resigned rather than face being fired.

Paterno's dismissal was met with violence from students and alumni. That night several thousand Penn State students chanting Paterno's name rioted in the streets, hurling rocks, tearing down street signs and overturning a news van.

Final resting place of the legendary coach who obviously has not been forgotten.

On November 18, Paterno's family announced that he was suffering from lung cancer. He was hospitalized on January 13, 2012, and nine days later died on January 22, 2012. Paterno's funeral was held in State College on January 25. About 750 mourners attended a private ceremony, after which thousands lined the route of the funeral procession. On January 26, a public memorial service was held at the Bryce Jordan Center and an estimated 12,000 people attended. JoePa is buried in a modest grave in Spring Creek Presbyterian Cemetery in State College, just a few short miles away from Beaver Stadium.

The scandal had far-reaching effects on the University and on Joe Paterno's legacy. On June 22, 2012, Sandusky was found guilty on all but three of the counts against him. On October 9, 2012 he was sentenced to a minimum of 30 years and maximum of 60 years in prison. Judge John Cleland stated that he intentionally avoided a sentence with a large number of years, saying it would be "too abstract" and also said to Sandusky that the sentence he handed down had the "unmistakable impact of saying 'the rest of your life.'"

In July 2013, a report on an investigation commissioned by Penn State Board of Trustees and conducted by former FBI director Louis Freeh was released. The report stated that Paterno, as well as the University's president, vice-president and athletic director, had known about allegations of child abuse on Sandusky's part as early as 1998, and were complicit in failing to disclose them. The report concluded that the four men had "concealed Sandusky's activities from the Board of Trustees, the University community and authorities." The report criticized Paterno for his failure to "alert the entire football staff in order to prevent Sandusky from bringing another child into the Lasch Building" [the football team's 89,000 square-foot indoor facility on the Penn State campus, just a short walk from Beaver Stadium].

A mere 11 days after the Freeh report, the NCAA announced sanctions against Penn State. The sanctions included a post-season ban, a large fine, the loss of scholarships and the vacating of all wins from 1998 to 2011. This amounted to 111 wins, including 6 bowl victories, and stripped Penn State of their shared Big Ten titles in 2005 and 2008. It also removed the 111 wins from Paterno's record, dropping him from first to 12th on the NCAA's all-time wins list (two wins behind legendary University of Delaware coach, Tubby Raymond). Penn State accepted the sanctions.

In the weeks that followed, Nike Inc. removed Paterno's name from the Joe Paterno Child Development Center at the company's headquarters in Beaverton, Oregon. Brown University, Paterno's alma mater, announced it would remove Paterno's name from its annual award honoring outstanding male freshman athletes. The NCAA revoked Paterno's 2011 Gerald R. Ford leadership award. The lifesize statue of Paterno outside Beaver Stadium was removed by the university.

The story continues to develop and will for some time to come. There are many arguments and disagreements about Paterno's role. Penn State's former president, vice-president and athletic director were all indicted and are awaiting trial at the time of this publication. There have been civil lawsuits and settlements, and there may be more. Additional investigations are ongoing, and there may be more. Books have been written, and there will be more. We may never know the full story. There has been much pain and much conflict over Paterno's role, his culpability, his treatment by Penn State, the grand jury investigation, the Freeh report, The Second Mile, and the NCAA's response. Of particular interest at the time of this writing is an ongoing lawsuit filed by the Paterno family (along with several members of the Penn State Board of Trustees, and a number of faculty, former players and coaches) against the NCAA. They assert that the Freeh report—which the NCAA relied for its actions—is fundamentally wrong, incomplete and inaccurate. They further allege that the consent decree with Penn State which set forth the various sanctions was hastily imposed on the University, completely disregarding the rights of the affected parties.

Just before his death, Paterno told the *Washington Post*, "I didn't know exactly how to handle it, so I backed away." Then he added, "I'm sick about it."

So too are a whole lot of others.

If You Go:
Union Cemetery in nearby Bellefonte has many interesting graves, including:

Pennsylvania's governor during the Civil War, Andrew Curtin, (See *Keystone Tombstones: Civil War*, Chapter 29);

James Adams Beaver, who was a Civil War general, later elected governor of Pennsylvania (1887-1891) and after whom Penn State's Beaver Stadium is named; and

Penn State's first president, Evan Pugh, who served in the University's highest post from 1859 until his death from typhoid in 1864 at the age of 36. An agricultural chemist, he was responsible for securing Penn State's designation in 1863 as a land-grant institution under the Morrill Land Grant Act. Today, the highest honor the University can bestow on a faculty member is the title "Evan Pugh Professor."

Governor Beaver

If you are looking for a great place to stop for refreshments, the area is full of wonderful eating and drinking establishments. The possibilities boggled our minds.

"The Voices of Pittsburgh"

BOB PRINCE and MYRON COPE

County: Allegheny
Towns: Pittsburgh, Carnegie
Cemeteries: Westminster Presbyterian Church, Cartiers
Addresses: 2040 Washington Road, 801 Noblestown Road

Bob Prince, known as "the Gunner", was an announcer who was the voice of the Pittsburgh Pirates for 28 years, from 1948 until 1975 and became a Pittsburgh institution. Yet he missed the greatest moment in Pirate history and one of the greatest moments in all of baseball history. The moment took place when Bill Mazeroski hit his World Series winning home run in the bottom of the ninth inning in the 1960 World Series against the New York Yankees that gave the Pirates their first championship in 35 years. He was making his way back from the Pirate Clubhouse where he had been sent to do postgame interviews when it appeared the Pirates would win 9-7. When the Yankees tied it up in the top of the ninth, he was ordered back to the booth. He was in the elevator when the historic and dramatic home run was hit and was told to return to the Pirate clubhouse just as he stepped off the elevator. He was broadcasting the World Series nationwide on NBC and the NBC production people were telling Prince what to do, but not telling him what happened. He had no idea when an NBC staffer directed Mazeroski toward Prince in the exuberant Pirate clubhouse. Prince merely asked Mazeroski how it felt to be a world champion and Mazeroski said "great." Then Prince moved on.

Robert Ferris Prince was born in Los Angelas on July 1 1916. His father, a former West Point football standout, was a career military man and thus young Prince, an army brat, went to many different schools before graduating from Schenley High School in Pittsburgh. He started college at the University of Pittsburgh where he lettered on the swimming team. When his father was transferred and the family moved to California, he transferred to Stanford. He hated Stanford and claimed he flunked out on purpose. Later, after another family move, he enrolled and graduated from the University of Oklahoma with a degree in Business Administration. He then went to Harvard Law School but quit after he landed a job in 1941 as host of "Case of Sports" on WJAS radio in Pittsburgh.

Prince sold insurance during the day and hosted his show in the evening. He made a name for himself among sports fans with his loud, opinionated rants. Once, Prince accused hometown boxer Billy Conn of

The official green weenie created by Bob Prince for use during Pirate games.

ducking tough opponents. Conn ran into Prince several nights later at the Pittsburgh Arena and slammed Prince against a wall and threatened to beat him senseless. Ironically, the two later became close friends.

In 1948, Prince was hired by the Pirates to work as the sidekick to beloved Pirate play-by-play man Rosey Roswell. He got along well with Roswell and was promoted to the top spot when Roswell died in February 1955. He became known as "The Gunner" because of his rat-a-tat-tat delivery. He had many descriptive phrases that became known as "Gunnerisms." Some of the most famous are "you can kiss it goodbye!" for a home run, "a bloop and a blast" which he would call when the Pirates were down a run or "by a gnat's eyelash" when describing a close play.

Prince enjoyed an unusual relationship with Pirate players and for many became a friend, confidant, and mentor. He also had a close relationship with former Pirate great and hall of fame outfielder, Ralph Kiner, that included outside business partnerships, and the two drove matching silver Jaguars around Pittsburgh. Prince, who spoke Spanish, became very close to Roberto Clemente, who in 1971, in a public ceremony in Puerto Rico, gave Prince the silver bat he had received in 1961 for winning the National League Batting title.

Prince believed that part of a broadcaster's job was to pull for the home team. He was an unabashed Pirate fan and after every Pirate win, regardless of how the game went, he would yell "We had 'em all the way!" In 1966, he popularized a good luck charm known as the "Green Weenie," a plastic rattle in the shape of an oversized pickle that Pirate fans used to jinx opponents. The idea was derived from pins distributed by the H.J. Heinz factory in Pittsburgh shaped like a pickle. In 1974, Prince invented a similar good luck charm encouraging female fans to wave their "babushkas" to spark a rally.

When he chose to stay focused, Prince could deliver a very accurate, exciting description of the game, but he usually rambled a lot and told stories about anything that popped into his mind. While most Pirate fans seemed to like this, some hated it. He also lived a wild lifestyle, drank a lot, wore colorful flashy clothes, and once in a hotel in St. Louis, leaped from a third floor window into the hotel pool to win a twenty dollar bet. Beneath all the bluster and flamboyance, Prince was a sensitive, caring, and generous man. He co-founded the Allegheny Valley School for Exceptional Children in 1960 to care for children with intellectual and developmental disabilities. Over the years, he raised four million dollars for the school and volunteered countless hours with students at the school.

Despite his popularity, Prince began to clash with his bosses after KDKA purchased the rights to the Pirate broadcasts in 1969. In 1975, Prince and his sidekick Nellie King were fired. Pirate fans and sponsors went berserk. Hundreds of supporters held a rally downtown to show support and several Pirate players including Willie Stargell and Al Oliver spoke to a crowd estimated at 10,000. Their efforts failed and KDKA hired Milo Hamilton to succeed Prince.

A broken hearted Prince had stints with the Houston Astros, Pittsburgh Penguins hockey team, and even on ABC's "Monday Night Baseball" but he wasn't himself and each ended after a short time. He drifted from job to job, many of which were considered small for a celebrity of his stature. Eventually, he returned to baseball when in 1982 a cable station hired him to do Pirate games. Exposure was limited since cable did not have many subscribers and they offered only a small selection of games.

In 1985, Prince, a smoker, was diagnosed with mouth cancer. Shortly after surgery to remove a tumor between his tongue and jaw, he was hired by the Pirates to return to fulltime duty as a member of the regular radio broadcast team. On May 3, 1985, Bob Prince returned to the Pirate radio booth. The crowd gave him a standing ovation and the Pirates scored nine runs in his first inning of broadcasting. Prince's return to the booth lasted just two more games. He became ill on May 20 while sitting through a rain delay and returned to the hospital. He died 21 days later on June 10, 1985 at the age of 68. Prince was posthumously awarded the Ford Frick Award by the Baseball Hall of Fame in 1986.

Bob Prince's remains are at the Westminster Presbyterian Church in Upper Saint Clair, just south of Pittsburgh. A book on Prince titled "We Had 'Em All the Way" by Jim O'Brien was published in 1998.

The Other famous voice of Pittsburgh is the "voice of the Pittsburgh Steelers," Myron Cope. He was born Myron Sidney Kopelman on January 23, 1929 in Pittsburgh to Jewish parents of Lithuanian descent. A graduate of Taylor Allderdice High School and the University of Pittsburgh in 1951, he was a journalist before becoming a broadcaster. His first job after college was with the Erie Times, but he was soon hired by the Pittsburgh Post-Gazette as a general assignment reporter. It was then that his byline became Myron Cope. During the 1960's, several of his freelance sports articles were published in magazines such as *The Saturday Evening Post* and *Sports Illustrated*. In 1963, Cope received the E.P. Dutton Prize for "Best Magazine Sportswriting in the Nation" for a piece on Cassius Clay. At its 50th anniversary, Sports Illustrated selected Cope's profile of Howard Cosell as one of the fifty best pieces ever published in the magazine. In 1964, Cope published his first book co-written with Jim Brown called "Off My Chest." It was a controversial book in which Jim Brown expressed his opinions about racial injustice in sports.

In 1968, a radio station in Pittsburgh hired Cope to do a brief sports show during the morning commute hours. Cope, who had a nasally voice, a Pittsburgh accent, and an unusual speech pattern did not get positive reviews at first, but gradually listeners realized the quality of his broadcasts and warmed to his style. His popularity grew.

Cope married Mildred Lindberg in 1965, and their son Daniel was born with severe autism. Cope devoted much of his energy to causes addressing autism and spoke candidly about his experiences as a parent of a child with autism and about his efforts to better educate the public about autism. His son lived most of his life at the Allegheny Valley School previously mentioned as having been co-founded by Bob Prince.

In 1970, he was hired as a color analyst for Pittsburgh Steelers radio broadcasts and remained in that role for thirty-five years, the longest term with a single team in NFL history. Over the years he became known for unique catch-phrases and nicknames. He often used Yiddish expressions and became known for his use of "Yoi" or sometimes "Double Yoi" during a broadcast. He is the creator of phrases such as "Steel Curtain" and "Immaculate Reception" and for nicknames such as "The Bus" for Jerome Bettis, "Jack Splat" for Jack Lambert and "Slash" for Kordell Stewart. He also used the term "Cincinnati Bungles" to describe the play of the Bengals during the 1990's.

In 1973, Cope began hosting his own radio talk show and in 1975, he invented the Pittsburgh Steelers' Terrible Towel, their famed good luck symbol. It is arguably the best known symbol of any pro sports team. In 1996, Cope gave the rights to the Terrible Towel to the Allegheny School. The proceeds have raised over three million dollars for the school.

In 2002, he published his autobiography, "Myron Cope: Double Yoi!", a touching and humorous memoir. In 2005, he announced his retirement citing health concerns. He had broadcast five Super Bowls and became the first pro football announcer elected to the National Radio Hall of Fame. He died of respiratory failure on February 27, 2008. Two days after his death, hundreds of people gathered in heavy snow in front of City Hall in Pittsburgh to honor Cope. Included in the ceremony was one minute of silent Terrible Towel waving. He is buried in Chartiers Cemetery just south of Pittsburgh. There were Terrible Towels on his grave when we visited.

A terrible towel rests on the tombstone of its inventor, the great Pittsburgh Steeler announcer, Myron Cope.

Here lay the remains of the "Gunner" Bob Prince voice of the Pittsburgh Pirates who announced the first World Series game telecast coast to coast in 1960.

If You Go:
Chartiers is a nice cemetery with friendly and helpful staff. Buried near Myron Cope are two Congressional Medal of Honor recipients, both from the Civil War. James H. Bronson was born a slave. He enlisted into Company D of the 5th U. S. Colored Infantry Regiment. He was awarded the Medal of Honor for his actions at the Battle of Chaffin's Farm, Virginia in 1864.

James Lemuel Carey is also buried nearby. He was awarded the Medal of Honor for action on April 9, 1865 at Appomattox Courthouse, Virginia. Also buried in Charters Cemetery is Edward Rynearson an educator and founder of the National Honor Society.

Here lies Edward Rynearson, founder of the National Honor Society. For some reason, neither of us was extended an invitation to apply for membership. We are as confused as you are.

23

"The Cop That Would Be King"

FRANK RIZZO

County: Philadelphia
Town: Philadelphia
Cemetery: Holy Sepulchre
Address: 3301 Cheltenham Avenue

Francis "Frank" Lazarro Rizzo was an American police officer and politician. He served two terms as mayor of Philadelphia from January 1972 to January 1980. He served as Police Commissioner for four years prior to becoming mayor. Mr. Rizzo was one of those seemingly larger than life figures, destined to be a hero to some and a villain to others.

He was born October 23, 1920 in Philadelphia to a police family. After a brief stint in the US Navy and three years working in a steel mill, he became a policeman in 1943, rising through the ranks to become Police Commissioner in 1967. He served in that role during the turbulent years of 1967-1971. Known as a cop's cop, he showed his mettle when, with a nightstick protruding from the cummerbund of his tuxedo, he left a black tie affair in order to lead "my men" to break up a riot. While serving as Commissioner, he expanded the police force, won the loyalty of his men, and kept the crime rate below that of any other major city. He was, however, accused of racism and police brutality. Supporters noted that in his five year tenure, Philadelphia had the lowest crime rate of the nation's ten largest cities. His detractors said the price for that order was intolerable. In 1970, shortly before he resigned to run for mayor, the police deeply embittered Philadelphia blacks by raiding the Black Panther headquarters, herding them into the street, and ordering them to strip naked in front of TV cameras and reporters. "Imagine the big Black Panthers with their pants down," Mr. Rizzo gloated at the time.

In 1971, Rizzo ran for mayor using "Firm but Fair" as his slogan and won as a law and order Democrat. As Mayor Rizzo continued to support the strong-arm tactics of the police department, he himself made use of them, forming a secret police force that investigated his political opponents. His rough edges and penchant for bombastic statements frequently inflamed his enemies. Two of his most famous quotes are: "Just wait until after November, I'm gonna make Attila the Hun look like a faggot" and "a liberal is a conservative who hasn't been mugged yet."

Rizzo had a controversial relationship with the media including Andrea Mitchell, who was one of the first female urban beat reporters. Almost immediately after he had been elected Mayor, *The Philadelphia Inquirer*

Statue of Frank Rizzo

began running a series of articles detailing Rizzo's years as police commissioner. The articles did not compliment the new mayor. In addition, Richard Dilworth, a former Philadelphia mayor, went public with allegations that Rizzo had used the police force for his own political purposes. Rizzo, by this time, had few supporters in the press, as he had hired about two dozen reporters who had written about him while he was commissioner in a positive manner. What Rizzo accomplished was the removal of his biggest supporters from the media.

Rizzo's problems with the press did not ease as he went further into his first term. In one incident, Rizzo was accused by the Democratic Party Chairman, Peter Camiel, of offering jobs in exchange for choosing certain candidates for other city offices. Rizzo responded by calling Camiel a liar. A reporter from the Philadelphia Daily News asked Rizzo if he would take a polygraph test to prove Camiel was lying. Both men agreed to take the test. "If this machine says a man lied, he lied," Rizzo said before taking the test. The test results showed that Rizzo appeared to be lying and Camiel appeared to be truthful. The scandal was widely reported and severely damaged his reputation and chances of becoming Governor. At this point, Rizzo severed his relationship with the media and didn't hold a press conference for almost two years.

Campaigning for a second term in 1975, Rizzo's slogan was, "He held the line on taxes." Almost immediately after his victory in the election, he convinced city council to raise the taxes. The move angered fiscal conservatives who had supported Rizzo during the campaign. Another development during his second term was the taking over by the city of the Philadelphia Gas Works. Formerly considered one of the best managed municipal utilities in the country, it soon became a long-running fiscal and management embarrassment to the city due to generous municipal labor contracts and the expansion of patronage hiring. Rizzo himself would serve as a security consultant at the Gas Works from 1983-1991.

Rizzo's actions during his second term resulted in a well organized effort for a recall election. As a matter of fact, the organizers of the effort collected well over the 250,000 signatures required to force the recall. Rizzo supporters responded by challenging the validity of the signatures and the constitutionality of the recall procedure. Polls showed that Rizzo would lose a recall election by a wide margin, but he managed to survive when the Pennsylvania Supreme Court, by a single vote, declared the recall process unconstitutional. The Supreme Court decision was written by Chief Justice Robert Nix. Nix had been elected to the court in 1971 with Rizzo's support.

As mayor, Rizzo continued to champion the idea that strong and severe law enforcement methods were necessary in light of rising crime rates. By 1979, the issue had been moved into the courtroom. The Justice Department filed suit in the United States District Court, charging Mayor Rizzo and other high ranking city officials with committing or condoning "widespread and severe" acts of police brutality. A federal judge later dismissed the suit saying the government had no grounds to have filed it in the first place.

Rizzo wanted a third consecutive term in 1979 but was facing a two term consecutive term limit in the City Charter. He got the City Council to place a question on the ballot that would have allowed him to run. In a record turnout, Philadelphians voted two to one against the change, thus blocking him from running in 1979. He ran again for Mayor in 1983 but lost the Democratic nomination to Wilson Goode. In 1985, he switched to the Republican Party and ran again in 1987, but lost the general election again to Wilson Goode. He was running for Mayor again in 1991 when on July 16, Frank Rizzo died of a massive heart attack. Frank Rizzo's funeral was large and carried on live television. He is buried with family members in Holy Sepulchre Cemetery in Cheltenham.

A statue of mayor Rizzo waving one of his arms in greeting, stands in front of Philadelphia's Municipal Services Building. A book by Joseph Daughen and Peter Binzen titled "The Cop Who Would Be King" is considered an authoritative account of Rizzo's rise to power.

If You Go:
See *Keystone Tombstones Volume 1* chapter 16 on Connie Mack. Also buried at Holy Sepulchre Cemetery are three other noteworthy Pennsylvanians:

Hizzoner Frank Rizzo.

John B. Kelly Sr., also known as Jack Kelly, was one of the greatest American oarsmen in the history of the sport. He was a triple Olympic Gold Medal winner and once won 126 straight races in a single scull, including six U.S. National Championships. He was also the father of Grace Kelly, the actress who became Princess of Monaco.

Robert N.C. Nix, Jr., was the first African American Chief Justice of any state's highest court and the first to be elected to statewide office in Pennsylvania. He served as a justice of the Supreme Court of Pennsylvania for 24 years, 12 of which were as Chief Justice.

Michael McKeever was awarded the Congressional Medal of Honor for his bravery at Burnt Ordinary Virginia (now Toano, Virginia) on January 19, 1836. His citation reads "was one of a small scouting party that charged and routed a mounted force of the enemy six times their number. He led the charge in a most gallant manner, going beyond the call of duty."

"Mister Rogers' Neighborhood" was a carefully structured show. The routine of walking through the door and changing his sneakers and sweater was a ritual designed to give children a sense of security.

"America's Favorite Neighbor"

FRED ROGERS

County: Westmoreland
Town: Latrobe
Cemetery: Unity
Address: 114 Chapel Lane

Fred Rogers was an American Treasure and icon. He had a profound effect on the lives of millions of people through his ministry to children and families. His message was simple; that you can be lovable just the way you are. He taught kindness and love over the course of four decades through his television program, books, and songs. He helped children deal with common fears such as starting school or going to the doctor. He became an American icon of children's entertainment and education as well as a symbol of compassion, patience, and morality. He received the Presidential Medal of Freedom, two Peabody awards for his life's work, and was inducted into the Television Hall of Fame.

It all began in Latrobe, Pennsylvania where Fred McFeely Rogers was born on March 20, 1928. He showed an early interest and aptitude for music fostered by his mother and maternal grandfather Fred McFeely. He graduated from Latrobe High School and attended Dartmouth College before transferring to Rollins College in Florida where he graduated with a degree in music in 1951.

He was fascinated with the new medium, television, so he put his plans to become a minister on a back burner and accepted a job with NBC in New York City. He worked on a number of shows but grew disillusioned and left to help found WQED, the nation's first community supported public television station. He married his college sweetheart Sara Joanne Byrd, moved back to the Pittsburgh area and began working at WQED.

He developed "The Children's Corner" a prototype for "Mister Rogers Neighborhood" and for the next several years developed many of the puppets, characters, and music used in his later work, such as King Friday XIII, Daniel Striped Tiger and X the Owl. During this time, Rogers was studying Theology at nearby Pittsburgh Theological Seminary and was ordained a Presbyterian minister in 1962. That year he created a fifteen minute version of "Mister Rogers' Neighborhood" for Canadian television, and in 1966 WQED launched the series as a half-hour show. In 1969, "Mister Rogers' Neighborhood" began airing on PBS stations across the United States.

"Mister Rogers' Neighborhood" was a carefully structured show. The routine of walking through the door and changing his sneakers and sweater was a ritual designed to give children a sense of security and to signal a time for a relaxed visit together. The trips between fantasy and reality had structured transitions, such as the summoning of the Neighborhood Trolley to take us from Mister Rogers living room through a tunnel and into the Neighborhood of Make Believe. Songs composed by Rogers, more than 200 in his career, were used to impart many of his messages through simple lyrics that speak to a child's concerns. Songs like Daniel Striped Tiger's "Sometimes I Wonder if I'm a Mistake" say it's okay for kids to be themselves and "What Do You Do?" offers a list of ways for a child to deal with anger.

Photo of Fred Rogers located at the Rogers Center on the campus of Saint Vincent's College in Latrobe.

Typically, each week's episode explored a major theme, such as going to school for the first time or a visit to the hospital to show children what to expect. The program became a huge success. From 1968 to 1999 eight hundred ninety-five episodes were produced, all of which Rogers wrote and executive produced. Often there were celebrity guests like Yo-Yo Ma, Tony Bennett, Julia Child, Lynn Swann, David Copperfield, and Pittsburgh native actor Michael Keaton who also worked on the show as a stagehand.

The popularity of the show and its repetitive format led to many parodies over the years. After Burger King used an actor impersonating Mister Rogers for a TV commercial ("Can you say 'Flame Broiled'? I knew you could"), Fred Rogers called the head of the company concerned that the ad was "confusing innocent children" into thinking he was promoting their fast food franchises. Rogers never did any commercial promotions of any kind. Burger King openly apologized, and the commercial was pulled. Johnny Carson once did a skit on "The Tonight Show" called "Mister Rambo's Neighborhood." When Rogers complained, Carson apologized and expressed admiration for Roger's work. Rogers did, however, have a good sense of humor and enjoyed Eddie Murphy's parody of his show on "Saturday Night Live" called "Mister Robinson's Neighborhood" ("Can you say 'Eviction Notice'? I knew you could.")

Rogers also published many books to supplement the messages on his television show. Among these were "Mister Rogers Talks with Parents," "You are Special," "The World According to Mister Rogers," "Important Things to

This large statue of Fred Rogers sits just outside Heinz Field in Pittsburgh. The site is called Tribute to Children.

Remember," and eight New Experiences titles such as "The New Baby," "Moving," and "When a Pet Dies."

In 1968, Rogers was appointed Chairman of the Forum on Mass Media and Child Development of the White House Conference on Youth. In 1969 he appeared before the United States Senate in support of funding for PBS and the Corporation for Public Broadcasting. He spoke on the need for social and emotional education that public television provided and argued that alternative television programming helped encourage children to become happy and productive citizens sometimes opposing less positive messages in the media and popular culture. He even recited lyrics to "What do you do?" The Chairman of the Subcommittee Sen. John Pastore said the testimony had given him "goose bumps." President Nixon had proposed cutting their budget to $9 million but after Rogers's testimony, Congress agreed on $22 million.

In 1979, Rogers testified in the case Sony Corp of America v Universal City Studios Inc. The Supreme Court considered his testimony and quoted him in the footnote in its decision that held that the Betamax video recorder did not infringe copyright.

At the 1998 Emmy's, Rogers was awarded the Lifetime Achievement Award. In accepting the award on stage he said, "All of us have special ones who have loved us into being. Would you just take, along with me, ten seconds to think of the people who have helped you become who you are. Ten seconds of silence." The gesture brought many of the star studded Hollywood crowd to tears and drew a standing ovation. Thereafter, Rogers frequently repeated this in his many speeches and appearances.

Production of "Mister Rogers' Neighborhood" ceased in December 1999 after a total of 895 episodes, and the last week of original episodes aired in August 2000. After production of the program ceased, Fred Rogers devoted his time to the "Mister Rogers' Neighborhood" website, writing books, and numerous speaking engagements.

Fred Rogers was laid to rest in this mausoleum in Latrobe, Pennsylvania.

Rogers was diagnosed with stomach cancer in December 2002. His last public appearance was as Grand Marshall of the Tournament of Roses Parade with Bill Cosby and Art Linkletter. He died on February 27, 2003 at his home with his wife by his side. He was just shy of 75 years old.

He never sought the spotlight, but the list of awards he was presented is enormous. The Presidential Medal of Freedom, the highest civilian award that can be bestowed, was awarded Rogers in 2002 by President George Bush. "Mister Rogers' Neighborhood" won four Emmy awards, and Rogers was given a Lifetime Achievement Award by the Academy of Television Arts and Sciences. He was awarded two Peabody Awards, was named one of the "50 greatest TV starts of all time" by TV Guide in 1996, was inducted into the Television Hall of Fame in 1999, had an asteroid named after him (Misterrogers), and got a star on the Hollywood Walk of Fame. The Smithsonian Institution in Washington, DC has his signature sweater on display. There is a large memorial statue of Fred Rogers just outside of Heinz Field, and St. Vincent College in Latrobe is home to The Fred M. Rogers Center for Early Learning and Children's Media. In 2003, the U.S. House of Representatives unanimously passed Resolution 111 honoring Rogers for "his legendary service to the improvement of lives of children, his steadfast commitment to demonstrating the power of compassion, and his dedication to spreading kindness through example."

Fred Rogers was a soft-spoken man of great modesty with a steady hand and a generous heart. His television persona was no act. This author had the privilege of meeting him a number of times and even seeing him record an episode of "Mister Rogers' Neighborhood." He was always patient, caring, humble, and kind with everyone. He is buried in historic Unity Cemetery in Latrobe, PA. He is buried in a mausoleum that does not bear his name. It has the name "Given", a relative of Rogers.

If You Go:
If you go to Latrobe, be sure to visit the beautiful inspiring campus of the community of scholars known as St. Vincent College. Esatablished in 1846, it has been turning out some of our best thinkers for over 150 years (This author went there). It's also the training camp of the Pittsburgh Steelers. If that's not enough stimulation, stop at Sharky's Café at 3960 Rt 30. Sharky's has been turning out some of our best drinkers for many years. It's the area's largest and most complete restaurant and sports bar. Even President Obama and Sen. Bob Casey stopped in for a beer when campaigning in the area. It's a festive, friendly atmosphere. We loved it.

Art Rooney with cigar

25

"The Chief"

ART ROONEY

County: Allegheny
Town: Pittsburgh
Cemetery: Christ Our Redeemer
Address: 204 Cemetery Lane

Arthur Joseph "Art" Rooney, often referred to as "The Chief," was a man who has come to represent the triumph of the underdog. He was the founding owner of the Pittsburgh Steelers and is a member of the Pro Football Hall of Fame. The Steelers were once known as the "lovable losers" after managing only 24 victories in their first eight years. Today, the Steelers have won more Super Bowls than any other team in the history of the National Football League.

Rooney was born on January 27, 1901, in the small mining town of Coulter, near Pittsburgh. His great-grandparents were Irish immigrants who came to Canada during the potato famine of the 1840's. His parents, Dan and Maggie, settled on Pittsburgh's North Side in 1913, where they bought a three-story building in which Dan opened a saloon and the family lived above on the second floor. Three Rivers Stadium would later be built on this very site.

Rooney attended St. Peter's Parochial School and Duquesne University Prep School. He then attended Indiana Normal School (now Indiana University of Pennsylvania), Georgetown and Duquesne. He was always an exceptional athlete. When he was done with school he dedicated himself to sports. He won the AAU welterweight boxing title in 1918, and was named to the U.S. Olympic boxing team in 1920 but did not participate. Years later, he became a close fan and friend of the boxer, who was light heavyweight champion at the time, the Pittsburgh Kid, Billy Conn (see Chapter 7, p. 45). As a matter of fact, it was Rooney who broke up the infamous fight between Billy Conn and his father-in-law that led to the cancellation of Conn's rematch with Joe Louis.

He played minor league baseball for the Flint (Michigan) Vehicles and Wheeling (West Virginia) Stogies. In 1925, he was the Wheeling player-manager and led the league in hits, runs, stolen bases and finished second in batting average.

He was twice offered football scholarships to Notre Dame by Knute Rockne but did not accept, and in the mid-1920's was offered baseball contracts with the Chicago Cubs and Boston Red Sox. He developed arm trouble while playing for Wheeling and that ended his major-league hopes.

Rooney's professional football career began with his founding an independent semi-professional football team based in Pittsburgh for which he coached and played. The team was originally called the "Hope-Harvey." The name was based on two things: (1) the firehouse where the team would dress and shower (which was located in the city's Hope ward); and (2) Dr. Walter Harvey, a physician who tended to the injured players. Dr. Harvey never charged for his services to the team and the uniforms were homemade by the players or their family members. After a few years, a sponsor (Loeffler's Electronic Store) renamed the team after one of its best-selling products: the "Majestic Radios."

The team played for seven years as the Majestic Radios, but prior to the 1931 season the affiliation with Loeffler's ended and the team became known as the J.P. Rooneys to promote Art's brother James P. Rooney, who was running for election to the Pennsylvania House of Representatives (a race which James easily won). Art's semi-professional teams won two Western Pennsylvania Senior Independent Football Conference titles and he began to think about adding a Pittsburgh team to the National Football League (NFL).

The NFL began operating in 1920 and wanted a team in Pittsburgh due to the city's history with football and the popularity of the University of Pittsburgh football team. Pennsylvania's "blue laws" were however a major barrier. The blue laws prohibited sporting events on Sundays, when most of the NFL's games took place. When Pennsylvania relaxed its blue laws in 1933, Rooney saw an opportunity. On July 8 of that year, he bought an NFL franchise for $2,500 and named it the Pittsburgh Pirates. They were a member of the Eastern Division in a 10-team league which included the Chicago Bears, Green Bay Packers and New York Giants.

It has been said many times that Rooney bought the franchise with his winnings from betting on the horses, but that is uncertain. He did however win big at the Saratoga Course in 1936, where he won an amount he never revealed but various reports place it between $160,000 and $358,000 Depression-era dollars (or in today's money between about $2.7- $6.0 million dollars). It was no fluke, as Rooney is said to have been one of the greatest handicappers in the sport. He always remained interested in racing, and attended the Kentucky Derby and Irish Derby regularly. He acquired Yonkers Raceway in 1972, was an owner of Liberty Bell Racetrack near Philadelphia, and owned and operated Shamrock Farm in Maryland where he bred and trained thoroughbreds.

In 1935, Rooney used some of his winnings to hire a coach for his new football team: Joe Bach. Bach, who was one of Notre Dame's famed "seven mules" on the 1924 national championship team, coached the Pirates in the 1935 and 1936 seasons.

In 1938, Rooney sent shockwaves through the NFL by signing Byron "Whizzer" White to a record-breaking $15,000 contract. White was a college football star at Colorado, where he acquired the nickname "Whizzer." He postponed attending Oxford University on a Rhodes Scholarship for one year to play for the Pirates. He led the league in rushing and then departed for England. After Oxford, White played two years for the Detroit Lions, joined the Navy, fought in World War II, became a lawyer and in 1962 was appointed by President Kennedy to the United States Supreme Court where he would serve for over 30 years. In 1940, Rooney renamed the team the Pittsburgh Steelers.

Rooney married Kathleen McNulty in 1931 and they had five sons. He was involved in many businesses and political enterprises over the years, including racing and boxing, and was a partner in the General Braddock Brewing Company which made "Rooney Beer." Rooney made one reluctant venture into elective politics that got him mentioned in *Time* magazine. He was persuaded by the Republican Party to run for Allegheny County Register of Wills. He gave only one speech during the campaign. Newspaper and magazine accounts of the story report that Rooney stood up and said that he didn't know the first thing about being Register of Wills. In fact, he didn't even know where the office was located. He said he would consult the phone directory to find the office and assured voters that if he won he would hire capable assistants to run the office. He lost and never ran for office again.

One of the most amazing and convoluted deals he ever made was after the 1940 football season involving the Steelers. Rooney was tired of losing on the field and at the gate. The owner of the Philadelphia Eagles, Bert Bell, shared those same feelings. A man named Alexis Thompson approached Bell about buying the Eagles intending to move the franchise to Boston. Bell contacted Rooney and brokered a deal in which Rooney sold the Steelers for $160,000 and invested $80,000 to become a partner in the Eagles. The sale was approved and the team was renamed the Ironmen, but the other owners refused permission for the team to leave Pennsylvania.

Rooney meanwhile had second thoughts. Thompson was a rich playboy who lived in New York and Rooney proposed that they now swap cities. Rooney and Bell would take their franchise back to Pittsburgh and renamed it the Steelers while Thompson could operate his franchise from Philadelphia and be closer to New York.

All sides agreed and from 1941 until 1946 when Bert Bell became NFL commissioner and gave up his interest in the Steelers, the teams operating name was Philadelphia Eagles Football Club Inc. The NFL considers the Rooney ownership reign unbroken because they never actually missed a game in Pittsburgh.

The Steelers had their first winning season in 1942 but then in 1943—when the loss of players due to World War II depleted their roster—they survived by forming a merger. Rooney sought out Thompson (who was serving in the Army) and they got the NFL to approve a merger known as the

Phil-Pitt Eagles-Steeler Combine. Within weeks they were dubbed the "Steagles." The two head coaches, Walt Kiesling and Earle Neale, hated each other, so Rooney had Neale coach the offense and Kiesling coached the defense. All of the players were required to keep full-time jobs in defense plants.

The Steagles finished the season 5-4-1, the first winning season in the history of the Philadelphia franchise and just the second for Pittsburgh. The team wore green and white and played six of its 10 games at "home": two at Forbes Field in Pittsburgh and four at Shibe Park in Philadelphia.

After the war, Rooney became team president and focused on trying to bring an NFL championship to Pittsburgh. He moved the Steelers' offices from the ground floor of the Fort Pitt Hotel to the fourth floor of an office building. Rooney loved to tell the story of how when the office was at the Fort Pitt Hotel, guests used to come in and leave through a window that opened onto the street instead of taking the long way around through the hotel lobby. Pie Traynor (See *Keystone Tombstones – Pittsburgh Region*, p. 43), the Pirate baseball Hall of Famer and a regular at nightly card games that were held at the Fort Pitt, refused to come to the new offices. He was sure that he would forget where he was and step out the fourth floor window some night.

Despite his efforts, the Steelers remained perennial also-rans and were known in the NFL as the "lovable losers." It did not help that they cut the then-unknown Johnny Unitas in training camp and traded their first round pick in 1965 to the Bears, who drafted Dick Butkus.

Finally, in the 1970's the team hit on the right combination of coaches and players. The Steelers became the most dominant team of an entire decade. They won four Super Bowls (1974, 1975, 1978 and 1979) during a streak of 13 consecutive winning seasons which included an eight-year run of playoff appearances.

After the 1974 season, Rooney relinquished day-to-day operation of the Steelers and named his oldest son, Dan, president. He did, however, remain Chairman of the Board until his death. With his family at his bedside, Art Rooney died on August 25, 1988 at Mercy Hospital in Pittsburgh, eight days after suffering a stroke. He was 87 years old.

Well before the Steelers won even a single title, Art Rooney's football achievements and contributions to the game were significant enough to warrant his election into the Pro Football Hall of Fame in 1964. There are tributes to him everywhere. A large statue of his likeness, built with donations of more than $371,000 from fans, sits just outside the Steelers' current home at Heinz Field, near "Art Rooney Avenue." Duquesne University plays football at Rooney Field, and there is a Rooney Middle School on Pittsburgh's North Side. St. Vincent College (where the Steelers hold training camp each summer) and Indiana University of Pennsylvania both have dormitories named "Rooney Hall." There are numerous books about Art Rooney, as well as a one-man play called "The Chief" in which Rooney is the only character. This author has seen "The Chief," and it was a sheer delight. Art Rooney is buried at Christ Our Redeemer Catholic Cemetery (sometimes referred to as "North Side Catholic Church") on his beloved North Side of Pittsburgh.

If You Go:

Also buried in Christ Our Redeemer Cemetery is one of Art Rooney's coaches, Walter Kiesling. Kiesling was inducted into the Pro Football Hall of Fame for his play with a number of teams from 1926 until 1939. He coached the Steelers from 1939 to 1944 and again from 1954 to 1956. Kiesling was head coach when a young Pittsburgh-born and bred Johnny Unitas was cut at the end of training camp in 1955. Kiesling never even let Unitas take a snap in practice. After being cut, Unitas hitchhiked home and took a job as a pile-driver at a construction job while continuing to play football for a semi-pro team on rock- and glass-covered fields in Pittsburgh for $6 a game. Unitas' rights were picked up the following year by the Baltimore Colts, and he went on to be one of the greatest quarterbacks ever to play.

Also buried in Christ Our Redeemer is Vietnam Medal-of-Honor recipient John Gary Gertsch. Staff Sergeant Gertsch was awarded the Medal of Honor for his bravery in the Republic of Vietnam's A-Shau Valley, during combat from July 15-19, 1969, when he was killed in combat.

This plot contains the remains of Art Rooney, the owner of the Pittsburgh Steelers, who was known as "The Chief."

Bessie Smith

"The Empress of the Blues"

BESSIE SMITH

County: Delaware
Town: Sharon Hill
Cemetery: Mount Lawn
Address: 84th Street and Hook Road

Bob Dylan and the Band recorded an album in 1967 titled "The Basement Tapes." The record wouldn't be released until 1975. One of the tracks is a song composed by Band members Robbie Robertson and Rick Danko on which Dylan provides the lead vocal. When he gets to the chorus he sings:

"I'm just going down the road to see Bessie
Oh, see her soon
Going down the road to see Bessie Smith
When I get there I wonder what she'll do."

The song is called Bessie Smith, and it pays homage to a woman that many consider to be the greatest blues singer of all time. Smith is buried in Sharon Hill, Pennsylvania not far from Philadelphia.

According to the 1900 census, Bessie Smith was born in Chattanooga, Tennessee in July 1892. When the 1910 census was recorded, her birth date changed to April 15, 1894. The latter date is the one she observed throughout her life. By the time Smith was nine, both of her parents had died and as a result, she was raised by an older sister. She was raised in poverty and in an attempt to bring some money into the household, Smith and one of her brothers formed a duo and began performing on the streets of Chattanooga. She would sing and dance to the music her brother supplied on his guitar.

In 1912 she auditioned for a job in a travelling show known as the Stokes troupe. She was hired as a dancer because the show already had a woman singer named Ma Rainey. Many believe that Ma Rainey helped Smith as she grew to become a stage performer. By 1913 she had developed her own act, and by 1920 she was well known throughout the south.

In 1920 a singer by the name of Mamie Smith (no relation) recorded and released a song titled "Crazy Blues." It turned out to be a hit and prompted the recording industry to search for other female blues singers. In 1923, Smith signed a recording contract with Columbia records. By that time, she had made Philadelphia her home and met and married Jack Gee a security guard. By all accounts, the marriage was rocky from the start with both partners having affairs. Gee couldn't come to terms with Smith's bisexuality, and when she learned that he was having an affair with another singer she ended the relationship in 1929. Smith would eventually enter into a common-law marriage with Richard Morgan who happened to be Lionel Hampton's uncle. Their relationship would endure until the day she died.

While her personal life wasn't going well, Smith's professional career could hardly have been improved upon. Her first record called "Downhearted Blues" was a major hit. She became the highest paid black performer in the 1920's as she headed her own show that featured as many as forty other entertainers. While touring, she lived and travelled in her own private railroad car. Columbia records called her the "Queen of the Blues", but newspapers gave her the upgraded title "Empress."

Smith was known for her powerful voice that was excellent for recording. She recorded more than 150 songs for Columbia backed by some of the greatest musicians at the time including Joe Smith, Fletcher Henderson and a young fella by the name of Louis Armstrong. Her career was cut short by the Great Depression and the advent of talking movies. The first event almost ended the entire recording industry, and "talkies" pretty much ended vaudeville shows.

In 1929, Smith appeared in the film "St. Louis Blues." She sings the title song in the movie accompanied by Fletcher Henderson's band, a choir and a string section. The combination produced a sound very different from anything found on her recordings.

In the early thirties Smith continued to tour and perform. In 1933, John Hammond had her record for Okeh records. She was paid $37.50 for each recording. Music had entered the "swing era" and she was backed by notable swing era musicians including pianist Buck Washington, tenor saxophonist Chu Berry and guitarist Bobby Johnson. This recording session, which took place on November 24th, would be her last. Billie Holiday, who cited Smith as a major influence, would make her first record three days later with these same musicians.

On September 26, 1937, Smith was travelling in a car, driven by Richard Morgan, on Route 61 between Memphis, Tennessee, and Clarksdale, Mississippi. Morgan failed to properly judge the speed of a truck that was ahead of him. He attempted to avoid hitting the truck by passing it on the left but was not successful as he hit the rear of the truck with the passenger side of his vehicle. Smith, sitting in the passenger seat, was badly hurt; Morgan had no injuries.

A Memphis surgeon by the name of Dr. Hugh Smith and his fishing partner, Henry Broughton, came upon the accident scene and stopped to offer assistance. Dr. Smith examined the injured singer and concluded that she had lost about a half pint of blood and that her right arm was almost completely severed at the elbow. Broughton and Dr. Smith moved Smith to the side of the road where he dressed the arm injury while Broughton went to a nearby home to summon an ambulance.

By the time Broughton returned to the scene, Smith was in shock. As time passed, with no ambulance arriving, Dr. Smith decided to take Smith to a hospital in his car. He had just finished clearing out his back seat when he heard a car approaching at a high rate of speed. The fast moving car hit the Doctor's vehicle sending it into Smith's car completely demolishing it. The oncoming car went into a ditch on the right side of the road barely missing Broughton and Bessie Smith.

The ambulance finally arrived, and Smith was taken to Clarksdale's G.T. Thomas Afro-American Hospital. Her right arm was amputated, but she remained in a coma. She died later that morning having never regained consciousness. After her death John Hammond circulated a rumor that she had died after being refused entrance to a whites only hospital. This was not the case for as Dr. Smith noted no ambulance driver in the south at that time "would even have thought of putting a colored person off in a hospital for white folks."

Smith's body was placed in the O.V. Catto Elks Lodge to handle the crowd who came to wish her farewell. It is estimated that 10,000 people filed past her coffin. She was laid to rest in Mount Lawn Cemetery on October 4, 1937. Though money was raised for a tombstone to mark her grave, her estranged husband Jack Gee pocketed the money, and Smith's grave remained unmarked until August 7, 1970. On that day a tombstone partially paid for by Janis Joplin was erected. Joplin also recorded a song called "Stone for Bessie Smith" on her album "Mythical Kings and Iguanas."

Three of Bessie Smith's recordings have been inducted into the Grammy Hall of Fame. The songs "Downhearted Blues", "St. Louis Blues" and "Empty Bed Blues" were recognized for their historical significance. "Downhearted Blues" is also in the Rock and Roll Hall of Fame having been selected as one of the 500 songs that shaped that genre of music. Smith herself was inducted into the Rock and Roll Hall of Fame in 1989. She is also a member of the Blues Hall of Fame and the Big Band and Jazz Hall of Fame.

A number of great female vocalists have acknowledged that Smith influenced them. These include Billie Holiday, Sarah Vaughn, Aretha Franklin and Janis Joplin who said of Smith, "She showed me the air and taught me how to fill it."

Of course her influence has not been confined to female singers. As noted in the beginning of this

This tombstone partially paid for by Janis Joplin marks Bessie Smith's final resting place.

chapter, Bob Dylan and the Band have also paid tribute to the great blues singer in the song "Bessie Smith." As Dylan sings in the songs last verse;

> "When she sees me will she know what I've been through?
> Will old times start to feeling like new?
> When I get there will our love still feel so true?
> Yet all I have, I'll be bringing it to you
> Oh Bessie, sing them old time blues."

If You Go:
Mount Lawn Cemetery is the final resting place of another entertainer, Lawrence Brown Sr. who was a vocalist with Harold Melvin and the Blue Notes. In the 1970's this popular group had hits with a number of songs including, "The Love I Lost", "If You Don't Know Me By Now" and "Wake Up Everybody." Brown performed until a few months prior to his death in 2008.

Hank "The Bankman" Gathers is also buried in this cemetery. Gathers was a college basketball star who became the second player in the history of the game to lead the nation in both scoring and rebounding. He died during a game on March 4, 1990. The cause of his death was heart failure.

Another basketball player, Guy Rodgers, was also laid to rest at Mount Lawn. Rodgers had a 12 year career as a guard in the National Basketball Association. During that time he played for San Francisco Warriors, the Chicago Bulls, the Cincinnati Royals and the Milwaukee Bucks. Rodgers passed away in 2001.

Not far from Mount Lawn is the town of Essington, Pennsylvania. We stopped for refreshments at Coaches Bar and Grill located at 350 Jansen Avenue. The food was excellent and reasonably priced. There is a large outdoor patio and numerous televisions for your viewing pleasure. The wait staff was friendly, courteous and efficient. If you are in the area, we recommend a visit.

"The Dictator of Congress"

THADDEUS STEVENS

County: Lancaster
Town: Lancaster
Cemetery: Shreiner's
Address: North Mulberry and West Chestnut Streets

There have been many powerful congressmen who have served in the United States House of Representatives. A majority have held the title Speaker of the house. Members who have held that lofty position include Henry Clay, Champ Clark, Sam Rayburn and Tip O'Neill. However, only one member of the House was ever called the "dictator" of Congress. His name was Thaddeus Stevens, and many historians hold the opinion that he wielded more power than any other congressman in the history of the country.

Stevens was born on April 4, 1792, in Vermont. He faced numerous hardships in his early life, including a club foot. In addition, his father was an alcoholic who found it impossible to hold a steady job. It is not known what happened to the elder Stevens, but it is clear that he left his wife and four sons in poverty. Stevens himself was ambitious and saw the value of education. He studied at Peacham Academy and afterwards entered Dartmouth as a sophomore from where he graduated in 1814. Stevens then moved to York, Pennsylvania where he worked as a teacher while he studied law. He was admitted to the bar and established himself first as a lawyer in Gettysburg and later in Lancaster.

Stevens would never marry, though he did have two boys, who were the sons of his mixed race housekeeper, Lydia Hamilton Smith, live with him. Smith would manage Steven's home and businesses in Lancaster for 24 years. She also served as his hostess during his days in Washington. During this time, society operated under a policy of segregation. As a result, rumors swirled about their relationship. Based on their correspondence and accounts by those who knew them, it appears that the relationship they established could best be described as a respectful friendship.

Stevens was deeply interested in politics. Initially he joined the Federalist Party, when that party faded he joined the Anti-Masonic Party, he then became a Whig before finding his final home as a Republican. In 1833 he was elected to the Pennsylvania State House of Representatives where he served on and off until 1842. His record during this time reflects beliefs he would carry forward throughout his political career. He was against secret societies, he favored funding to Pennsylvania colleges and he wanted a constitutional limit established on the state debt. His support for black

Thaddeus Stevens

citizens surfaced when he refused to sign the Pennsylvania constitution of 1838 because it failed to allow those citizens to vote. He also championed the establishment of free public schools. Though Stevens had been elected by a constituency that favored repeal of the public education act, he fought to preserve it. He was instrumental in persuading the Pennsylvania Assembly to vote overwhelmingly in favor of keeping the new law.

Those who knew Stevens agreed that he was a man who could be counted on to employ his considerable energies toward furthering those causes he believed in. It was his view that slave owners were attempting to gain control of the federal government in order to ensure that slavery would be permitted to grow. He vowed to fight to further the cause of liberty. He was first elected to Congress in 1848 and he served until 1853. In 1859 he returned to Congress as a republican and would continue to serve until his death in 1868. As a member of Congress, he supported Native Americans, Mormons, Jews and women. However no cause was dearer to him than that of the abolition of slavery. He was an active member of the Underground Railroad, and he assisted in helping runaway slaves make their way to Canada. A possible Underground Railroad site has been discovered under his office in Lancaster, Pennsylvania.

When the Civil War broke out, Stevens used his political skills to enhance his influence and power. He became the chairman of the Ways and Means Committee, and combining the power of this position with his oratorical skills, he soon became the leader of a group that would be known as the Radical Republicans.

Stevens was outraged in July of 1861 when Congress passed the Crittenden-Johnson Resolution which held that the war would be won by restoring the Union while preserving slavery. Stevens worked hard for its repeal which occurred that December. In that same month he was calling for the emancipation of the slaves as a means to weaken the Confederate states. In early 1862 he was calling for total war. On January 22nd he addressed the House and declared that the war would not end until, "...one party or the other be reduced to hopeless feebleness and the power of further effort shall be utterly annihilated." In that same speech he again urged the immediate emancipation of all slaves arguing that such a move would assist in crippling the Confederate economy that relied on slave labor to raise cotton, rice, tobacco and grain.

That January Lincoln also took action within his cabinet. He appointed his embattled Secretary of War, Simon Cameron (see Chapter 5, p. 30) to the post of United States Minister to Russia. Upon hearing this news Stevens said, "Send word to the Czar to bring in his things of the night." In addition, prior to his departure to Russia, the House censured Cameron for adopting policies that flagrantly damaged the public service.

By the time the war was drawing to a close, Stevens was the acknowledged leader of the Radical Republicans. The elections of 1866 put this group in firm control of the Congress. Stevens became the architect of the country's policies governing the Reconstruction of the Southern states. His plan was to use military power to force the South to recognize the equality of the freed slaves. Lincoln's successor, President Andrew Johnson, opposed the vast majority of Steven's plans. Stevens was up for the fight in August of 1866 during a Congressional speech. He proclaimed,

> "You will remember in Egypt he sent frogs, locusts, murrain, lice and finally demanded the first born of everyone of the oppressors. Almost all these have been taken from us. We have been oppressed with taxes and debts, and he has sent us worse than lice, and has afflicted us with Andrew Johnson."

It was Stevens who proposed the resolution for the impeachment of Johnson in 1868. Every Republican voted in favor of the measure, and Stevens made it a point to put members of both the House and Senate on notice relative to their ultimate decision on the matter. After the articles of impeachment were adopted he said,

> "Let me see the recreant who would vote to let such a criminal escape. Point me to one who would dare do it and I will show you one who would dare the infamy of posterity."

FORMAL NOTICE OF THE IMPEACHMENT OF ANDREW JOHNSON, BY THE HOUSE COMMITTEE, THADDEUS STEVENS AND JOHN A. BINGHAM, AT THE BAR OF THE SENATE, WASHINGTON, D. C., ON THE 25th FEB.

The tomb of a man that would not accept slavery in the United States.

That man turned out to be a Republican Senator Edmund Ross from Kansas who found Johnson to be not guilty and as a result the President's impeachment failed by one slender vote. Rather than daring the infamy of posterity Ross was hailed for his stand and vote in John F. Kennedy's "Profiles in Courage."

While Stevens failed in his efforts to impeach the President, he was largely successful in having his policies adopted in terms of the Reconstruction of the South. In terms of historical judgment, Reconstruction is largely viewed as having failed. Historians differ as to the reasons for this outcome and that remains a matter of controversy to this day.

Three months after the acquittal of Johnson on August 11, 1868, Thaddeus Stevens died in Washington. He was 76 years of age. His coffin lay in state in the Capitol Rotunda attended by a Black Honor Guard. His funeral in Lancaster was attended by over 20,000 people, half of which were African Americans. He decided to be buried in the Shreiner Cemetery because it would accept people without regard to race. Stevens composed the inscription on his headstone. It reads,

"I repose in this quiet and secluded spot, not from any natural preference for solitude, but finding other cemeteries limited as to race, by charter rules. I have chosen this that I might illustrate in my death the principles which I advocated through a long life, equality of man before his Creator."

In death Stevens attempted to carry on the causes he worked for during his life. He left $50,000 to establish the Stevens School. The school provided refuge and education to homeless orphans. The students were admitted without regard to their race or the religion of their parents. The school is now the Thaddeus Stevens College of Technology, and its goal remains to provide the underprivileged with opportunities they would otherwise be denied.

If You Go:

In *Keystone Tombstones Volume One* we identified a number of sites worth visiting in Lancaster. We would urge you to review Chapters 2, 20 and 24 in that publication which cover the careers of President James Buchanan, the Pennsylvania Patriot Thomas Mifflin and general John Fulton Reynolds.

"The Greatest Athlete of the 20th Century"

JIM THORPE

County: Carbon
Town: Jim Thorpe
Cemetery: Jim Thorpe Memorial
Address: 101 East 10th Street

The man who many consider to be the greatest athlete of his time is buried in Pennsylvania in the town that bears his name. Jim Thorpe excelled at multiple sports, though he is best remembered for his accomplishments in football and in track and field. It was as a direct result of his play in these two areas that from 1996-2001 he was awarded ABC's Wide World of Sports Athlete of the Century award.

Thorpe was born on May 22, 1888 in Oklahoma on a Sac-and-Fox Indian reservation. Thorpe's youth, not unlike his adult life, was filled with ups and downs. His father recognized his athletic ability and encouraged young Thorpe to develop it. Among his favorite childhood games was chasing (on foot) and catching wild horses. He was also a big fan of follow the leader, though when he was the leader you would have to do things like climb trees and jump to the ground as well as swim across rivers. Thorpe was also known to run the 20 miles home from school each day. He thrived at competing with others.

As mentioned above, there were also childhood disappointments. Few in his family were blessed with long lives. His twin brother passed away when he was 8. Both of his parents died when he was in his teens. He took his father's death extremely hard.

When Thorpe was 16 he was recruited to attend the Carlisle Indian School in Carlisle, Pennsylvania. It was here that his athletic ability caught the attention of the legendary coach Glen "Pop" Warner. One day Thorpe was walking past the field where the track team was practicing. He stopped to watch and noticed how no one could clear the high bar that was set at 5 feet 9 inches. Despite the fact that he was in his street clothes, he walked onto the field and cleared the height easily.

Thorpe enjoyed great success in track and field while attending Carlisle. For example, in 1909 he almost beat the Lafayette team by himself when he won six events. The Lafayette coach, Harold Anson Bruce, said he had never seen such a natural athlete. But it was on the football field where Thorpe really made a name for himself. Pop Warner was initially against Thorpe playing football because he felt his star track and field athlete might get hurt. Finally, Thorpe convinced him to let him run a few plays in practice.

Jim Thorpe

On two successive plays Thorpe galloped for touchdowns untouched. After the exhibition, Thorpe walked over to Warner tossed him the football and said, "Nobody is going to tackle Jim."

By 1911, Pop Warner was calling Thorpe "the greatest all-around athlete in the world." That year, Carlisle was to play the powerful Harvard football team in Cambridge. Thorpe was outstanding at running the ball, using his strength and remarkable speed to consistently advance its position. One reporter noted that he was amazing at avoiding tacklers in the open field. Thorpe was responsible for all of Carlisle's points. While scoring a touchdown and kicking four field goals, he led his team to a 18-15 upset win. Thorpe's play during the season earned him All-American honors.

While 1911 was a great year for Thorpe, it could not compare to his accomplishments in 1912. The 1912 Olympics were held in Stockholm that summer and Thorpe was a member of team USA. First he won the pentathlon a competition that included five different events. Six days later he competed in the decathlon where he set a world record with 8,412 points. What is remarkable about this total is that if Thorpe had posted the identical marks in the 1948 Olympics he would have won the silver medal. In fact his time of 4 minutes 40.1 seconds in the 1500 meter race would not be beaten until the 1972 Olympics.

After his Olympic performance he was congratulated by King Gustav V of Sweden. The king told Thorpe, "Sir, you are the greatest athlete in the world." Thorpe replied, "Thanks, king."

Thorpe returned to the United States as a national hero. New York City honored him with a ticker tape parade. At the conclusion of the parade Thorpe remarked, "I heard people yelling my name and I couldn't realize how one fellow could have so many friends."

That fall he returned to Carlisle to resume his football career playing for Pop Warner. One of the teams he faced was Army, whose roster included a cadet named Dwight Eisenhower. Carlisle won easily 27-6, and Thorpe put on a spectacular performance. On one play, he galloped 92 yards for a touchdown only to have the play nullified due to a penalty. On the next play he went 97 yards for the score. His play obviously impressed the future president who spoke of Thorpe in a 1961 speech. Ike said, "Here and there, there are some people who are extremely endowed. My memory goes back to Jim Thorpe. He never practiced in his life, and he could do anything better than any other football player I ever saw."

Carlisle went undefeated in 1912 and was widely acknowledged as the national champion. Thorpe won All-American honors again and he found himself sitting on top of the athletic world. There was, however, trouble on the horizon.

A writer for the Worcester Mass. Telegram named Roy Johnson published a story stating that Thorpe had been paid to play semi-pro baseball in 1909 and 1910. During this time, it was not unusual for college athletes to play

Jim Thorpe as a member of the New York Giants.

semi-pro, but most played under different names to avoid losing their amateur status. Thorpe made the mistake of playing under his real name.

As a result of this revelation, the Amateur Athletic Union asked Thorpe for an explanation. Thorpe replied in writing saying, "I hope I will be partly excused by the fact I was simply an Indian schoolboy and did not know about such things. I was not very wise in the ways of the world and did not realize this was wrong." There was not at the time any good reason for not accepting Thorpe's explanation. The Athletic Union thought otherwise and withdrew Thorpe's amateur status retroactively. The International Olympic Commission followed suit by declaring Thorpe a professional athlete. As a result, Thorpe was stripped of his Olympic titles and his gold medals. Almost immediately Thorpe began receiving offers from professional teams.

In 1913 baseball was the most popular sport in the country. It was also, arguably, Thorpe's weakest sport. He signed with the New York Giants where he played in the outfield for three seasons. Thorpe played six seasons of professional baseball, from 1913 to 1915 and from 1917 to 1919. His career totals in baseball are unimpressive. He played in 289 games and had a career batting average of .252. He scored 91 runs and drove in another 82. His career in the big leagues was over though he did continue to play minor league ball until he hung up his bat and glove for good in 1922.

Professional football was in its infancy and nowhere near as popular as it is today. That didn't stop Thorpe from signing with the Canton Bulldogs in 1915. The Bulldogs paid Thorpe $250 per game an amount that in current dollar terms would exceed $5,000. This was considered a very lucrative wage. At the time, Canton's average attendance per game was about 1,200 fans. When Thorpe made his debut, 8,000 paying customers attended the game. Thorpe and the Bulldogs were successful in winning league titles in 1916, 1917, and 1919. With little time left in the 1919 title game, the Bulldogs were forced to punt from deep in their own territory. Thorpe, with the wind at his back, took the snap and kicked a 95 yard punt sealing the victory and the championship.

While playing for the Bulldogs, Thorpe was named the league's President, a post he held for one year. He continued to coach and play for Canton until he joined the Oorang Indians in 1921. He was with this team, made up of all Native Americans, through 1923. While the team did poorly, Thorpe played well enough to be named to the first ALL-NFL team in 1923. Thorpe never won an NFL championship and retired from football in 1928 at the age of 41.

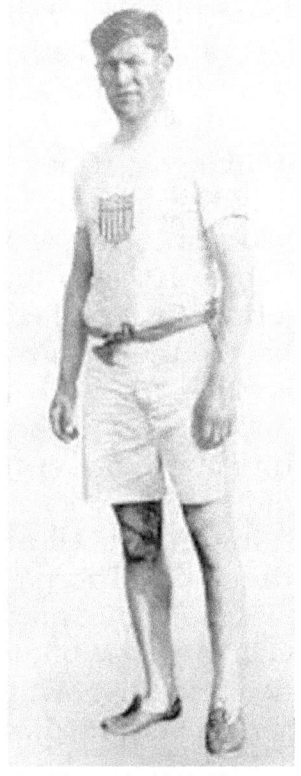

Jim Thorpe at 1912 Olympics

Here is the final resting place (at least for now) of the man that was called the greatest athlete in the world.

It was recently discovered that Thorpe also had a basketball career. In 1926, he was the star player for the "World Famous Indians" of Larue. His team played exhibitions in New York, Pennsylvania, and Ohio. The fact that he was a basketball player came to light in 2005 when a ticket to one of his games was discovered in an old book.

After Thorpe's athletic career ended, he led a troubled life. His first two marriages, which produced eight children, ended in divorce. One son, Jim Jr. died at the age of two. Thorpe's drinking, which had always been a problem, grew worse. It was not unusual for his drinking binges to end in fights. He also found holding a steady job difficult. He worked many odd jobs that included painting, digging ditches, serving as a deck hand, and a bar bouncer. In the 1930's he appeared in a few short films, usually playing an Indian.

By 1950, Thorpe was broke. That same year, the nation's press named him the most outstanding athlete of the first half of the 20th Century. He did receive about $15,000 from Warner Brothers in 1951 when the movie "Jim Thorpe All-American" was released. The film starred Burt Lancaster in the role of Thorpe and was a big hit.

In 1953, Thorpe was living with his third wife in a trailer in Lomita, California. While eating dinner on March 28th Thorpe suffered his third heart failure. Artificial respiration was used, and it revived him for a short time before he died. He was 64.

Another section of the Jim Thorpe Memorial that tells the story of his life.

Thorpe's athletic achievements have been recognized by many organizations. In 1951, he was elected to the College Football Hall of Fame. In 1963 he was named a Charter Enshrinee in the Pro Football Hall of Fame. He is also a member of the Track and Field Hall of Fame. In 1986, the Jim Thorpe award was created. It is awarded annually to the best defensive back in college football.

After his death, supporters of Thorpe pushed to have his Olympic titles reinstated. Thirty years later their efforts proved successful. On January 18, 1983, commemorative medals were presented to Thorpe's children. He was once again declared an Olympic champion.

In 1954, the towns of Mauch Chunk and East Mauch Chunk merged to form the town now known as Jim Thorpe. Town leaders made a deal with Thorpe's third wife to have his remains moved there in 1954. The town erected the Jim Thorpe Memorial which currently house the great athlete's remains. In June of 2010, Thorpe's son Jack filed a federal lawsuit seeking to have his father's remains retuned to Oklahoma. The case is pending.

If You Go:
Jim Thorpe is a quaint town with lots of nice shops and restaurants. We chose the Molly Maguire Pub and enjoyed it immensely. The old county jail in Jim Thorpe, where four alleged Mollie Maguires were hung at one time (see chapter 19), is now a museum.

RMS Titanic sea trials, April 2, 1912

29

Titanic Victims and Survivors

41°43.5' N 49°56.8' W
15 April 1912

For more than 100 years, the story of the sinking of the RMS *Titanic* has fascinated people all over the world. On the night of April 14 and the morning of April 15, 1912, four days into her maiden voyage, the largest passenger liner in the world hit an iceberg and sunk in the icy North Atlantic Ocean. Two hours and forty minutes after hitting the iceberg, she disappeared beneath the sea. She was carrying an estimated 2,224 people from Southampton, England to New York City, 1,500 of whom lost their lives in the tragedy, making it one of the deadliest peacetime maritime disasters in history.

Once the British passenger liner hit the iceberg and started taking on water, much chaos ensued and many controversies have endured for over a century. The evacuation was chaotic and controversial. Those who survived were rescued by the RMS *Carpathia*, which arrived about an hour and a half after the sinking. Less than a third of those aboard survived the disaster. Some survivors died shortly afterwards from injuries or the effects of exposure. Statistics compiled after the disaster show that 49% of the children and 26% of the female passengers died. The percentages for male passengers and crew were 82% and 78%, respectively. However, the figures show stark differences in the survival rates of the different classes. Only 3% of first-class women were lost, but 54% of those in third class died. Similarly, five of six first-class and all second-class children survived, but 52 of the 79 in third class perished. The figures for men show one-third of first-class men were saved but only 8% and 16% of second- and third-class men survived, respectively.

As the great ship went down, over a thousand passengers and crew members were still on board. Hundreds more were left dying in the icy 28°F sea, due to insufficient lifeboats and an inefficient, chaotic evacuation. Most lifeboats had empty seats. As the occupants sat and watched the horror around them, they could hear those freezing to death in the water as they yelled, screamed and pled for their lives.

Only a few of those in the water survived. Occupants of the lifeboats debated and argued about attempting to help those in the water. In all but two of the boats the occupants decided against trying to help, fearing that they would be capsized by the desperate, panicked swimmers. After about 20 minutes, the cries for help began to fade as the swimmers lapsed into unconsciousness and died. One of the *Titanic's* officers in Lifeboat No. 14

gathered together five of the lifeboats and transferred the occupants between them to free up space and headed back to the site of the sinking. Almost all of those in the water were already dead. They found four men still alive, one of whom died shortly afterwards. The *Carpathia* took the survivors to New York where the full scope of the disaster was just becoming known.

For years after, controversies and investigations would ensue. Issues like the speed and course of the *Titanic*, the failure to heed six warnings, the insufficient number of lifeboats, the chaotic evacuation, poor radio communication between ships at sea, and the survival of J. Bruce Ismay, managing director of the White Star Line (owner of the *Titanic*) who was aboard, were just a few of the subjects that came under close scrutiny following the disaster.

Pennsylvania, while welcoming home its share of *Titanic* survivors, also shared in the grief and sorrow of this horrible event. These are the remarkable stories of several such Pennsylvanians.[1]

Austin Van Billiard (35)
James Van Billiard (10)
Walter Van Billiard (9)
County: Montgomery
Town: Flourtown
Cemetery: Union Cemetery of Whitemarsh
Address: 654 Bethlehem Pike

Imagine the shock and despair of James Van Billiard and his wife, who learned in several days after the accident that their son Austin Van Billiard and two of their grandsons - James (age 10) and Walter (age 9) - were passengers on the *Titanic* and were missing.

This monument marks the final resting place of two Titanic victims the Van Billiards Austin, and his son James. Another son named Walter also perished but his body was never found.

Austin had been working in the diamond mining industry in South Africa for 10 years, living there with his wife and four children. During that time he was not able to see his brother or parents, who lived in Pennsylvania (North Wales Borough, Montgomery County). After much success, Austin decided to return to the U.S. to be a diamond merchant there. The family left South Africa and on their way to America they stopped to visit his wife's parents who lived in London. Austin then decided to take

---

[1] A number in parenthesis after an individual's name in each heading indicates that person's age at the time he or she perished on April 14-15, 1912. If no number is present after a person's name, that indicates the person survived the disaster.

his two eldest sons with him ahead of the rest of the family for a surprise visit. He took with him at least 12 uncut diamonds - diamonds which would soon be found on his body when it was recovered from the icy Atlantic.

The senior Van Billiards received a cablegram from their daughter-in-law informing them that Austin and the boys were on the *Titanic*. It was the first they knew of it.

Austin's body and that of his son Walter were recovered. James' body was never found (or, if it was recovered, was never identified). The family speculates that the boys would not have left their father to get on a lifeboat. The bodies of Austin and Walter are buried in Union Cemetery in Whitemarsh, Montgomery County. The headstone also lists James.

William Loch Coutts
County: Allegheny
Town: Penn Hills
Cemetery: Sunset View (a/k/a, Riverview Memorial Park)
Address: 2023 Lincoln Road

Unlike the Van Billiards, the situation was different for two other little boys who accompanied a parent aboard the *Titanic*. Mrs. Winnie "Minnie" Coutts and her two sons, William (age 9) and Neville (age 3) were third-class passengers on the *Titanic* heading to be reunited with her husband who was working in Brooklyn as an engraver. He had been sending money to Winnie for a year to pay for the trip.

The night of the disaster, she was awakened by the commotion outside her stern cabin. She dressed her boys but found only two life preservers in her cabin. She put them on her boys and entered the hallway. She quickly found herself lost but soon encountered a crewman who gave her his life preserver and directed her up to the lifeboats, all the while asking her to pray for him if she was saved. After finding their way to the boat deck, Winnie and her sons encountered a problem: the officer in charge of the lifeboat refused to let Willie board because he looked too old. Apparently the straw hat he was wearing made him look older. Nevertheless, Winnie finally persuaded the officers to let the 9-year old join her and Neville in Lifeboat No. 2. All three Coutts were picked up by the *Carpathia*. There were only 17 in the lifeboat, which was designed to hold at least 40-60 people.

Life As *Titanic* Survivors: The family moved to Pittsburgh in 1920, and Mrs. Coutts and Neville moved to California about 20 years later. William became a professional musician, got married, and had two daughters. On Christmas Day 1957, he was found dead in the street in Steubenville, Ohio. His death was attributed to natural causes. He is buried at Sunset View Cemetery in Penn Hills Township near Pittsburgh. He was 55 years old.

His mother, Winnie, died in New Jersey in 1960, at the age of 84.

On December 16, 1958, his brother Neville was one of a dozen or so *Titanic* survivors who attended the New York City premiere of the movie "A Night to Remember" (a 1958 British drama film adaptation of Walter Lord's 1955 book *A Night to Remember*, which recounts the *Titanic's* fateful final night). Neville died in Florida in 1977, at the age of 78.

Victorine Chaudanson
County: Delaware
Town: Springfield
Cemetery: Saints Peter and Paul
Address: 1600 South Sproul Road

The grave of Victorine Chaudanson a woman who survived the sinking.

At the Philadelphia premiere of "A Night to Remember," a woman named Victorine Chaudanson was honored. Miss Chaudanson was a maid for the Ryersons, a wealthy Philadelphia family, and was traveling with them on the *Titanic*. Arthur Ryerson, along with his wife (Emily) and their children (Emily, John and Suzette), were hurrying back to the U.S. after learning of the death of their son, Arthur Jr., who died in a car accident at the age of 20. Mr. Ryerson gave Victorine his life preserver when he saw that she had none. She and Mrs. Ryerson and the children were rescued in Lifeboat No. 5. Mr. Ryerson was lost in the sinking.

Life As a *Titanic* Survivor: Victorine Chaudanson later became Mrs. Henry Perkins and lived in Ridley Park, Pennsylvania. She died on August 13, 1962 (age 87), and is buried as Victorine Perkins at Saints Peter and Paul Cemetery in Springfield, Delaware County.

Sophie Halaut Abraham
County: Westmoreland
Town: Greensburg
Cemetery: Westmoreland County Memorial Park
Address: 150 Eastside Drive and West Newton Road (Route 136)

Another survivor, 18-year old Sophie Halaut Abraham, was returning from Syria where she was visiting family, witnessed some panic. When she arrived near the lifeboats, men were fighting for an opportunity to get in. Several of the ships' officers had to command them to stand back and make way for the women and children. The first sailor who tried to help Mrs.

Abraham into the lifeboat lost his grip on her, and she was tossed into the sea. She was lucky enough to be taken into a crowded lifeboat, but those fortunes quickly changed when that lifeboat was upset by a big wave, dumping everyone on board into the water. Yet another lifeboat picked Mrs. Abraham and a few others out of the water. Four sailors in her lifeboat rowed away from the *Titanic* to safety.

Life As a *Titanic* Survivor: Sophie returned to Greensburg, Pennsylvania, where she lived until her death in December 1976, at the age of 82. She is buried in Westmoreland County Memorial Park in Greensburg.

Lily Potter
Olive (Potter) Earnshaw
County: Philadelphia
Town: Philadelphia
Cemetery: Laurel Hill
Address: 3822 Ridge Avenue

Things went relatively smoothly for Lily Potter and the two passengers who accompanied her aboard the *Titanic*: her daughter (Olive Earnshaw); and her friend (Margaret Hays). Olive was going through a divorce and Lily, now a widow, thought a vacation would be good for her. They invited Margaret to join them. After touring Italy and the Middle East, they booked passage home on another ship. However, after hearing about the *Titanic* and how grand it would be to sail on her, they changed their reservations. Following the collision with the iceberg, Olive and Margaret went to see what had happened. They returned to their cabin and reported to Lily that a steward had told them not to worry and to go back to bed. Lily was upset and did not believe the steward. They dressed quickly and warmly and were put on the first lifeboat launched. All three survived in Lifeboat No. 7.

Life As *Titanic* Survivors: Lily and Olive spent the rest of their lives as huge supporters of the Red Cross. Lily helped found the Southeastern Pennsylvania Chapter of the American Red Cross. She received the Gimbel Award as Philadelphia's outstanding woman in 1939 and gave the $1,000 prize to the Red Cross. She died in January 1954, at the age of 98. Olive remarried and had two sons. She was a Red Cross volunteer for the rest of her life, which ended when she died of cancer in 1958 (age 69). Olive and Lily are buried together at Laurel Hill Cemetery in Philadelphia.

Benjamin Guggenheim (46)
Died at sea
Atlantic Ocean (375 miles South of Newfoundland, and 963 miles northeast of New York City)
Aboard RMS *Titanic*
Body never recovered

Benjamin Guggenheim

"Women and children first!" was the order, but as the situation became more obvious and more desperate, there was some not-so-noble behavior. Many men, however, did act heroically in the face of death. One such notable person was Benjamin Guggenheim, a fabulously wealthy industrialist from Philadelphia. He was traveling with his mistress, a French singer named Leontine Aubart. He went to the boat deck and helped Aubart and her maid into Lifeboat No. 9 (both of whom survived), and then helped other women and children into lifeboats. Once they were loaded, Guggenheim and his valet, Victor Giglio, returned to their cabin and changed into evening wear. Guggenheim was heard to say "we've dressed up in our best and are prepared to go down like gentlemen." He then told a steward:

"If anything should happen to me, tell my wife in New York that I've done my best in doing my duty. No woman shall be left aboard because Ben Guggenheim was a coward."

Guggenheim and Giglio were last seen seated in deck chairs in the foyer of the Grand Staircase, sipping brandy and smoking cigars. The steward survived and delivered the message to Mrs. Guggenheim. Benjamin Guggenheim and Victor Giglio went down with the ship. Their bodies were never recovered. Guggenheim was one of the most prominent Americans lost in the disaster and has been depicted in numerous movies about the *Titanic*.

William C. Dulles (39)

County: Philadelphia
Town: Philadelphia
Cemetery: Laurel Hill
Address: 3822 Ridge Avenue

Another prominent Philadelphian who perished in the disaster was William C. Dulles, a relative of long time CIA director John Foster Dulles, and a prominent Philadelphia lawyer in his own right. Dulles, a bachelor, had been traveling with his mother in Europe. His body was recovered by the Cable Ship (CS) *MacKay-Bennett*, and he was buried at Laurel Hill Cemetery. He was 39.

Final resting place of William Dulles who died when the great ship went down.

Henry Blank

County: Delaware
Town: Drexel Hill
Cemetery: Arlington
Address: 2900 State Road

Mr. Henry Blank, a successful jeweler from New Jersey, was also 39 as he sat aboard the *Titanic* en route for New York. He was traveling alone, returning from a business trip to Europe. On the night of the tragedy at the moment when the *Titanic* hit the iceberg, Blank was playing cards with two men he had befriended on the ship. Someone yelled that the ship had hit an iceberg and all three went up to the Promenade Deck to catch a look at an iceberg, but the berg had passed and was not in sight. The men returned to their game.

Here is the grave of Henry Blank, a Titanic survivor, who found a place in a lifeboat because women who were offered seating refused to leave their husbands.

We will never know how lucky Blank was at cards that night, but he was extremely lucky at life. The *Titanic* came to a stop shortly after the men resumed their game and curiosity got to them. They went below to look for trouble and saw seawater entering the squash court. They hurried to prepare to evacuate. Blank was among the first to arrive on the starboard Boat Deck. He and his friends and the women they were traveling with were assisted into Lifeboat No. 7. It was the first lifeboat lowered into the water. Here, Blank was extremely lucky.

The Captain's order of put "women and children in and lower away" was interpreted differently by *Titanic* Officers Charles Lightoller and William Murdoch, who each took charge of a side (Lightoller the port side; Murdoch the starboard side). Lightoller took the Captain's order to mean women and children *only*; Murdoch took it to mean women and children *first*. Initially, few passengers were willing to board lifeboats. Many women refused to leave the *Titanic* without their husbands and male companions. In an effort to move the evacuation along, Murdoch allowed several men into Lifeboat No. 7. It was lowered with 28 passengers on board despite a capacity of 65. Neither officer knew the capacity of the lifeboats nor that there weren't enough lifeboats for everyone.

Blank helped row away from the sinking ship. After a while, revolver shots could be heard coming from the *Titanic*. As the massive ship began to sink, the lifeboat occupants could hear the screams and cries from those left on board.

Several hours later, Blank and the other occupants of Lifeboat No. 7 were pulled from the icy Atlantic by the *Carpathia*.

Life As a *Titanic* Survivor: Blank returned to his business and prospered for many years. He died from pneumonia on St. Patrick's Day 1949, at the age of 76. He is buried in the family plot in Arlington Cemetery, in Drexel Hill, Pennsylvania.

Richard Williams
Charles Duane Williams (51)
County: Chester
Town: Wayne
Cemetery: Old St. David's Churchyard
Address: 763 South Valley Forge Road

Mr. Charles Williams and his son, Richard, weren't quite so lucky. Charles (sometimes referred to as "C. Duane") was a lawyer originally from Radnor, Pennsylvania, and a direct descendant of Benjamin Franklin. Richard, a 21-year-old accomplished tennis player, had won the Swiss Championship while being tutored privately at a Swiss boarding school, and after playing in some summer tournaments in the U.S., would be entering Harvard in the Fall. The two men were traveling from Geneva back to the U.S.

Final resting place of Richard Williams a Titanic survivor who became a tennis champion.

After the collision, both men left their stateroom and encountered a steward trying to open the door of a cabin behind which a panicking passenger was trapped. The younger Williams broke through the door with his shoulder. The steward threatened to report him for damaging White Star Line property. This event inspired a scene in the 1997 film "Titanic."

The two men wandered the decks as the ship sank under them. They went to the bar and the elder Williams tried to get a steward to fill his flask with whiskey. The steward refused, stating that the bar was closed and it would be against the rules. Charles handed the flask to Richard, which remains a Williams' family heirloom.

As the *Titanic* sunk, Richard and Charles found themselves in the water - swimming for their lives. There was a loud cracking sound, and Richard turned to see his father crushed by the forward smokestack as it crashed down. It almost got Richard too. The resulting wave pushed him towards a lifeboat referred to as "Collapsible A," which was upright but partly flooded as its sides had not been properly raised. Richard clung to the side for some time, as the occupants were being very careful not to take on any more water. Even after being hauled aboard, the occupants had to sit in a foot of freezing water. Many died of hypothermia during the night.

The *Carpathia* arrived near dawn. Richard Williams and those still alive in Collapsible A were lifted aboard. When a doctor on board examined Richard, the doctor recommended amputation of both legs, fearing gangrene. Williams refused permission and instead walked every two hours around the clock, hoping to save his legs.

The decision worked out well for Williams. Three days later when the *Carpathia* arrived in New York, he walked off the ship. Three months later at the Philadelphia Cricket Club, he won the U.S. Mixed Doubles Tennis Championship.

Life As a *Titanic* Survivor: "Dick" Williams (as he was sometimes referred to) continued his tennis career and entered Harvard as planned. He went on to win the U.S. Singles Championship in 1914 and again in 1916, the U.S. Men's Doubles Championship twice (1925 and 1926), and the Wimbledon Men's Championship in 1920. In 1914, he played with another *Titanic* survivor, Karl Behr (rescued on Lifeboat No. 5) on the U.S. Davis Cup team. He subsequently captained the Davis Cup team from 1921 through 1925. At the 1924 Olympics in Paris, Williams and Hazel Wightman won the gold medal in mixed doubles.

Richard Williams served with distinction in the U.S. Army during World War I and was awarded the Croix de Guerre for heroism as well as the Chevalier de la Legion d'Honneur (Legion of Honor), two of France's highest military honors.

Williams went on to be a successful investment banker in Philadelphia and for 20 years served as President of the Historical Society of Pennsylvania. He died of emphysema in 1968, at the age of 77. He is buried in Old St. David

Church Cemetery in Wayne, Pennsylvania. Next to his grave is a memorial marker for his father, C. Duane Williams, whose body was never recovered.

George Dunton Widener (50)
Harry Elkins Widener (27)
Eleanor Elkins (Widener) Rice
County: Philadelphia
Town: Philadelphia
Cemetery: Laurel Hill
Address: 3822 Ridge Avenue

Reports say that one of the people seen with C. Duane Williams during the last moments of the *Titanic* was 50-year-old George Dunton Widener, one of the wealthiest men in Philadelphia. George and his wife (Eleanor) and son (Harry) were returning from a trip to Paris, where they had gone with the intention of finding a chef for George's new Philadelphia hotel, The Ritz Carlton.

Their fate was more in line with what was expected. After the evacuation began, George and Harry escorted Eleanor to Lifeboat No. 4 and helped her in. John Jacob Astor IV, who was one of the richest men in the world, did

The Widener mausoleum honors both George and Harry Widener. Father and son, who perished on the voyage. The wife and mother Eleanor who was a survivor was laid to rest here.

the same with his wife. The men were refused entry themselves by Officer Lightoller, who launched the boat with 20 of the 60 seats unoccupied.

George and Harry died, and Eleanor was rescued by the *Carpathia*. Harry's body was never recovered. George's body was recovered by the *MacKay-Bennett*, but its condition was such that it was buried at sea. A memorial service for the two of them was held at St. Paul's Episcopal Church in Elkins Park, Pennsylvania, where stained-glass windows were dedicated in their memory.

Life As a *Titanic* Survivor: Eleanor presented Harvard University with a two million dollar library in memory of her son Harry, a 1907 Harvard graduate. She also rebuilt St. Paul's Episcopal Church as a memorial to her husband, and in 1929 gave $300,000 to the Hill School at Pottstown for a general science building in memory of Harry, a 1903 Hill School graduate.

In 1915, Mrs. Widener married explorer Dr. Alexander Hamilton Rice and traveled extensively in South America, Europe and India. In July 1937, while shopping in a Paris store, she died of a heart attack, at the age of 76.

Eleanor Elkins Rice is buried in the Widener mausoleum in Philadelphia's Laurel Hill Cemetery. Her crypt makes no mention of the *Titanic*. Harry and George Widener have cenotaphs in the mausoleum, both of which reference the ship.

William Ernest Carter
Lucile Polk Carter Brooke
Counties: Montgomery, Berks
Towns: Bala Cynwyd, Birdsboro
Cemeteries: West Laurel Hill, St. Michael's[2]
Addresses: 227 Belmont Avenue, Mill and Church Streets

William Thornton Carter
Lucile Carter Reeves
County: Montgomery
Towns: Bala Cynwyd, King of Prussia
Cemeteries: West Laurel Hill, Valley Forge Memorial Gardens
Addresses: 227 Belmont Avenue, 352 South Gulph Road

Things turned out differently for the Carter clan from Philadelphia, who ironically on the night of the accident were together with the Wideners at a dinner party in honor of the ship's Captain. William Carter, 36 years old, was traveling with his wife, Lucile (also 36), and his children (11-year-old son, William, and 13-year-old daughter, Lucile). Also traveling with them were their maid (Auguste Serreplan), Mr. Carter's servant (Alexander Cairns) and his chauffeur (Charles Aldworth).

---

2 Now known as the New First Baptist Church of Birdsboro

The original story was that Cairns, Aldworth, and Mr. Carter escorted his wife, two children and maid to Lifeboat No. 4. The three men then left, accompanied by George Widener, John Astor and John Thayer (see page 205 for more on Thayer). Mrs. Carter, her son and daughter, and the maid were all rescued. The men all died, *except for Mr. Carter.* Carter escaped on the Collapsible "C" lifeboat, along with Bruce Ismay. Ismay was the President of White Star Lines, the company that owned the Titanic. In the tragedy's aftermath, Ismay was savaged by both the American and British Press for deserting the ship while women and children were still on board. Some papers called him the "Coward of the Titanic." There are accounts that Ismay and the elder Carter stepped into Collapsible C at the last minute. By other accounts, Carter was swimming in the water and then picked up by the lifeboat. Whatever happened, Carter actually ended up on board the *Carpathia* before his family members. More than two hours after his arrival, his wife and children reached the *Carpathia* in Lifeboat No. 4, which Mrs. Carter had helped row.

Grave of William Ernest Carter and his son William Carter both of whom survived the sinking.

Two years later, Mrs. Carter sued for divorce and testified that her husband had left her and their children to fend for themselves. She said that after the *Titanic* hit the iceberg at 11:40 p.m., Mr. Carter came to the stateroom, told her to get up, get herself and the children dressed, and then he essentially ... vanished. According to her, from that moment until the time she arrived at the *Carpathia* around 8:00 a.m. the next morning, she did not once see Mr. Carter.

Life As *Titanic* Survivors: After the divorce, Lucile married George Brooke in 1914. She died in 1934 at the age of 58 and is buried in St. Michael's Cemetery in Birdsboro, Pennsylvania. Her tombstone reads: "Lucile Polk Brooke."

William Ernest Carter died in 1940, at the age of 65. He was buried in a huge mausoleum in West Laurel Hill Cemetery. His son, William Thornton Carter, died in 1985, at the age of 84. He was buried alongside his father.

The daughter, Lucile, married a man named Samuel J. Reeves. She died in 1962, at the age of 64. Lucile Carter Reeves is reportedly buried in Valley Forge Memorial Gardens, but when the authors visited there, the staff could not find any record of her being there.

John Borland Thayer, Jr. (49)
Marian Thayer
John B. ("Jack") Thayer III

County: Montgomery
Town: Bryn Mawr
Cemetery: Church of the Redeemer
Address: 230 Pennswood Road

Memorial to Marian and John Thayer who were both passengers on the great ship. Only Marian survived the voyage.

Also at that dinner party hosted by the Wideners were John and Marian Thayer of Philadelphia, along with their 17-year-old son, Jack. Mr. Thayer was the second Vice President of the Pennsylvania Railroad. They were preparing for bed when the collision occurred. Jack at first went to investigate and returned to put on warm clothes and alert his parents. They went up to the "A" Deck where things were crowded and noisy. Jack and his parents were separated in the confusion, but John saw Marian safely into Lifeboat No. 4.

Jack encountered a friend he had met earlier that evening over coffee, Milton Long, and tried to board a lifeboat, but they were turned away because they were men. They discussed jumping overboard and swimming to a lifeboat, but decided against it for the moment.

John watched as Lifeboat No. 4 was lowered and his wife, Marian, helped row away from the *Titanic*. He then joined his friends, Charles Duane Williams, George Widener, and George's son, Harry, to await their fate. His body was never recovered.

Jack and Milton had watched the last lifeboats being lowered and realized they were not full. They now felt that jumping and swimming to a boat was their best chance. At 2:15 a.m. – just minutes before the *Titanic* slipped beneath the ocean's surface – the two men along with hundreds of other passengers made their way towards the stern of the ship. As the water rushed up the sinking deck, Long and Thayer stood at the starboard rail near the second smokestack, shook hands and prepared to jump into the water, now just 12 to 15 feet below them. It was the last time the two of them would ever see each other.

It was fortunate that Jack Thayer was a stronger swimmer. He struggled in the numbing cold but ultimately did manage to successfully swim against the suction of the sinking liner. Long did not fare as well. In subsequent interviews, Jack said that although he never actually saw Long again after the two of them jumped, it was his belief that Long had "been sucked into the deck below" and drowned.

Jack swam until he reached the Collapsible "B" lifeboat, which was overturned as a result of having been improperly launched. About 35 men were clinging precariously to the hull of the capsized boat. A few of those men helped pull Jack (who by that time was too exhausted to help himself) from the frigid water. Realizing the danger to the boat of being swamped by the mass of swimmers trying to reach them, the men who had found refuge on Collapsible B slowly paddled away from them.

Grave of Titanic survivor Jack Thayer who later committed suicide.

They drifted all night, trying to remain motionless so as not to slip off into the icy water. After daylight, Lifeboat Nos. 4 and 12 came to their aid. Thayer was so distracted trying to get into boat 12 that he did not notice his mother in boat 4 nearby. Likewise, his mother was so numbed by the cold that she did not see him either. When Lifeboat No. 12 finally was rescued by the *Carpathia*, Jack and his mother were reunited and discovered that the senior Thayer, John, had not made it.

Life As *Titanic* Survivors: Marian Thayer never remarried. She died on April 14, 1944, the 32nd anniversary of the disaster, at the age of 72. She is buried in the Church of the Redeemer Cemetery in Bryn Mawr, Pennsylvania.

Jack Thayer went on to graduate from the University of Pennsylvania, served as a captain in the artillery during World War I, got married and had five children, and had a career in banking and finance. In 1940, he described his experiences with the *Titanic*'s sinking in vivid detail in a self-published pamphlet printed for family and friends. This paper was published again in 2012 as "A Survivor's Tale: The Titanic by John B. Thayer."

Both of Jack's sons, Edward and John the IV, enlisted in the armed forces during World War II. In October 1943, Edward was killed in action in the Pacific. Jack had survived the *Titanic,* but he could not survive the death of a son. He committed suicide on September 20, 1945. He was found in an automobile at 48th and Parkside Avenue with his wrists and throat cut. He was 50 years old. He too is buried at the Church of the Redeemer Cemetery.

Charlotte Cardeza
Thomas Cardeza
County: Montgomery
Town: Bala Cynwyd
Cemetery: West Laurel Hill
Address: 227 Belmont Avenue

Another Pennsylvanian who survived the disaster was Mrs. Charlotte Cardeza. Her father, Thomas Drake, was a co-founder of Fidelity Insurance. Mrs. Cardeza - a lover of big-game hunting - was returning home to Germantown, Pennsylvania with her 36-year-old son (Thomas), after an African safari and a visit to Thomas' hunting reserve in Hungary. They were accompanied on board the *Titanic* by Mrs. Cardeza's personal maid (Anna Ward) and Thomas' servant (Gustave Lesueur). The Cardeza entourage brought fourteen trunks, four suitcases, and three crates of baggage. They stayed in the most expensive suite on the *Titanic*, which featured two bedrooms, a sitting room, and a private 50-foot promenade.

In a strange twist of fate, all four members of their party - including two males - were allowed to board Lifeboat No. 3, and all four were rescued by the *Carpathia*.

Life As *Titanic* Survivors: Mrs. Cardeza died on August 1, 1939, at the age of 75. She is buried in a mausoleum in West Laurel Hill Cemetery. Thomas went on to be a director of his grandfather's company, Fidelity Insurance, from 1922-1951. Thomas died in June 1952, at the age of 77, and is buried with his mother in West Laurel Hill Cemetery.

Anna Ward, who had a premonition that something bad was going to happen, had to be persuaded to make the trip by her mother. She went on to marry Mrs. Cardeza's gardener, William Moynahan. She died on Christmas Day 1955, at the age of 81, and is buried with her husband in West Laurel Hill Cemetery.

Fortunately for chocolate lovers all over the world, Milton Hershey and his wife, Kitty, who had put a $300 deposit down for tickets on the *Titanic*, did not make the journey.

Milton Hershey c. 1905

The Hersheys were on a lengthy trip to Nice, France, and had planned months in advance to make their return voyage home aboard the supposedly-unsinkable luxury vessel. However, urgent (and ultimately, life-saving!) business matters arose in the U.S. for which Mr. Hershey was needed. He and Kitty thus had to cancel their *Titanic* reservations and return to America a few days earlier than planned, ironically aboard the German ship, *Amerika*. They arrived back home several days before the *Titanic* sunk.

The check for the transaction, made out to White Star Lines, is still in the Hershey Community Archives. See chapter 14 within on Milton Hershey.

If You Go:

We have said many times in our various volumes what treasures Laurel Hill Cemetery and West Laurel Hill Cemetery are. They contain hundreds of graves of interesting and important historical figures, many of whom are mentioned in our books.

Some other graves of interest in other cemeteries mentioned in this chapter are:

At Old Saint David Church Cemetery, you will find one of the graves of Anthony Wayne (see *Keystone Tombstones Volume 3* chapter 29), a Revolutionary War hero who is buried in two places.

Also at Old Saint David Church Cemetery is the grave of William Atterbury, who was vice president of the Pennsylvania Railroad when he was abruptly commissioned a Brigadier General in the United States Army during World War I. He was appointed Director General of Transportation for the Armed Services in Europe. His reorganization of the European Railroad Network contributed to the victory for the Allies. He was nicknamed "The Railroad General" and received medals from many nations, including the Distinguished Service Medal and the French Legion of Honor.

The Church of the Redeemer Cemetery has the grave of artist Mary Cassatt, who became the sole American artist at the forefront of the Impressionist movement. She is widely recognized as one of the most important figures in the development of American culture and an inspiration to a generation of women in the arts. You will also find the grave of George Earle, the Governor of Pennsylvania from 1935-1939, and a confidant and advisor to President Franklin D. Roosevelt.

Three interesting sports figures can be found at Saints Peter and Paul Cemetery:

Danny Murtaugh, who was a major league baseball player and manager. He was named National League Manager of the Year in 1944 with the Pittsburgh Pirates. He later led the Pirates to the famous upset of the heavily-favored New York Yankees in the 1960 World Series, and won the championship again in the 1971 World Series versus the Baltimore Orioles.

John Facenda, who was a sports newscaster for WCAU-TV in Philadelphia for 25 years and the voice of NFL Films for two decades.

Jack "Blackjack" Ferrante, who played for eight seasons as a wide receiver for the Philadelphia Eagles in the 1940's, despite never having attended college. He was discovered in the sandlots of Philadelphia and wound up being named an All-Pro two times and scored 31 touchdowns over his career.

At Arlington Cemetery are the graves of:.

Morris "Morrie" Rath, who was a major league baseball player for the Philadelphia Athletics (1909-10), the Cleveland Naps (1910), Chicago White Sox (1912-13) and Cincinnati Reds (1919-1920). Batting leadoff for the Reds in the 1919 World Series, Rath became a key figure in the ensuing "Black Sox" scandal when he was hit by White Sox pitcher Eddie Cicotte with the second pitch of the Series. This was believed to be a signal to gamblers that the White Sox had agreed to throw the series.

Morrie Rath baseball card

Theodore Smith, who was an Indian Wars Medal of Honor recipient.

"The Pope of Pop"

ANDY WARHOL

County: Allegheny
Town: Bethel Park
Cemetery: Saint John the Baptist Byzantine Catholic
Address: Intersection of Connor Road and State Route 88

He was known as the "Pope of Pop." He was famous worldwide as a painter, filmmaker, record producer, and author. He was the first to come up with the phrase "fifteen minutes of fame." He was also well known because of the people with whom he associated. These groups included intellectuals, celebrities, the very wealthy, and street people living a Bohemian life style. He is buried in Pennsylvania, about five miles outside of his hometown of Pittsburgh.

Andy Warhol was born and named Andy Warhola on August 6, 1928. Warhol's father immigrated to the United States from Slovakia in 1914. His mother arrived in the States in 1921. Warhol's father found employment in a coal mine. Warhol had two older brothers and the family attended a Byzantine Catholic Church.

At an early age, Warhol exhibited talent in drawing and painting. However, he was not a healthy child. He was often bed-ridden, and he had few friends at school. Because of the time he spent at home, his relationship with his mother was a close one. On days when he couldn't make it to school, he passed the time listening to the radio. During this period, he also began collecting pictures of movie stars. Warhol would come to believe that this period in his life was very important in developing his personality. When he was thirteen, his father was killed in a work accident.

After he graduated from high school, Warhol studied commercial art at the Carnegie Institute of Technology in Pittsburgh. He graduated in 1949 and found employment in New York City doing magazine illustrations and advertising. The magazines he worked for included "Vogue" and "Harper's Bazaar." He quickly became one of the most sought after commercial artists in New York City.

It was in the fifties that Warhol began exhibiting his own work. His New York shows were met with much success. By the early 1960's, he was ready to take his work across the country to the west coast. On July 9, 1962, he opened an exhibition in Los Angeles that marked the premiere of his pop art out west. Later in that same year he opened another exhibit in New York City. This show included the works titled "Marilyn Diptych", "100 Soup Cans", and "100 Coke Bottles." It was during this time that Andy began to

Andy Warhol

paint celebrities such as Marilyn Monroe, Elvis, and Muhammad Ali. He also founded "The Factory," the studio that became the center of his work. Other artists, musicians, and underground celebrity types were drawn to him. His work while popular was controversial.

In December of 1962, New York's Museum of Modern Art held a conference on pop art. Warhol was attacked for surrendering to consumerism. Such attacks on Warhol and his work became common during the sixties. Warhol was changing the way people viewed art. In fact he was raising the question "What is and what isn't art?" As the leader of the pop movement, he became an inviting target to critics.

It was during this time that Warhol branched out into filmmaking. He made more than 60 films between 1963 and 1968. Warhol discovered his own stars for his films and named them superstars. This group included Edie Sedgwick, Jackie Curtis, Nico, Viva, and Ultra Violet among others. An emerging young singer by the name of Bob Dylan did screen tests for Warhol. There is speculation that Dylan's relationship with Edie Sedgwick ended any chance of Dylan and Warhol working together. Why this proved a strain is anybody's guess as Warhol was a homosexual. The films themselves were often unusual. For example the movie "Sleep" monitors a sleeping man for six hours. Another film titled "Empire" is eight hours long and treats the viewer to scenes of the Empire State Building at dusk. His most successful film was "Chelsea Girls" which was released in 1966. His last film was 1968's "Blue Movie," which stars Viva, shows the star having sex and fooling around in bed with a man for about 33 minutes. In the seventies, Warhol pulled the films he had directed out of circulation. After his death, some of the films were restored and are shown occasionally at film festivals.

On June 3, 1968 a woman, Valerie Solanas, showed up at the Factory and attempted to retrieve a script she had given to Warhol. When the script couldn't be located, she was turned away. Solanas was known at the Factory, having appeared in Warhol's 1968 film "I, A Man." Later that day, Solanas returned to Warhol's studio and shot him and art critic Mario Amaya. While Amaya received only minor injuries, Warhol was seriously wounded. Surgeons had to open his chest and massage his heart to save him. Solanas was arrested the next day. She said she shot Warhol because he had too much control over her life. He would suffer physical effects from the shooting until the day he died and the incident also had an effect on his art. News coverage of the assault ended quickly when Senator Robert F. Kennedy was assassinated two days later.

Compared to the turbulent sixties, Warhol's life aroused much less controversy in the following decade. During the seventies, Warhol worked at lining up the rich and famous for portrait commissions. His clients included the Shah of Iran, John Lennon, Diana Ross, and Mick Jagger. In 1975, he published the book "The Philosophy of Andy Warhol." One of the ideas he sets forth in the book is "Making money is art, and working is art and good business is the best art." During this period Warhol could be found at high profile New York nightspots including the famous Studio 54. Those who observed him described him as quiet and shy.

In the eighties, Warhol aligned himself with young and upcoming artists. Partially due to this, he had a re-emergence in terms of critical and financial success. By this time, the critics were calling Warhol a "business artist,"

BEST OF KEYSTONE TOMBSTONES

The noted artist lies buried in the family plot outside of Pittsburgh. Note the grave goods left by visitors, including Campbell Soup cans, coins, and a guitar pick.

and they didn't mean it in a good way. The critics jumped on his seventies portraits of celebrities describing them as commercial and without any depth. Since then, other art critics have come to admire the images calling them, among other things, a brilliant mirror of those times. Warhol, who always had a special place in his heart for Hollywood, summed it up himself by saying, "I love Los Angeles. I love Hollywood. They're so beautiful. Everything's plastic, but I love plastic. I want to be plastic."

In February of 1987, Warhol entered a New York hospital for routine gallbladder surgery. By all reports, the surgery was a success and he was on the road to recovery. However, at around 6:30 in the morning on February 22, 1987, Warhol died in his sleep. The cause of death was a sudden cardiac arrhythmia.

Warhol's brothers arranged to have his body returned to Pittsburgh for burial. In the coffin Warhol was dressed in a black suit, a paisley tie, a platinum wig, and he was wearing sunglasses. Yoko Ono made an appearance at the service. At the conclusion of the Mass, Warhol's body was taken to Saint John the Baptist Byzantine Catholic Cemetery in Bethel Park. Warhol was laid to rest next to his mother and father. However, before the coffin was lowered into the grave, a bottle of Estee Lauder perfume called "Beautiful" was laid beneath him. New York City didn't forget Andy. On April 1, 1987 a memorial service was held at Saint Patrick's Cathedral. More than 20,000 people attended.

If You Go:
The cemetery is divided into two levels. Warhol is buried on the upper half approximately a quarter of the way through the cemetery from the upper entrance. The burial site is on the right side of the road and should be easy to spot. Look for Campbell soup cans.

There are plenty of things to do and see in Pittsburgh, but if you make this trip you may want to visit the Andy Warhol Museum located on the north side of the city at 117 Sandusky Street. While you are on the north side, should you be in need of refreshment, we made a stop at a nearby spot called "The Tilted Kilt." The establishment features a very attractive work staff who provide excellent service.

INDEX

Aaron, Hank, 75
Abrams, Cal, 3
Acevedo, Kirk, 28
Albright, Charles, 122
Ali, Muhammad, 48, 58, 61 - 64, 211
Allen, Steve, 107
Amaya, Mario, 212
Ambrose, Stephen, 26
Anderson, Loni, 107
Anderson, Willie, 64
Angleton, James, 116, 117
Apostoli, Fred, 47
Archer, Jules, 21
Arena, James, 102
Armistead, Lewis, 81, 83, 84
Armstrong, Louis, 76, 176
Arnold, Everett (Busy), 143
Arthur, Chester, 86
Ashburn, Richie, 1 - 7, 10
Bach, Joe, 170
Barber, Samuel, 22
Barton, Clara, 96
Beaver, James Adams, 150
Bell, Bert, 171
Bell, Cool Papa, 76
Bennett, Tony, 164
Benny, Jack, 107
Berry, Chu, 176
Bettina, Melio, 47
Bergman, Maurice, 77
Bettie, Jerome, 154
Binzen, Peter, 160
Bissell, Richard M., 112
Blades, Bennie, 144
Booth, John Wilkes, 43
Borden, Joseph Emley, 22
Boyle, James, 103
Boyle James, 124, 125, 127, 129
Boyle, Thomas, 41
Bradlee, Ben, 112, 116
Brandeis, Louis, 110
Brodhead, Daniel, 117
Bronson, James H., 156
Broughton, Henry, 176
Brown, Jerome, 144
Brown, Jim, 154
Brown, Jordan, 28
Brown Sr., Lawrence, 178
Brua, Margaret, 30
Bruce, Harold Anson, 185
Buchanan, James, 30, 69, 184
Buell, Don Carlos, 88
Burleigh, Nina, 112, 113
Burns, George, 79
Butkas, Dick, 172
Butler, Smedley, 18 - 22
Butler, Thomas Stalker, 19
Byrd, Sara Joanne, 163
Cagney, Jimmy, 77
Cameron, Simon, 30 - 34, 71, 181
Camiel, Peter, 158
Campbell, Alec, 120, 124, 126, 127, 131, 132
Campbell, Bill, 7
Campbell, John, 130
Campbell, Patrick, 132
Cappelletti, John, 144
Capone, Al, 21
Carey, James Lemuel, 156
Carnegie, Andrew, 94, 97, 98
Carroll, James, 124, 125, 127, 129
Carson, Johnny, 1, 164
Carter, Jimmy, 103
Casey, Bob, 167
Charleston, Oscar, 76
Cheslock, Michael, 35, 38, 39, 41, 43
Child, Julia, 164
Clark, Champ, 179
Clark, John, 11
Clay, Cassius, 154
Clay, Henry, 179
Cleland, John, 148
Clemente, Roberto, 152
Clifford, Clark, 112
Clinton, Bill, 17
Cochrane, Eddie, 105
Collins, Joan, 105
Conn, Billy, 45 - 50, 80, 151, 152, 169
Connor, Ned, 136
Connery, Sean, 132
Coolidge, Calvin, 20
Cope, Myron, 151, 153 - 155
Copperfield, David, 164
Cosby, Bill, 166
Cosell, Howard, 58, 62, 63, 154
Couch, Darius, 83
Crowley, Jim, 104
Crump, Ray, 116
Curtin, Andrew, 150
Curtis, Jackie, 212
Curtis, Tony, 79
Dailey, Dan, 105
Daly, Dan, 20
Daniels, Terry, 62
Danko, Rick, 175
Dark, Alvin, 1
Daughen, Joseph, 160
Davis, David, 32
Davis, James, 20
Davis, Miles, 76
Deringer, Henry, 10
Domino, Fats, 105
Donahue, John, 127, 131
Donnelly, Thomas, 124
Doyle, Michael, 122 - 124, 127
Dougherty, Neil, 130
Duffy, Thomas, 124, 125, 127, 129, 131
Dulles, Allen, 112
Dunn, Harry, 22
Duranko, Pete, 99
Durant, Michael, 17
Durham, Yank, 60
Dylan, Bob, 175, 178, 212
Eisenhower, Dwight, 187
Ellis, Jimmy, 61
Elvis, 211
Engle, Rip, 143
English, William Hayden, 86
Estoppey, Ethel, 26
Ewbank, Weeb, 143
Farrar, Jim, 102, 103
Feldman, Myer, 113
Fisher, John, 127
Fisher, Thomas, 131, 132
Flood, Dan, 44, 104
Ford, Gerald R., 149
Foreman, George, 58, 62, 63
Fornance, Joseph, 81
Foster, Bob, 62
Foster, Stephen, 76

Franklin, Aretha, 177
Franklin, Benjamin, 51 - 56
Franklin, Josiah, 51
Frazier, Joe William, 58 - 64
Frazier, Tommy, 146
Freeh, Louis, 148
Frick, Henry Clay, 94
Frum, Elsie, 98
Furillo, Carl, 28
Futch, Eddie, 60 - 62, 64
Garfield, James, 86
Gargan, Joseph, 102
Gasparon, Ann, 14
Gathers, Hank, 178
Geary, John White, 34, 65 - 71
Geary, Richard, 65
Gee, Jack, 175, 176
Gertsch, John Gary, 173
Geyer, Frank, 139
Gibson, Josh, 72 - 76
Gillespie, Dizzy, 76
Gleason, Jackie, 107
Goode, Wilson, 160
Gorshin, Frank, 50, 77 - 80
Goss, Woody, 60
Gowen, Franklin, 64, 119, 121, 125, 129, 130 - 132
Graham, Katherine, 112
Grant, Cary, 77, 105
Grant, Ulysses, S., 85, 86
Greenlee, William (Gus), 76
Guarnere, William, 27
Hall, David, 54
Hamilton, Milo, 153
Hammond, John, 176, 177
Hampton, Lionel, 176
Hancock, John, 55
Hancock, Winfield Scott, 81 - 87
Hanks, Tom, 26
Hargitay, Mariska, 107
Harris, Richard, 132
Harris, William, 76
Harrison, Ronnie, 107
Hartranft, John Frederick, 87
Harvey, Walter, 170
Henderson, Fletcher, 176
Henderson, Mary Church, 69
Hendrix, Jimi, 107
Hershey, Milton S., 89 - 93

Hess, John, 95, 98
Highsmith, Alonzo, 144
Holiday, Billie, 176, 177
Holiday, Judy, 79
Holmes, Henry H., 133, 135 - 140
Holton, E. S., 135
Hooker, General, 83
Hope, Bob, 107
Huber, Hans, 60
Ickes, Harold, 110
Irvin, Michael, 144
Irvin, Monte, 75
Jackson, Andrew, 30
Jackson, Stonewall, 20, 69
Jagger, Mick, 212
James, Gomer, 36, 37
Janney, Peter, 114, 116
Jardine, Clark, 11
Jefferson, Thomas, 55
Johnson, Andrew, 85, 182, 183
Johnson, Bobby, 176
Johnson, George, 61
Johnson, Jimmy, 144
Johnson, Julius (Judy), 72, 76
Johnson, Roy, 187
Jones, Davy, 79
Jones, John P., 122 - 124, 126, 127
Joplin, Janis, 177
Jordan, David, M., 87
Kahn, Roger, 29
Kalas, Harry Norbert, 1, 3, 5, 7 - 10
Keaton, Michael, 164
Kehoe, Jack, 44, 118, 119, 125, 126, 128 - 132
Keith, William, 51
Kelly, Edward, 122, 123, 125, 127
Kelly, Grace, 161
Kelly Sr., John B., 161
Kendrick, W. Freeland, 20
Kennedy, Edward Moore, 100 - 103
Kennedy, Jackie, 113
Kennedy, John F., 100, 107, 110, 112 - 115, 117, 171, 183

Kennedy, Robert, 100, 101, 115, 212
Kerrigan, James, 121 - 125, 127 - 129
Kiesling, Walt, 172, 173
Kiner, Ralph, 152
King, Nellie, 153
Kingseed, Cole, 26
Knox, Philander Chase, 94, 98
Kohner, Paul, 77
Kopechne, Mary Jo, 44, 100 - 104, 109
Kuhn, Bowie, 75
Kurowski, George (Whitey), 28
LaFauvre, Anna, 14
Lambert, Jack, 154
Lancaster, Burt, 77, 190
Langdon, Frank, 129, 130
Lawrence, David, 50
Leary, Timothy, 113, 114
Lee, Robert E., 85
Lennon, John, 212
Leonard, Buck, 75
Lewis, Damien, 26
Lewis, Dewitt Clinton, 22
Lincoln, Abraham, 30, 32 - 34, 85, 117, 181
Lindbergh, Mildred, 154
Linden, Robert, 121, 124
Linkletter, Art, 166
Logan, Margaret Ann, 65
Lombardi, Vince, 141, 143
Look, Christopher (Huck), 103
Louis, Joe, 45, 47 - 49, 58, 169
Lumet, Baruch, 105
Lumet, Sidney, 105
L'Velle, Martin, 130
MacArthur, Douglas, 20
Mack, Connie, 64, 160
Mallon, Brian, 87
Malm, 102
Mansfield, Jayne, 105 - 109
Mantle, Mickey, 1
Marciano, Rocky, 58
Markham, Paul, 102
Martin, Dean, 79

Martin, Sheriff, 38, 39, 41, 42
Mason, Helen, 72
Mathis, Buster, 60
Mays, Willie, 1, 75
Mazeroski, Bill, 151
McAllister, James, 124
McCallister, Charles, 124, 125
McCallister, Ellen, 124, 125, 131
McCarron, Barney, 121, 122
McCrory, John, 99
McFeely, Fred, 163
McGehen, Hugh, 123 - 125, 127, 129
McKeever, Michael, 161
McKenna, James, 121
McNulty, Kathleen, 171
McParlan, James, 121 - 125, 129, 130, 132
McQueary, Mike, 147
Meade, George, 84, 86
Melvin, Harold, 64, 178
McClellan, George, 83
Mellon, Andrew, 94
Mencken, H. L., 45
Menotti, Carlo, 22
Meyer, Cord, 110, 112, 117
Meyer, Mary Pinchot, 110 - 117
Mifflin, Thomas, 184
Minick, John W., 17
Mitchell, Andrea, 157
Moffitt, George, 13
Monroe, Marilyn, 211
Morgan, Richard, 176
Mudgett, Herman Webster, 133, 134
Mudgett, Jeff, 139
Mudgett, Robert Lovering, 135
Munley, Thomas, 124, 127, 129
Murphy, Eddie, 164
Murtha, John, 99
Musial, Stan, 5
Mussolini, Benito, 20
Naugle, John, 12
Neale, Earle, 172
Neville, John, 76

Newcombe, Don, 3
Nico, 212
Nix, Robert, 158, 161
Nixon, Richard, 144, 165
Noakes, Cordella, 11 - 15
Noakes, Dewilla, 11 - 15
Noakes, Elmo, 11 - 16
Nobile, Phillip, 113
Obama, Barack, 167
O'Brien, Jim, 153
O'Donnell, Charles, 124, 125, 131
O'Donnell, James, 124
O'Donnell, Kenneth, 114, 115
Oliver, Al, 153
O'Neill, Tip, 115, 179
Ono, Yoko, 214
Osbourne, Tom, 146
Oswald, Lee Harvey, 115
Page, Ted, 75, 76
Paige, Satchel, 74 - 76
Parisi, Jack (the Dandy), 44
Pastor, Bob, 47
Pastore, John, 165
Paterno, Joe, 141 - 149
Penn William, 54
Penrose, Boies, 10
Peters, Ethel Conway, 19
Peterson, Robert W., 75
Pierce, Franklin, 67, 69
Pierce, Winifred, 11 - 15
Pinchot, Gifford, 110, 114, 117
Pitcher, Molly, 17
Pitezel, Benjamin, 136, 138, 139
Poland, Suzanne, 143
Polk, James K., 67
Powell, Morgan, 127
Powers, Dave, 115
Prince, Bob, 47, 151 - 153 - 155
Pugh, Evan, 150
Rainey, Ma, 175
Rankin, Oscar, 47
Ray, Johnny, 45
Rayburn, Sam, 179
Rayford, Linwood L., 116
Raymond, Tubby, 149
Reed, Deborah, 53, 55

Reed, George W., 99
Reed, James, 98
Reese, Harry, 93
Reese, Pee Wee, 3
Reynolds, John, 83, 184
Richard, Little, 105
Rickles, Don, 78
Rizzo, Frank, 64, 157 - 160
Roarity, James, 123, 124, 127, 129
Roberts, Robin, 3, 4
Robertson, Robbie, 175
Robinson, Edward G., 77
Robinson, Ray (Sugar), 58
Rockne, Knute, 169
Rodgers, Guy, 178
Rogers, Fred, 162 - 167
Rooney, Art, 49, 168 - 173
Rooney, James P., 170
Roosevelt, Franklin D., 20, 21
Rosenbaum, Ron, 113
Ross, Betsy, 57
Ross, Diana, 212
Ross, Edmund, 183
Roswell, Albert (Rosey), 76, 152
Royer, Joseph, 89
Roth, Alice, 4
Russell, Almira (Allie), 81, 83
Russell, Lillian, 76
Ruth, Babe, 72, 75
Rynearson, Edward, 156
Sam, Vilbrun, 20
Sandusky, Jerry, 147 - 149
Sanger, Thomas, 124, 125, 127
Schwarzenegger, Arnold, 107
Scott, Winfield, 81
Sedgwick, Edie, 212
Sedgwick, Norma, 11, 13 - 15
Seward, William, 32
Shaara, Michael, 83
Shapp, Milton, 130, 131
Shomo, Frank, 98
Shughart, Randall d., 17
Sickles, General, 84
Sinatra, Frank, 7
Sinex, Robert H., 43
Siney, John, 119
Sisler, Dick, 3

Slemmer, Adam Jacoby, 87, 88
Smathers, George, 100
Smith, Bessie, 174 - 178
Smith, Hugh, 176, 177
Smith, Jimmy, 47, 49
Smith, Joe, 176
Smith, Lydia Hamilton, 179
Smith, Mamie, 175
Smith, Mary Louise, 47
Snider, Duke, 1
Solanas, Valerie, 212
Spielberg, Steven, 26
Stander, Ron, 62
Stargell, Willie, 75, 153
Stassen, Harold, 112
Stengel, Casey, 4
Stevens, Thaddeus, 179 - 184
Stewart, Kordell, 154
Stone, Oliver, 115
Stuhldreher, Harry, 50
Sullivan, Ed, 79, 107
Surratt, Mary, 85
Sweeney, Catherine (Kitty), 91
Tarantino, Quenton, 79
Taylor, Zachary, 67
Testaverde, Vinny, 144
Thaw, Benjamin, 94
Thaw, Harry, 76, 94
Thompson, Alexis, 171
Thorpe, Jim, 44, 185 - 191
Tilden, Bill, 64
Tinker, Harold, 76
Titanic Victims and Survivors, 192 - 209
Toye, Joe, 23, 26 - 28
Traynor, Pie, 172
Truitt, Ann, 115, 116
Unitas, Johnny, 172, 173
Uren, William, 124, 125, 127
Van Buren, Martin, 30, 32
Vanderbilt Jr., Cornelius, 20
Van Wyck, Charles Henry, 117
Vaughn, Sarah, 177
Violet, Ultra, 212
Wagner, Boyd (Buzz), 99
Walker, Jimmy, 79
Walton, William, 115
Warhol, Andy, 210 - 214
Warner, Pop, 185, 187
Washington, Buck, 176
Washington, George, 55, 117
Webb, Jack, 105
Welsh, Oliver, 37
White, Byron (Whizzer), 170, 171
Whyte Jr., William Hollingsworth, 22
Wiggins, Henry, 116
Williams, Marion, 64
Williams, Minnie, 136
Williams, Ted, 3, 75
Wilson, James, 56
Winters, Dick, 23 - 28
Wood, Natalie, 105
Woodland, Woody, 115
Worts, Henry, 71
Yemelyyanov, Vadim, 60
Yo-Yo Ma, 164
Yost, Benjamin, 121 - 125 - 127, 129
Zivic, Fritzie, 47
Zook, Samuel Kosciuszko, 87

Cemeteries
Allegheny Cemetery, 72, 75, 76
Bergstrasse Cemetery, 23, 27
Calvary Cemetery, 45, 50, 77, 79, 80
Charles Evans Cemetery, 29
Chartiers Cemetery, 151, 155, 156
Christ Church Burial Ground, 51, 57
Christ Our Redeemer Cemetery, 169, 173
Fairview Cemetery, 105, 107
Forest Hills Memorial Park, 28
Gethsemane Cemetery, 23, 28
Gladwyne United Methodist Church Cemetery, 1, 7
Grandview Cemetery, 94, 98, 99
Harrisburg Cemetery, 30, 34, 65, 70, 71
Hazleton Cemetery, 35, 43
Hershey Cemetery, 14, 92, 93
Holy Sepulchre Cemetery, 157, 160
Holy Cross Cemetery, 133, 139, 140
Ivy Hill Cemetery, 58, 64, 119, 132
Jim Thorpe Memorial, 185, 191
Laurel Hill Cemetery, 1, 8 - 10
Milford Cemetery, 110, 117
Montgomery Cemetery, 81, 87
Most Precious Blood Cemetery, 44
Mount Lawn Cemetery, 175, 177, 178
Oaklands Cemetery, 19, 22
Old Public Graveyard, 17
Old Saint Jerome's Cemetery, 119, 131
Saint John the Baptist Byzantine Catholic Cemetery, 210, 214
Saint Joseph's Catholic Cemetery, 120, 131
Saint Stanislaus's Polish Catholic Cemetery, 43, 44
Saint Vincent's Cemetery, 100, 103
Shreiner's Cemetery, 179, 183
Spring Creek Presbyterian Cemetery, 141, 148
Union Cemetery, 150
Unity Cemetery, 163, 167
Westminster Memorial Gardens, 11, 14, 17
Westminster Presbyterian Church, 151, 153

Cities and Towns
Allentown, 107
Altoona, 12, 15, 16
Andersonville, 71
Ann Arbor, 133
Atlantic City, 27
Audenried, 129
Bastogne, 25, 27

Beaufort, 58, 63
Beaverton, 149
Bellefonte, 150
Berchtesgaden, 25
Bethel Park, 210, 214
Biloxi, 107
Boston, 1, 51, 138, 139
Brest, 20
Brooklyn, 1, 141, 144
Bryn Mahr, 105
Buena Vista, 72
Cambridge, 187
Campbelltown, 27
Canonsburg, 65
Carentan, 25
Carlisle, 11, 13, 17, 69, 185, 187
Canton, 189
Carnegie, 151
Cambridge, 112
Chancellorsville, 69, 83
Chappaquiddick Island, 101, 102
Chattanooga, 175
Cheltenham, 160
Chicago, 32, 89, 135, 136, 138 - 140
Clarksdale, 176, 177
Cleveland, 107
Coaldale, 123
Coleraine, 38
Concord, 55
Coulter, 169
Denver, 89, 132
Dallas, 105
Duncansville, 12
East Mauch Chunk, 191
Eckley, 132
Edgartown, 102, 103
Englewood, 141
Ephrata, 23
Essington, 178
Foy, 25
Fredericksburg, 26, 83
Gettysburg, 65, 69, 81, 83 - 87, 179
Girardville, 129, 131
Gladwyne, 1
Harpers Ferry, 69
Harrisburg, 22, 30, 65, 83
Harwood, 38
Hazleton, 35, 38 - 41, 43
Hershey, 26, 89 - 93
Hollywood, 77, 214
Honeybrook, 37
Hughestown, 27
Hurtgen, 117
Indianapolis, 138
Jim Thorpe, 122, 131, 132, 185, 191
Johnstown, 94, 95, 97 - 99
Lancaster, 23, 89, 121, 179, 181, 183, 184
Lansford, 122
Larksville, 100, 103
Latrobe, 143, 163, 164, 166, 167
Lattimer, 35 - 39, 41 -43
Laureldale, 23, 28
Leesburg, 69
Lemoyne, 83
Lexington, 55
London, 51, 54, 133
Los Angeles, 60, 77, 79, 151, 214
Manila, 63
Mauch Chunk, 122, 126, 127, 132, 191
Maytown, 30, 34
McVeytown, 12, 15
Mechanicsburg, 93
Memphis, 176
Mexico City, 81
Milford, 110, 113
Milnesville, 38
Monessen, 72
Montgomery, 100
Mount Airy, 121
Mount Pleasant, 65
Naperville, 7
New Cumberland, 12, 65
New York City, 1, 6, 47, 58, 63, 86, 89, 110, 125, 141, 163, 171, 187, 210 - 212, 214
Norristown, 81, 84, 86
Paris, 55
Pen Argyl, 105, 107 - 109
Petersburg, 85, 99
Philadelphia, 1, 10, 13, 19, 20, 22, 54, 56 - 58, 63, 64, 65, 69, 86, 89, 119, 136, 139, 147, 157, 159, 160, 170 - 172, 175
Pittsburgh, 45, 47, 49, 50, 65, 72, 75 - 77, 79, 80, 151 - 155, 163 - 165, 169 - 173, 210, 213, 214
Pottsville, 121, 123, 127, 129 - 132
Quantico, 20
Reading, 27 - 29
Reiffton, 28
Roseville, 12, 15
Salt Lake City, 13
San Francisco, 65, 67, 110
Shanghai, 18
Sharon Hill, 175
Springville, 13
State College, 141, 143, 148
St. Come-du-Monte, 27
St. Louis, 81, 153
St. Marie Du-Mont, 28
Stockholm, 187
Stony Creek Mills, 29
St. Petersburg, 5
Summit Hill, 131
Tamaqua, 119, 121, 122, 127, 131
Tilden, 1
Tokyo, 60, 63
Toronto, 138
Valley Forge, 117
Veracruz, 19, 67
Washington, 20, 30, 86, 100, 112, 113, 116, 166, 183
West Chester, 19, 22
West Hazleton, 44
West Reading, 28
Wilkes-Barre, 27, 42, 100
Williamsburg, 83
Yeadon, 133
York, 179

Pubs and Restaurants
Battered Mug, 44
Black N Blue, 93
Brother Paul's, 87
Coaches Bar and Grill, 178
Devon Seafood Grill, 93
Fire Alley, 93
Hershey Hotel, 93
Houlihan's, 93

Iberian Lounge, 93
Molly Maguire Pub, 132, 191
Overtime Sports Bar, 93
Rustic Tavern, 17
Sharky's Cafe, 167
Stella Blue and the Star Bar, 10
Subway Cafe, 34
The Third and Spruce Cafe, 28
The Tilted Kilt, 214
Timbers, 44
Trolley Car Cafe, 10
Winghart's, 50